OUR
GOD
IS
TRIUNE

ESSAYS IN
BIBLICAL THEOLOGY

EDITED BY

MICHAEL R. BURGOS JR.

Published by

CHURCH MILITANT PUBLICATIONS
Artillery Support for the Local Church
Torrington, Connecticut, USA

ISBN: 0692422919
ISBN-13: 978-0692422915

CONTENTS

Apart from the incarnation and the Trinity, it is possible to know that God is, but not who God is.

−Timothy George[*]

[*] *Is the God of Muhammed the Father of Jesus*, (Grand Rapids: Zondervan, 2002), 70.

EDITOR'S NOTE TO THE READER

I am greatly pleased and honored to have worked with these brothers to produce this volume, as this work is the distillation of many years of biblical study and critical theological evaluation. The book you hold in your hands is like many others since it is intended to provide you with a robust understanding of key areas of biblical theology. However, it is also different in that its content is, frankly, rare among books that deal with trinitarianism. In addition to careful biblically-driven theology, we have sought to interact with the best non-trinitarian interpreters, using them as a foil from which to reflect the effulgence of God's truth. We'd like you to know from the outset that all of the contributors to this volume affirm the Nicene, Chalcedonian, Athanasian and Apostle's creeds, the five *Solas* of the Protestant Reformation, and the *Chicago Statement on Inerrancy*. It is our hope that this volume serves you well.

Ave Sanctae Trinitatis!
M. R. Burgos Jr.
Torrington, CT
August 2018

PROTO-TRINITARIAN CHRISTOLOGY

Michael R. Burgos Jr.[1]

I have labored elsewhere to demonstrate the progressive nature of biblical revelation and the trinitarian conception of God within the New Testament, and the New Testament's conception of the Old Testament.[2] Since the depiction of God within the New Testament is the supreme revelation of the nature of God, an inerrantist view of the biblical text demands that the Old Testament

---

[1] Michael serves as Pastor at Northwest Hills Community Church in downtown Torrington, Connecticut. He and his wife Marion have seven children. He holds a BS in Bible and Theology (Lee University), an MA in Biblical Studies (Andersonville Theological Seminary), and a PhD in Polemic Theology (Forge Theological Seminary). Michael also serves as Prof. of Systematics at Forge Theological Seminary.

[2] Burgos Jr., Michael R., *Against Oneness Pentecostalism: An Exegetical-Theological Critique*, 2nd Ed., (Winchester: Church Militant Pub., 2016). See also Ram, Bernard, *Protestant Biblical Interpretation*, (Grand Rapids: Baker, 1956), 111-117, Beale, G. K., *Handbook on the New Testament Use of the Old Testament: Exegesis & Interpretation*, (Grand Rapids: Baker Academic, 2012), 53ff and Poythress, Vern S., *Reading the Word of God in the Presence of God: A Handbook of Biblical Interpretation*, (Wheaton: Crossway, 2016), 226-228.

agree. Despite this, it is a common tactic of subordinationist[3] and Oneness Pentecostal apologists to claim that the Old Testament, especially the many monotheistic decrees within the "Trial of the False Gods" (Isaiah 40-45),[4] preclude a trinitarian conception of God. However, a careful reading of the Old Testament text divulges robust support of the doctrine of the Trinity, and particularly trinitarian Christology. The Old Testament's theology of God is thoroughly proto-trinitarian,[5] and can only be reconciled

---

[3] The term "subordinationism" refers to the "teaching about the Godhead which regards either the Son as subordinate to the Father or the Holy Spirit as subordinate to both." We are here using that term primarily in its Christological sense. Cross, F. L., Livingstone, E. A. Eds., *The Oxford Dictionary of the Christian Church*, (New York: Oxford Univ. Press, 1997), 1552.

[4] E.g., Buzzard, Anthony, Hunting, Charles F., *The Doctrine of the Trinity: Christianity's Self Inflicted Wound*, (Lanham: International Scholar's Press, 1998), 19ff, Chang, Eric H. H., *The Only True God: A Study of Biblical Monotheism*, (Bloomington: Xlibris, 2013), 64-65, 142-144, Gill, J. Dan, *The One: In Defense of One God*, (Nashville: 21st Century Reformation Pub., 2016), 203-289, and Norris, David, *I Am: A Oneness Pentecostal Theology*, (Hazelwood: WAP Academic, 2009), Kindle, loc. 514.

[5] The phrase "proto-trinitarian" is here meant to indicate the Triune nature of God as revealed partially in the text of the Old Testament. We agree with Berkhof who wrote,

> Some of the early Church Fathers and even some later theologians, disregarding the progressive character of God's revelation, gave the impression that the doctrine of the Trinity was completely revealed in the Old Testament. On the other hand Socinians and Arminians were of the opinion that it was not found there at all. Both were mistaken. The Old Testament does not contain a full revelation of the trinitarian existence of God, but does contain several indications of it. And this is exactly what might be expected.

4

with unitarianism[6] by way of ignoring large portions of key narratives *and* an intensely eisegetical hermeneutic.

The Son of God in the Old Testament

Throughout the Old Testament there are appearances of an individual known as the Angel of the LORD.[7] The term "angel," in Hebrew, refers not to a specific ontology, but rather the function of an individual.[8] Therefore the phrase "Angel of the LORD" does not in and of itself communicate the nature of the messenger, but instead his relation to Yahweh. Some subordinationists claim the term "angel" can only refer to a creature. For instance, one unitarian claimed, "For one to be an angel 'of God' ("of the

---

The proto-trinitarian theology of the OT is to be distinguished from the unbiblical unitarianism of interpreters both ancient and modern. That is, the proto-trinitarian theology of the OT is enough to completely preclude unitarianism. Berkhof, Louis, *Systematic Theology*, New Comb. Ed., (Grand Rapids: Eerdmans, 1996), 85. See also Grudem, Wayne, *Systematic Theology: An Introduction to Biblical Doctrine*, (Grand Rapids: Zondervan, 2000), 227-229.

[6] The term "unitarianism" refers to "A Christian thought and religious observance which rejects the doctrines of the Trinity and the Divinity of Christ in favour of the unipersonality of God." Cross, Livingstone Eds., *The Oxford Dictionary of the Christian Church*, 1659. Unitarianism finds expressions among Christian cults (e.g., Jehovah's Witnesses, Oneness Pentecostals, The Way Intl., Christadelphians, *Iglesia Ni Cristo*) and non-Christian world religions (e.g., Islam, Judaism).

[7] Wenham has noted that the phrase occurs 58 times within the OT, and the "Angel of God" 11 times. Wenham, Gordon J., *Word Biblical Commentary: Genesis 16-50*, (Grand Rapids: Zondervan, 2000), 9.

[8] See Koehler, Ludwig, Baumgartner, Walter, *Hebrew & Aramaic Lexicon of the Old Testament*, (Leiden: Brill, 1999), 585-586. Harris, R. L., Archer Jr., Gleason L., Waltke, Bruce K. Eds., *Theological Wordbook of the Old Testament*, (Chicago: Moody Press, 1980), 464.

5

LORD") means by definition that one is not God."[9] This statement however, cannot account for the fact that Yahweh is himself said to be a *mal'āk*.[10] Moreover, to say that the genitival phrase "of the Lord" necessitates that "one is not God," is to assume unitarianism from the outset.

The Angel of Yahweh, while personally distinct from Yahweh, is Yahweh himself. That is, the Angel of Yahweh is the Son of God who, while possessing complete deity, is personally distinct from his Father. In order to demonstrate this claim, I will provide a consideration of two varieties of texts. First, I will assess those passages which demonstrate the absolute deity of the Angel and the impossibility of his ontological inferiority to God. These texts show the deity of the Angel of Yahweh in the same way the New Testament identifies Jesus to be God; by attributing to him actions, titles, and characteristics that belong only to God. Second, passages which show a personal distinction between the Angel of the LORD and the LORD, both in communication and economy, will demonstrate the presence of trinitarian relationships in the Old Testament. This argument may be consolidated into the following premises and conclusion:

> **Premise 1:** The Angel of Yahweh is LORD and God just as the Son of God is LORD and God.
> **Premise 2:** The Angel of Yahweh is personally distinct from Yahweh just as the Son of God is personally distinct from his Father.
> **Conclusion:** There exists a thorough proto-trinitarian Christology in the Old Testament that is akin to the divine Christology in the New Testament.

Below I have outlined the biblical evidence for each of the

---

[9] Gill, *The One*, 169.

[10] Gen 48:16; Ecc 5:6; Mal 3:1.

above premises. However, before a consideration of the relevant passages, an assessment of the phrase מַלְאַךְ יהוה (*mal'āk* Yahweh) is necessary. Traditionally the phrase *mal'āk* Yahweh has been understood definitely (i.e., "the Angel of the LORD"), thereby indicating a particular individual whose presence occurs throughout the Old Testament. However, some have argued that the phrase is better rendered indefinitely and is subsequently a phrase that is indicative of a number of individuals who act as an angel of the LORD at various times.

The general determiner as to whether a Hebrew noun is definite is that of its modifiers. Waltke and O'Connor note, "In Hebrew the definiteness of a noun and that of its modifiers are in agreement" and, "The largest class of intrinsically definite nouns is names."[11] Lopez has noted that this rule has its exceptions, and has argued that *mal'āk* Yahweh is one:

> While 'every proper noun is determinate per se,' this may not always apply to nouns in construct with a proper noun. This is corroborated by Gesenius: 'In a few instances [when] the *nomen regens* appears...it often is so before a proper name,' as in ...a feast of the Lord (Exod 10:9)... an abomination unto the Lord (Deut 7:29) ... a virgin of Israel (Deut 22:19) ... a man of Benjamin (1 Sam 4:12), etc.' Hence, it may be correct to translate the anarthrous construct noun (מַלְאַךְ) as indefinite.[12]

The key component that distinguishes *mal'āk* Yahweh from the indefinite phrases cited by Lopez is the consistent utilization of

---

[11] Waltke, Bruce K., O'Connor, M., *An Introduction to Biblical Hebrew Syntax*, (Winona Lake: Eisenbrauns, 1990), 239 and 156 resp.

[12] Lopez, René A., 2010. "Identifying the 'Angel of the Lord' in the Book of Judges: A Model for Reconsidering the Referent in Other Old Testament Loci," *Bulletin for Biblical Research* 20, 2.

mal'āk Yahweh throughout the Old Testament. While there are many abominations unto the LORD, there is only one Angel of the LORD. This is evident due to the several Old Testament realities. First, the Angel of Yahweh is explicitly identified as Yahweh himself, and this within a monotheistic context.[13] Hence, if one were to suppose that there was a multiplicity of Angels of Yahweh, then one would necessarily be asserting multiple Gods. Second, there exists no place within the Old Testament wherein *mal'āk* Yahweh occurs in plural form. The lack of a plural points toward a particular individual who is distinguished from other angels.[14] The Angel of Yahweh is no longer mentioned upon the arrival of Jesus Christ, and the equivalent phrase in the New Testament only appears indefinitely.[15] So too, there are two implicit identifications of Jesus as the Angel within the New Testament. Jude 1:5 states,

---

[13] See Gen 31:13.

[14] The same observation may be levelled at the lack of a plural in the NT. Although, Luke 2:9-15 implies plurality.

[15] E.g., Matt 1:20, v. 24; 2:13, v. 19; 28:2. The only possible exception is Gal 4:14. Wallace has argued for taking ἄγγελος κυρίου definitively in the NT, saying, "Although most scholars treat ἄγγελος κυρίου in the NT as 'an angel of the Lord,' there is no linguistic basis for doing so." He went further to suggest that "a particular angel is in view." Wallace, Daniel B., *Greek Grammar Beyond the Basics* [*GGBB*], (Grand Rapids: Zondervan, 1997), 252, n. 97. While there may not be a grammatical basis, there are robust contextual reasons. For example, the identification of the divine Angel with the Christ (see below) demands that the lesser ἄγγελος be distinguished via an indefinite rendering. Such a distinction however, is necessitated by the incarnation and therefore only appears in the NT. That is, if the divine angel is in the tomb, *an angel of the Lord* must role away the stone (Matt 28:2). The identification of Gabriel as an ἄγγελος κυρίου in Luke 1:19 also presupposes an indefinite rendering.

Now I want to remind you, although you once fully knew it, that Jesus, who saved a people out of the land of Egypt, afterward destroyed those who did not believe.[16]

In identifying the Son of God's involvement in the exodus, the New Testament has provided an inspired identification of the Angel of Yahweh's identity. The Angel of Yahweh who is credited with saving a people out of Egypt is none other than Jesus Christ,[17] and therefore the phrase *mal'āk* Yahweh depicts a single individual consistently.

The reading "Jesus" appears in the critical editions of the Greek New Testament as it possesses superior attestation by both manuscript and versional witnesses and patristic literature. The Byzantine reading "Lord" occurs in Siniaticus, 044, and a correction of Ephraemi Rescriptus. The reading "Jesus" is present in Alexandrinus, Vaticanus, a number of important minuscules,[18] and among Coptic MSS. Additionally, it is attested by Origen, Cyril, Jerome, and Bede. In observation of this, Comfort rightly notes that the critical reading is backed by "an impressive collection of witnesses."[19] "Jesus" is also the most difficult reading, which, ironically, is the rationale given by former members of the editorial committee of the United Bible Societies for its omission. Metzger has noted that "a majority of the Committee was of the opinion that the reading was difficult to the

---

[16] In this volume, unless otherwise indicated, I have utilized the venerable *English Standard Version*, (Wheaton: Crossway, 2001).

[17] Judges 2:1.

[18] 33, 81, 88, 1739, 1881, and 2344. It is noteworthy that P^{72} possesses the reading θεός Χριστός (God Christ). This reading indirectly supports Ιησούς.

[19] Comfort, Philip W., *New Testament Text and Translation Commentary*, (Carol Stream: Tyndale House Pub., 2008), 802.

point of impossibility."[20] Metzger concluded that while committee formally rejected the reading, the "Critical principles seem to require the adoption of Ἰησοῦς."[21]

Some unitarians have rejected the critical reading upon the basis of dubious reasoning. For example, Schoenheit, Graeser, and Lynn wrote,

"…the Lord delivered his people out of Egypt…" was changed to "Jesus delivered" in a few manuscripts to make Jesus exist in the Old Testament.[22]

These authors have provided no external or internal evidence supporting their rejection of the reading. Yet, they have the temerity to thank "the honest scholars who work the texts and draw their conclusions from the textual evidence rather than from tradition."[23]

A similar sentiment to that of Jude is communicated by Paul:

For I do not want you to be unaware, brothers, that our fathers were all under the cloud, and all passed through the sea, and all were baptized into Moses in the cloud and in the sea, and all ate the same spiritual food, and all drank the same spiritual drink. For they drank from the spiritual Rock that followed them, and the Rock was Christ. (1 Corinthians 10:1-4)

Paul went on to exhort the Corinthians not to "put Christ to the test, as some of them did and were destroyed by serpents" (v. 9).[24]

---

[20] Metzger, *A Textual Commentary on the Greek New Testament*, (New York: United Bible Societies, 2005), 724.

[21] Ibid.

[22] Graeser, Lynn, Schoenheit, *One God & One Lord*, 627.

[23] Ibid.

[24] The reading "Christ" in 1 Cor 10:9 is strongly attested and appears in the critical editions as well as the best English translations.

Clearly, Paul saw the Son of God as the God of Israel and yet distinct from the Father.[25]

Further identification of the Son of God as the Angel of Yahweh occurs within the Septuagint's rendering/interpretation of Isaiah 9:6.

ὅτι παιδίον ἐγεννήθη ἡμῖν, υἱὸς καὶ ἐδόθη ἡμῖν, οὗ ἡ ἀρχὴ ἐγενήθη ἐπὶ τοῦ ὤμου αὐτοῦ, καὶ καλεῖται τὸ ὄνομα αὐτοῦ Μεγάλης βουλῆς ἄγγελος, ἐγὼ γὰρ ἄξω εἰρήνην ἐπὶ τοὺς ἄρχοντας, εἰρήνην καὶ ὑγίειαν αὐτῷ.[26]

Because a child was born for us, and a son was given for us, whose rulership was upon his shoulders, and his name is called Angel of Great Counsel. (Author's translation)

For those Jews who translated the Tanakh into the tongue of the diaspora, the Messiah, who is the mighty God,[27] is also the Angel of Great Counsel, who is none other than the Angel of Yahweh who led his people out of Egypt and counseled the prophets. In light of the above, there is robust evidence which supports the traditional contention that the phrase mal'āk Yahweh ought to be rendered definitely.

Premise 1: The Angel of Yahweh is LORD and God just as the Son of God is LORD and God.

In the New Testament, Jesus is identified as God by explicit statements thereof,[28] and by the attribution of actions and

---

There is no variant reading in v. 4. See Comfort, 506-507.

[25] Cf. 1 Cor 8:6.

[26] 9:5, LXX.

[27] Cf. Isaiah 10:21.

[28] John 1:1; 1:18; 20:28; Acts 20:28; Rom 9:5, Col 2:9; Heb 1:9; 2

statements that belong to deity alone.[29] Similarly, there exists bountiful evidence that the Angel of Yahweh is God throughout the Old Testament:

- Moses identifies the Angel of Yahweh who appeared to Hagar as "Yahweh who spoke to her" (Gen 16:13), and Hagar characterizes the Angel saying, "You are a God of seeing."

- It was the Angel who appeared to Moses in the bush, and said, "take the sandals off your feet, for the place on which you are standing is holy ground" (Exodus 3:4). The Angel then identified himself saying, "I Am Who I Am" (v. 14).

- The Angel of the LORD swears by himself—an action that Wenham notes is the "First and only divine oath in the patriarchal stories, though it is frequently harked back to (Gen 24:7; 26:3; 50:24; Exod 13:5)."[30] This action is similar to the covenant established with Abram, a covenant predicated upon only the character and faithfulness of Yahweh.[31]

- The Angel of Yahweh said to Jacob, "I am the God of Bethel, where you anointed a pillar and made a vow to me" (Gen 31:13). When Jacob made that vow he stated, "If God will be with me…then the LORD shall be my God, and this stone, which I have set up for a pillar shall be God's house" (Gen 28:20-22). Hosea identifies the Angel saying Jacob "met God at Bethel" (Hos 12:4), and went on to identify

---

Pet 1:1.

[29] Mark 2:5-12; 1 Cor 8:6; Col 1:16; Heb 1:2-3.

[30] Wenham, *Gen 16-50*, 111.

[31] See Gen 15:1-21.

him as "the LORD, the God of hosts, the LORD is his memorial name" (v. 5).

- Jacob prayed to the Angel of Yahweh when he blessed Ephraim and Manasseh. He stated, "The God before whom my fathers walked, the God who has been my shepherd all my life long to this day, the angel who has redeemed me from all evil, bless the boys…" (Gen 48:15).

- The Angel of Yahweh does not merely speak in the name of God, but rather God's "name is in him" and he is the one who will not pardon Israel's sins (Exod 23:21).[32]

- It is the Angel of Yahweh who calls himself Yahweh (Gen 22:16),[33] and who is credited with saving Israel out of Egypt (Judges 2:1).

- When God was angry at Balaam, the Angel of Yahweh appeared. After correcting Balaam by means of his donkey, the Angel told Balaam, "Go with the men, but speak only the word that I tell you." Balaam interpreted this command

---

[32] Ausloos, Hans, 2008. "The 'Angel of YHWH' in Exod. Xxiii 20-23 and Judges ii 1-5. A Clue to the Deuteronom(ist)ic Puzzle?," *Vetus Testamentum*, 58.1, 9-10.

[33] The Angel of the LORD is used by Yahweh exactly as a means unto ensuring his hearers of the certainty of his words. E.g., Exodus 3:2; Ezekiel 37:14. Huijen has noted, "The angel is both distinct from and identified with the Lord. The clearest exemplary text for this phenomenon is the narrative of Akedah in Genesis 22… First God addresses Abraham (Gen 22:1), but later on in the narrative, the Angel of Yahweh not only speaks on behalf of Yahweh (Gen 22:11), but also as if he were Yahweh himself, promising Abraham God's blessing in the first person singular (Gen 22:16-17)." Huijen, Arnold. 2017. "Traces of the Trinity in the Old Testament: From Individual Texts to the Nature of Revelation," *International Journal of Systematic Theology*, 19.3, 260.

by saying, "The word that God puts in my mouth, that I must speak" (Num 22:22-38).

- The Angel of Yahweh identified himself as the "commander of the LORD's army" and said to Joshua, "Take off your sandals from your feet, for the place where you are standing is holy" (Joshua 5:15). Just a few verses later, the commander of Yahweh's army is identified as Yahweh by Joshua (6:2).

- It was the Angel of Yahweh, having a "wonderful" name, who heralded the coming of Samson's birth, and who received an offering from Manoah (Judges 13:15-25).[34] Manoah concluded his interaction with the Angel of Yahweh saying, "We shall surely die, for we have seen God" (v. 22).

- Whereas in 1 Samuel 21:15-16 the Angel of Yahweh appeared to David, 2 Chronicles 3:1 states that it was Yahweh himself who appeared.

- Barker has noted that the Hebrew text of Ecclesiastes 5:6 reads "Let not your mouth lead you into sin, and do not say before the angel that it was a mistake." The Septuagint renders this to say, "Do not say before the Lord." Similarly the Hebrew of Isaiah 63:9 states, "The angel of his presence saved them." The Septuagint renders this, "Not a messenger nor an angel but he himself saved them."[35]

- Zechariah 12:8 states that to "be like God" is to be "like the Angel of Yahweh."

In virtually every defining moment in Israel's history, the Angel of Yahweh played a primary role and was characterized and

---

[34] Cf. Isaiah 9:6-7.

[35] Barker, *The Great Angel*, 32.

treated as Yahweh himself. Compare this to the treatment in other
angelic encounters within Scripture. For instance, when John fell
down at the feet of an angel to worship him (Rev 19:10), the angel
responded saying, "You must not do that! I am a fellow servant
with you and your brothers who hold to the testimony of Jesus."

In an effort to mitigate the deity of the Angel of Yahweh,
some unitarians have argued that the Angel of Yahweh isn't
Yahweh at all, but rather a created agent.[36] The agent-sender
theory most often relies upon the so-called "law of agency"
defined below:

> Agent (Heb: *Shaliah*): The main point of the Jewish law of
> agency is expressed in the dictum "a person's agent is
> regarded as the person himself"… Therefore any act
> committed by a duly appointed agent is regarded as having
> been committed by the principal, who therefore bears full
> responsibility for it with consequent complete absence of
> liability on the part of the agent.[37]

Using the term שָׁלִיחַ (*shaliah*) as a means of identifying the
Angel of Yahweh as a created agent is a tactic typical of
subordinationists who are desirous to defend the notion that the
God of Israel is one person. Explaining the identity of the Angel of
Yahweh as a created agent poses an array of logical, theological,
and exegetical problems. In the first place, proponents of this
theory merely assume that the Angel of Yahweh is created agent
without providing any positive biblical evidence to support such an
assertion. Subordinationists must assume their conclusion when

---

[36] Graeser, Lynn,, Schoenheit, *One God & One Lord*, 563ff. Barron,
David, *God and Christ: Examining the Evidence for a Biblical Doctrine*,
(Self Published: 2009), i-iv. Gill, *The One*, 165.

[37] Werblowsky, R. J. Zwi, Wigoder, Geoffrey Eds., *Encyclopedia of
Jewish Religion*, Rev. Ed., (New York: Adama Books, 1996), 15.

they equate agency with finitude, as agency is a category of function and not ontology. Jesus Christ served as the Father's agent in creation, and yet, he resides on the eternal side of the Creator/Creature divide.

The Angel of Yahweh is never called a *shaliah*. One would expect the use of the term in any one of the dozens of passages that describe the Angel of Yahweh as the primary salvific actor. Additionally, the above definition does not possess an accurate depiction of the biblical agent-sender relationship in several important ways. In *every* account within the Old Testament wherein an emissary acts on behalf of his sender, the agent is immediately identified as distinct from the one who sent the agent. For instance, even when God said to Moses, "See, I have made you like God to Pharaoh, and your brother Aaron shall be your prophet" (Exodus 7:1), there was never an acceptance by Moses of the kind of honor belonging to Yahweh. Moses did not start receiving worship and calling himself Yahweh. Rather, Moses spoke the words that Yahweh gave him while still communicating a tacit distinction between himself and Yahweh. No one who saw Moses believed that they had seen Yahweh and lived, as in Judges 13:22. Clearly therefore, even in the Old Testament's quintessential agent-sender narrative, there is a sharp distinction made between the sender and the one sent.[38] Unlike Moses, the Angel of Yahweh *never* identifies himself as a representative or Yahweh's inferior.

By the time of the New Testament, *shaliah* was the general equivalent of the Greek term ἀπόστολος.[39] While the apostles represented Christ, they were never called "Jesus" or "Christ," or worshiped as Christ. Even though Paul was an apostle and was

---

[38] See also Gen 24:1-67 and 1 Sam 25:39-42.

[39] Kittel, Gerhard, Ed. *Theological Dictionary of the New Testament* [*TDNT*], Vol. 1, (Grand Rapids: Eerdmans, 1964), 413.

given the power to conduct miracles, he refused to be worshipped as if he was Christ.[40]

If the agency theory is adopted to explain the identity of the Angel of Yahweh, there would exist no meaningful way to distinguish the function of God from his agent. That is, since the Angel is identified so often as the salvific actor within the Old Testament, and if the Angel is actually a created agent, there exists no legitimate means to avoid idolatry. When Yahweh asks the rhetorical question, "Who is like me?" (Isaiah 44:7), consistency demands that those who hold the agency view say, 'Your created Angel is exactly like you. He even says that he is God Almighty and receives worship and prayer.' With the agency view, the prohibition in the Decalogue against idolatry is effectively obliterated.

> **Premise 2:** The Angel of Yahweh is personally distinct from Yahweh just as the Son of God is personally distinct from his Father.

There are several passages in which the Angel of Yahweh and Yahweh communicate directly. For example, Yahweh spoke to the Angel of Yahweh saying, "It is enough, now stay your hand" (2 Sam 24:16). In Zechariah's prophecy the Angel of Yahweh is depicted as saying, "O LORD of hosts, how long will you have no mercy on Jerusalem…" (Zec 1:12).[41] Lopez and those who hold to a subordinationist agency theory seem to think these third person references demand an ontological distinction between the Angel of Yahweh and Yahweh.[42] Lopez relies heavily upon Zechariah 1:12 and states that the passage implies "that the angel of the Lord is not

---

[40] Acts 14:11-16. Cf. Acts 10:25.

[41] Cf. 3:7.

[42] See for example Gill, *The One*, 169-170, n. 6.

the Lord himself."[43] This statement is wrong on two counts. First, those who understand the Angel of Yahweh in a traditional sense also assert a personal distinction between the Angel and another person named Yahweh (i.e., the Father). Second, the text of Zechariah itself prohibits understanding the third person references as implying that the Angel of Yahweh isn't himself also Yahweh.

> Then he showed me Joshua the high priest standing before the Angel of the LORD, and Satan standing at his right hand to accuse him. And the LORD said to Satan, "The LORD rebuke you, O Satan! The LORD who has chosen Jerusalem rebuke you! Is not this a brand plucked from the fire?" Now Joshua was standing before the angel, clothed with filthy garments. And the angel said to those who were standing before him, "Remove the filthy garments from him." And to him he said, "Behold, I have taken your iniquity away from you, and I will clothe you with pure vestments." And I said, "Let them put a clean turban on his head." So they put a clean turban on his head and clothed him with garments. And the Angel of the LORD was standing by. (Zechariah 3:1-5)

Within the above passage, the Angel of Yahweh is called Yahweh, and in v. 2 the Angel (i.e., "the LORD") states, "The LORD rebuke you, O Satan" (v. 2). Clearly therefore, the personal distinction of the Angel of Yahweh is not intended to communicate that the Angel isn't himself Yahweh.[44] The Angel of Yahweh is both divine and personally distinct from Yahweh in the same manner that Jesus Christ is divine and personally distinct from his Father. This is made more evident in that Zechariah 3:1-5 typically displays the salvific work of Jesus' people by the imputation of his righteousness. For Jesus is the one who cleanses sinners, removing

---

[43] Lopez, 16.

[44] See also Gen 21:17.

their iniquity, clothing them in the spotless robes of his own righteousness.[45]

> **Conclusion:** There exists a thorough proto-trinitarian Christology in the Old Testament that is akin to the Christology in the New Testament.

Given the above, especially in light of the New Testament's characterization of Christ, it is clear that there existed a personal relationship between two divine persons, namely the Angel of the LORD and the LORD (i.e., the Son and the Father).

---

[45] See Rom 4:1-12.

JUSTIFIED: A PROTO-TRINITARIAN READING OF GENESIS 1:26-27

Michael R. Burgos Jr.

Then God said, "Let us make man in our image, after our likeness. And let them have dominion over the fish of the sea and over the birds of the heavens and over the livestock and over all the earth and over every creeping thing that creeps on the earth." So God created man in his own image, in the image of God he created him; male and female he created them. (Genesis 1:26-27)

Since the New Testament teaches that God the Father and the Son of God were involved in creation,[1] and since the Holy Spirit is depicted as active in creation (Gen 1:3), it is apparent that the plural verb נַעֲשֶׂה ("Let us make") and plural nouns בְּצַלְמֵנוּ ("in our image") and כִּדְמוּתֵנוּ ("according to our likeness") refer to the Triune God. However, many interpreters have sought to offer an alternative explanation. Aside from a trinitarian explanation, Hamilton has cited five explanations for the plural forms:[2]

---

[1] See John 1:1-3; 1 Cor 8:6; Col 1:16; Heb 1:2.

[2] Hamilton, Victor P., *The New International Commentary on the Old Testament: The Book of Genesis Chapters 1-17*, (Grand Rapids:

1. According to the so-called "mythological" interpretation, the "us" is said to refer to other gods.

This interpretation neither coheres with the theology of Genesis or an inerrantist reading of Scripture. God alone created the heavens and the earth.[3]

2. The plural pronouns refer to a heavenly court of angelic hosts.

While it is popular to explain the utilization of the plural pronouns by appealing to created angels, such an interpretation would necessarily mean that humankind was not only created in the image of God, but also other creatures, namely angels.[4] The emphasis in v. 27 itself (i.e., "God created man in his own image, in the image of God he created him..."), rules out the *ad hock* appeal to angels. Judging by Moses' commentary, he clearly believed that humankind was created in God's image alone. Moses wrote, "When God created man, he made him in the likeness of God" (Gen 5:1).[5] Further, nowhere in Scripture is it said that God created with any creatures. Rather, the Father created through his Son. A case in point is the argument made within the prologue of the epistle to the Hebrews. There, the Son is identified as the one

---

Eerdmans, 1990), 134.

[3] Isaiah 45:18.

[4] See for example the interpretation offered by Heiser, Michael, *The Unseen Realm: Recovering the Supernatural Worldview of the Bible*, (Bellingham: Lexham Press, 2015), 41, 52. Heiser never really deals with the emphatic structure of the text, or the other texts which reaffirm a single image giver. See also Gill, *The One*, 199.

[5] Cf. Gen 9:6 wherein the punishment for murder is predicated upon man's possession of the *imago Dei*.

"through" (διά) whom the Father created the world. In that same pericope the writer has given a prosponic application of Psalm 102 wherein the Father says to the Son, "You, Lord, laid the foundation of the earth *in the beginning,* and the heavens are the work of your hands" (v.10).[6] Therefore, God wasn't speaking to angels, but to his Son.

3. "God speaks to something he has recently created, and the most likely addressee would be the earth."

There is nothing within the context of the creation account that affords such an interpretation. Even if one were to, for some reason, countenance this option, it is apparent that it finds to parallel within the Old Testament.

4. A literary device known as the "plural of majesty."

If one accepts its presence in the Hebrew Bible, the *pluralis majestatis* or "plural of majesty" is a feature of nouns and adjectives, but never pronouns and only certain participles. The *Encyclopedia of Hebrew Language and Linguistics* states,

The *pluralis majestatis* appears most frequently in nouns…, but may also be used with some nominalized adjectives…[and] some participles. There are no undisputed examples of a pronoun or a verb displaying the *pluralis majestatis*… 'Let us make man in our image (Gen 1:26), has occasionally been explained as a *pluralis majestatis*, but comparative Semitic and

---

[6] Ellingworth has noted that "κατ' ἀρχάς is a classical synonym, rare in the Greek Bible (Ps. 119 [LXX 118]; 152 for ἐν ἀρχῇ (Gn. 1:1; Jn. 1:1)." Ellingworth, Paul, *The New International Commentary on the Greek Testament: The Epistle to the Hebrews,* (Grand Rapids: Eerdmans, 1987), 111, also n. 71.

contextual factors favor other explanations.[7]

Even if one were to insist that Genesis 1:26 is an example of the plural of majesty, the existence of the cohortative plural would result in a confusing sentiment. Baker has explained:

The plural of majesty (in effect singular) would not make sense of God's call for unanimity in the endeavor. Such a meaning on God's part would have required a singular cohortative voice (singular in the verb even if a plural of majesty were used for the noun/pronoun) rather than a plural cohortative. Even if it were here to be understood as a singular cohortative (difficult as that would be), we then would have the problem of understanding why God was trying to psyche himself up to some great feat.[8]

Some have sought to offer examples of the plural of majesty being used with pronouns in the Old Testament.[9] The two typical texts cited are Ezra 4:18 and Daniel 2:36. In Ezra a plural pronoun is utilized, but in Daniel a plural verb used, and both of these occurrences are better explained by a consideration of their respective context. The so-called "royal we" is simply not a feature of the Hebrew Bible, and is instead an invention of the 4th century AD.[10]

---

[7] Khan, Geoffrey Ed., *Encyclopedia of Hebrew Language and Linguistics*, (Leiden: Brill, 2013), 146.

[8] Baker, Doug P., *Covenant and Community: Our Role as the Image of God*, (Eugene: Wipf & Stock, 2008), 19.

[9] See Graeser, Lynn,, Schoenheit, *One God & One Lord*, 434-435.

[10] See Brown, R., Gilman, A., 1960. "The Pronouns of Power and Solidarity," *Style and* Language, MIT Press, 254. See also Baumgarten, Nicole, Du Bois, Inke, House Juliane Eds., *Subjectivity in Language and Discourse*, Leiden: Brill, 2012), 326.

5. The pronouns are a kind of self-deliberation akin the statement, 'Let's see.'

This option finds no linguistic parallel within the canon. Wenham notes that this option "is uncertain, for parallels to this usage are very rare."[11] While there are places within Scripture wherein people engage in self-deliberation (e.g., Ps 42:5), plural nouns are never utilized. If self-deliberation were a viable interpretation, we would expect non-Christian Jews within antiquity to utilize the such an explanation in their response to their Christian interlocutors. Instead, Sarfati has noted that,

Early Jewish Christians were using this passage [i.e., Gen 1:26] as evidence of plurality, because the establishment rabbis were already trying to get around this. E.g. the *Midrash Rabbah* (8.8) on Genesis tries to answer:

Rabbi Samuel Bar Hanman in the name of Rabbi Jonathan said, that at the time when Moses wrote the Torah, writing a portion of it daily, when he came to the verse which says, "And Elohim said, let us make man in our image and after our likeness," Moses said, "Master of the universe, why do you give herewith an excuse to the sectarians?" God answered Moses, "You write and whoever wants to err, let him err."[12]

Given these alternative interpretations, there exists good reason to accept the traditional trinitarian explanation. Wenham has

---

[11] Wenham, Gordon J., *Word Biblical Commentary: Genesis 1-15*, (Grand Rapids: Zondervan, 1987), 28.

[12] Sarfati, Jonathan D., *The Genesis Account: A Theological, Historical, and Scientific Commentary on Genesis 1-11*, (Powder Springs: Creation Book Publishers, 2015), 73.

objected saying, "It is now universally admitted that this was not what the plural meant to the original author."[13] Upon the basis of this objection Wenham resorted to two untenable interpretations. He wrote, "The choice then appears to lie between interpretations...'us' = God and Angels or...plural of self-exhortation."[14] The trouble with Wenham's appeal to authorial intent is that he fails to adequately observe the prominence of proto-trinitarianism within the Pentateuch. The Angel of Yahweh is a persistent presence in Genesis and is both identified as Yahweh/God and as personally distinct from Yahweh.[15] Hence, if one takes into account the mention of the Spirit within the creation account, and the heavy involvement of the divine Angel within the books of Moses, there remains little basis for using authorial intent to dismiss the interpretation that is all but explicitly indicated by the New Testament.

Elohim and Other Plural Forms Used of God

Beyond the plural verbs of Genesis 1:26, there are a variety of plural nouns and adjectives that are used of God throughout the Hebrew Bible. Most relevant to this discussion is the plural noun "God" (אֱלֹהִים). *Elohim* has been understood historically by many interpreters as evidence of God's triunity.[16] Typically, these

---

[13] Wenham, 27.

[14] Ibid., 28.

[15] Gen 16:7-14; 28:20-22; 31:13; 48:15; Exodus 3:4; Num 22:22-38; Joshua 5:15.

[16] This is true at least from the work of Lombard in the 12th c. Unlike the aforementioned interpretation of Gen 1:26, I cannot find any evidence of patristic writers using *elohim* as a trinitarian proof. See Benjamin R. Merkle's wonderful study, *Defending the Trinity in the Reformed Palatinate: The Elohistae*, (New York: Oxford Univ. Press, 2015). See also the absence of patristic consideration of the plural form in Bates, Matthew W., *The Birth of the Trinity: Jesus, God, and Spirit in New Testament & Early Christian Interpretations of the Old Testament,*

interpreters say that the plural noun combined with accompanying singular verbs and adjectives are indicative of the fact that God is three persons in one being.[17] Deriving a conclusion regarding God's nature from the grammatical number of a noun is not completely foreign to protestant exegesis. A similar understanding has been offered by some regarding the singular ὄνομα in Matthew 28:19. For instance, Warfield wrote,

> It does not say, "In the names [plural] of the Father and of the Son and of the Holy Ghost;" nor yet (what might be taken to be equivalent to that),"In the name of the Father, and in the name of the Son, and in the name of the Holy Ghost," as if we had to deal with three separate Beings. Nor, on the other hand, does it say, "In the name of the Father, Son and Holy Ghost," as if "the Father, Son and Holy Ghost" might be taken as merely three designations of a single person. With stately impressiveness it asserts the unity of the three by combining them all within the bounds of the single Name.[18]

(New York: Oxford Univ. Press, 2015), 80-81. See also bro. Dalcour's comments in this volume in "The Preexistence of the Person of the Son."

[17] Harris, Archer, and Waltke argue against understanding the plural form as derivative saying, "More probable is the view that *elohim* comes from *eloah* as a unique development of the Hebrew Scriptures and represents chiefly the plurality of persons in the Trinity of the godhead." *Theological Wordbook of the Old Testament*, Vol. 1, 41. Davidson has sought to have his cake and eat it too. He has argued for "'Plural of fullness,' implying 'within the divine being the distinction of personalities, a plurality within the deity.'" Klingbeil, Gerald A., *The Genesis Creation Account: & Its Reverberations in the Old Testament*, (Berrien Springs: Andrews Univ. Press, 2015), 106. See also Sarfati, *The Genesis Account*, 71, 95.

[18] Warfield, B. B., *Biblical Doctrines*, (Portland: Monergism Books, undated), Kindle Ed., loc. 2227.

The normative objection of finding the Trinity in *elohim* is to invoke the plural of majesty. Indeed, most Hebrew grammars and many good interpreters affirm the existence of this literary device, seemingly rejecting the aforementioned theological interpretation as a dead option.[19] Interpreters defending the Trinity in *elohim* have retorted by denying the existence of the plural of majesty, characterizing it as a novel concoction alien to the Hebrews. One often cited example of this kind of rejection is provided by Pauli:

Everyone who is acquainted with the rudiments of the Hebrew and Chaldee languages, must know that God, in the holy Writings, very often speaks of Himself in the plural. The passages are numerous, in which, instead of a grammatical agreement between the subject and predicate, we meet with a construction, which some modern grammarians, who possess more of the so-called philosophical than of real knowledge of the oriental languages, call *pluralis excellentiae*. This helps them out of every apparent difficulty. Such a *pluralis excellentiae* was, however, a thing unknown to Moses and the prophets. Pharaoh, Nebuchadnezzar, David, and all of the other kings, throughout התנ"ך (the Law, the prophets, and the Hagiographa,) speak in the singular, and not as modern kings in the plural. They do not say we, but I command; as in Gen.

---

[19] E.g., Henry, Carl F. H., *God, Revelation, & Authority Vol. II: God Who Speaks & Shows*, (Waco: Word Books, 1976), 185. Murphy, Bryan, 2013. "The Trinity in Creation," *Master's Seminary Journal*, 24/2, 168-172. Joüon, P., Muraoka, T., *A Grammar of Biblical Hebrew*, 2nd Ed., (Rome: Gregorian Press, 2011), 469-473. Blau, Joshua, *A Grammar of Biblical Hebrew*, 2nd Ed., (Wiesbaden: Harrassowitz, 1993), 66. Bornemann, Robert, *A Grammar of Biblical Hebrew*, (Eugene: Wipf & Stock, 1998), 220-221.Waltke, O'Connor, *An Introduction to Biblical Hebrew Syntax*, 122. Waltke and O'Connor identify the plural forms as "Honorifics and the Like," over and against the traditional language of the plural of majesty.

xli. 41; Dan. iii. 29; Ezra i. 2, etc., etc.[20]

Interestingly, in his own Hebrew grammar, Pauli articulates the opposite view:

It must be observed, that the Hebrew often uses the plural to express power, might, excellency, &c., or a superlative where other languages would use a singular only with an adjective. This plural is, both by ancient and modern grammarians, called *pluralis excellentiae*, not only applied to God, but also to inanimate and profane objects, e.g. Judg. v. 26..., *a lordly dish*; Ezek. xlvi. 6..., *a young bullock without blemish*. Great stress has been wrongly laid upon passages where אֱלֹהִים is joined to a verb in the singular, as Gen i. 1.[21]

Either Pauli changed his mind, since his denial of the plural of majesty (i.e., *pluralis excellentiae*) was written thirty-four years before his support of it, or Pauli gave one opinion in his academic work, and another in his popular level work.

---

[20] Pauli, C. W. H., (aka. Rabbi Tzvi Nassi), *The Great Mystery or How Can Three Be One?*, (London: William Macintosh, 1863), 7-8. See also Morey, who after providing the above quotation, goes on to identify the plural of majesty as "An Amazing Hoax" propagated by Gesenius as a "*ruse de guerre* against Christianity." Morey, Robert, *The Trinity: Evidence & Issues*, (Las Vegas: Christian Scholar's Press, undated), 94-95.

[21] Pauli, C. W. H., *Analecta Hebraica: With Critical Notes and Tables of Paradigms of the Conjugations of the Regular and Irregular Verbs*, (Oxford: J. H. Parker, 1829), 164. As an aside, while some unitarians have attempted to discredit Pauli, claiming that he wasn't a Hebraist and never taught at Oxford University, Foster's roster of Oxford instructors demonstrates that he was. See Foster, Joseph, *Alumi Oxonienses: The Members of University of Oxford 1715-1886*, Vol. 3, (London: Foster, 1888), 1030.

Knight, in his *A Biblical Approach to the Doctrine of the Trinity*, has marshaled a defense of the theological interpretation of *elohim*. Knight claims that those who advance the plural of majesty as an explanation are "firmly planted on the speculative approach of the Greeks."[22] Like Pauli, Knight has appealed to the royalty present in the OT, all of which are "addressed in the singular." However, unlike Pauli, Knight has provided a positive grammatical explanation as to how we ought to understand the plural form:

> There exists another usage in Hebrew which may help us to understand the term in question. The words for "water" and "heaven," for example, both happen to be in the plural. Grammarians have called this a quantitative plural. Such a term well describes the concept with which we are dealing. Water is a peculiar substance. It can be thought of in terms of individual rain drops or in terms of the mass of water in the ocean. Yet in both cases it is equally water. In like manner, and in all probability, can we account for the plural vowelling upon the word *Adhonai*, used as a parallel to the plural concept behind the word אֱלֹהִים. We should note that the word, though written as a plural, may be construed with a singular verb. That is to say, what we have before us is an example of this diversity in unity in regard to the nature of God... [23]

Aside from the *ad hominem*, there are several difficulties with this kind of argumentation, and the theological interpretation of *elohim* in general. The term is used of singular individuals, even the Davidic king/Messiah.[24] If therefore, *elohim* is an indication of

---

[22] Knight, G. A. F. 1953. "A Biblical Approach to the Doctrine of the Trinity," *Scottish Journal of Theology Occasional Papers*, No. 1, 20.

[23] Ibid.

[24] Psalm 45:7.

"diversity in unity," then is Christ Triune?[25] Is the Spirit of *elohim* in Genesis 1:2 somehow the Spirit of himself and the other two divine persons? While some might counter this objection by asserting that Yahweh is the archetypal *elohim* and that the term is applied in a secondary manner (i.e., a generic sense) to either singular divine persons or pretenders such as Baal,[26] such a defense is circular.

Other grammatical observations push the point. In Isaiah 45:14-15 the singular form *el* and the plural *elohim* are used interchangeably. The same is true for Ezekiel 28:2 and Daniel 11:36-38. Moreover, those like Knight who promote the theological interpretation have, like Warfield regarding Matthew 28:19, wrongly attributed theological, indeed even ontological significance to grammatical forms without exegetical warrant. In the same way in which it is inappropriate to see the singular "name" of Matthew 28:19 having anything to do with God's essential being, it is arbitrary and a massive leap to attribute this kind of theological significance to *elohim*.[27]

The question remains however, is the plural of majesty a legitimate concept within the Hebrew Bible? Refreshingly, Burnett identifies the plural of majesty as a persistent "nebulous concept."[28] In his study, Burnett assesses a variety of comparative

---

[25] Calvin argued that the logical conclusion of the theological interpretation of *elohim* results in modalism (i.e., "the error of Sabellius"), saying, "If we suppose three persons are to be here denoted, there will be no distinction between them." Calvin, John, *Commentaries on the Book of Genesis*, Vol. 1, 500th Anniv. Ed., (Grand Rapids: Baker, 2009), 70-72.

[26] E. g., 1 Kings 18:21.

[27] Matt 28:19 uses the singular "name" in a distributive sense, relying upon Sharp's rule (#6). See Burgos, *Against Oneness Pentecostalism*, 101-112.

[28] Burnett, Joel, *A Reassessment of Biblical Elohim*, (Atlanta: Society of Biblical Literature, 2001), 3.

linguistic data (e.g., Phoenician, Aramaic, and Akkadian). He notes that "If a 'plural of majesty' was operative in the language of the Canaanite rulers of the Armana period, it lacks unambiguous evidence."[29] Burnett has observed that rather than the plural of majesty *et al.*, the plural form is better understood via its near eastern counterparts as "a variety of the abstract plural, which sums up the 'conditions or qualities inherent in the idea of the stem."[30] An abstract plural "pertains not to the object denoted but to the meaning of the substantive itself."[31] Thus, the plural form *elohim* refers not to plurality in God, but is instead a qualitative reference to God's deity.[32] Thus, "It is the application of this abstract expression in a concretized sense that makes it suitable in reference to a single god ('deity')."[33]

There are however, passages within the Hebrew Bible which buck the normative utilization of *elohim*[34] and display a genuine plurality that cannot be explained as an abstraction.

> And when God caused (lit. Gods they caused) me to wander from my father's house... (Gen 20:13)

The plural of majesty, if accepted as a genuine feature of

---

[29] Ibid., 20.

[30] Ibid., 21.

[31] Ibid., 22.

[32] *The Pulpit Commentary* proposes either a *pluralis trinitatis*, or a *pluralis intensitatis*, which it defines as "expressive of the fulness of the Divine nature, and the multiplicity of powers." It is this second interpretation which comes closest to what Burnett has proposed. Spence, H. D. M., Exell, Joseph S. Eds., *The Pulpit Commentary: Genesis & Exodus*, Vol. 1, (Grand Rapids: Eerdmans, 1961), 2.

[33] Ibid., 26.

[34] The other plural abstract nouns used of Yahweh ought to be understood similarly (e.g., "Makers" in Job 35:10; Ps 149:2; Is 45:5; "Creators" in Ecc 12:1; "Lord" in Ps 8:1-9; Mal 1:6; etc.).

biblical Hebrew, is not present among verbs. Genesis 20:13 displays an absolute grammatical plurality that requires the reader to acknowledge intended plurality on behalf of Moses and Abraham. While there is not specific involvement of the divine Angel in the account of calling Abram from Ur, given the heavy involvement of the Angel in the balance of the Abrahamic narrative his inclusion is virtually expected. Thus the likely reason for the plural forms in Genesis 20:13 is the personal distinction Abraham discerned between the divine Angel and Yahweh.

> He built an altar and called the place El-bethel, because there God had revealed (lit. Gods had revealed themselves) himself to him when he fled from his brother. (Gen 35:7)

Again, we have both the absolute plural *elohim* joined with a plural verb. Looking at the narrative of Jacob wrestling with God in Genesis 32:22-32, it is apparent that only the Angel of Yahweh was interacting with Jacob. However, Genesis 35:1 adds a fascinating element to the narrative:

> God said to Jacob, "Arise, go up to Bethel and dwell there. Make an altar there to the God who appeared to you when you fled from your brother Esau."

Using the third person, God distinguishes himself from God (i.e., the Angel of Yahweh). Given Moses' recognition of this distinction, the plural noun and verb in v. 7 refer to Yahweh and his divine Messenger. Evidently, Moses understood the divine Angel to be the revealer of Yahweh, and subsequently included him in v. 7.[35]

A similar third person reference occurs at Amos 4:11:[36]

---

[35] Cf. John 1:18; Col 1:15.

[36] Cf. Isa 13:19; Jer 50:40. Within both of these texts Yahweh

"I overthrew some of you, as when God overthrew Sodom and Gomorrah, and you were as a brand plucked out of the burning; yet you did not return to me," declares the LORD.

Malone has attempted to explain the third person reference via illeism.[37] However, the explicit personal distinction in Genesis 19:24 annuls such a reading: "Then the LORD rained on Sodom and Gomorrah sulfur and fire from the LORD out of heaven." The prepositional phrase מֵאֵת יהוה מִן־הַשָּׁמָיִם ("from Yahweh from heaven") indicates via spatial and functional distinction that two persons who are both Yahweh are in view, namely, Yahweh and the Angel of Yahweh.[38] Aside from these examples, there are several other passages which indicate trinitarian plurality, if taken in tandem with the other biblical data.[39]

Whereas Protestant interpreters have persistently, although not universally, opted for a theological interpretation of *elohim*, there remains poor reasons to do so. Deriving trinitarianism from the grammatical plurality of *elohim* serves to detract from the genuine Old Testament evidence for trinitarianism.

---

retains the third person distinction.

[37] Malone, Andrew S. 2009. "God the Illeist: Third Person Self-References and Trinitarian Hints in the Old Testament," *JETS*, 52/3, 501. Elledge follows Malone here, and in his dissertation on the subject he completely neglects to assess the significance or impact of the divine Angel. Elledge, E. Roderick, *The Illeism of Jesus and Yahweh: A Study of the Use of the Third-Person Self-Reference in the Bible and Ancient Near Eastern Texts and its Implications for Christology*, PhD Diss., 2015, The Southern Baptist Theological Seminary, 4-5; 85-86.

[38] Cf. Gen 18:1; vv. 22-33.

[39] E.g., Gen 3:22; 11:7; Exod 32:4; 1 Sam 4:7; 2 Sam 7:23; 1 Kings 12:28; Psalm 58:11; Isa 6:8.

THE "HEAVENLY" & "EARTHLY" YAHWEH: A PROTO-TRINITARIAN INTERPRETATION OF GENESIS 19:24

Anthony Rogers[1]

Part I

Introduction

וַיהוָה הִמְטִיר עַל־סְדֹם וְעַל־עֲמֹרָה גׇּפְרִית וָאֵשׁ מֵאֵת יְהוָה מִן־הַשָּׁמָיִם:

Then Yahweh caused to rain on Sodom and Gomorrah sulfur and fire from Yahweh out of heaven. (Genesis 19:24)[2]

Among the many passages of the Old Testament that provide support for the doctrine of the Trinity, passages that have been

---

[1] Anthony is married and has four children. He has written for AnsweringIslam.org, numerous journals and publications, and he works with Dr. David Wood, producing content for Acts 17 Apologetics. He holds an AA in Christian Thought (Christ College), and a BDiv (Greenville Presbyterian Theological Seminary).

[2] My translation and all Scriptural citations, unless otherwise indicated, are from the ESV.

looked upon as significant in this regard by Christians from the earliest days of the Church, such as Genesis 1:26, 3:22, 11:7,[3] *et alia*, is the passage above that attributes the overthrow of Sodom and Gomorrah to the activity of more than one personal agent,[4] each designated LORD or Yahweh. Just as surely as this and other Old Testament passages have illumined the church's understanding of the Trinity, so those outside of the Church have attempted to view them in a different light. Some modern Christians, especially since the 19th century, have capitulated on this as well, not by

---

[3] Q.v. Barnabas (*The Epistle of Barnabas*, ch. VII); Ignatius (*To the Antiochians*, ch. II); Justin Martyr (*Dialogue With Trypho*, ch. LXII, CXXIX); Irenaeus (*Against Heresies*, preface, sec. 4; bk. 4, ch. XX, sec. 1); Clement of Alexandria (*Exhortation to the Heathen*, ch. X); Tertullian (*Resurrection of the Flesh*, ch. V; *Against Praxeas*, ch. XII); Novatian (*Treatise Concerning the Trinity*, ch. XXVI); Eusebius (*Church History*, Bk. 1, ch. 2, sec. 4); Socrates Scholasticus (*Ecclesiastical History*, Bk. 2, ch. 19); Athanasius (*Against the Heathen*, ch. 46, sec. 1-8; *Four Discourses Against the Arians*, ch. XVIII, sec. 31; ch. XXVI, sec. 29); Gregory of Nyssa (*On the Making of Man*, ch. VI, sec. 3; ch. XVI, sec. 5); Basil (*Hexaemeron*, homily IX, sec. 6); Augustine (*City of God*, Bk. XVI, ch. VI; and *On the Trinity*, Bk. I, ch. VII; Bk. VII, ch. VI, sec. XII; Bk. XII, ch. VI, sec. VI).

[4] E.g. Ignatius (*To the Antiochians*, II), Justin Martyr (*Dialogue with Trypho*, LVI, CXXVII), Irenaeus (*Against Heresies*, 3.6.1; *The Demonstration of Apostolic Preaching*, 44), Tertullian (*Against Praxeas*, XIII), Cyprian (*Treatises*, 3.33), Novatian (*Treatise Concerning the Trinity*, XVIII.15-17, XXVI), *Constitution of the Holy Apostles* (5.20), Chrysostom (*Homily on 2 Timothy*, III), Eusebius of Caesarea (*Church History*, 1.2.9), Ambrose (*Exposition of the Christian Faith*, 1.3.22-25), Athanasius (*Four Discourses*, 2.15.13), Hilary of Poitiers (*On the Trinity*, 5.16), Gregory of Nazianzen (*Oration*, 29.17), Basil (*On Proverbs* 7:22), Ambrose (*Exposition of the Christian Faith*, 1.2.22-23), Augustine (*Tractates on John*, 51.3), Cyril of Jerusalem (*Comments on 1 John 1:2*), Socrates Scholasticus (*Ecclesiastical History*, 5.20).

denying that the doctrine of the Trinity is found in the Bible as a whole, but by denying that any of these verses in their Old Testament setting provide certain of the necessary *indicia* for trinitarianism.[5] Some have gone so far as to deny that these Old Testament texts speak to the issue at all, even when the fuller revelation of the doctrine as given in the New Testament shines

---

[5] This denial on the part of some Reformed, Evangelical, and otherwise orthodox Trinitarians largely has its beginnings in the 19th century with B. B. Warfield, who taught that the Trinity was not and could not have been revealed apart from the incarnation of the Son and the outpouring of the Spirit. See Warfield, "Antitrinitarianism," in *Selected Shorter Writings*, Vol. 1 (Philipsburg: Presbyterian & Reformed, 1970), 88, and "The Biblical Doctrine of the Trinity," in *Biblical Doctrines*, (Carlisle: The Banner of Truth Trust, 1988), 139-142. Warfield's view overlooks the analogous and proto-typical realities of the OT centering upon the person, activity, and theophanic appearances of the Angel of the Lord, which anticipate the incarnation of the Son, and God setting His Holy Spirit in the midst of His Old Covenant people, which anticipates the outpouring of the Spirit at Pentecost (q.v. Isaiah 63:7-14; cf. Galatians 4:4-6), a view expressed by Calvin, *Institutes of the Christian Religion*, McNeill, John T. Ed., Trans. by Battles, Ford L., (Philadelphia: Westminster, 1960), 1.13.10. Orthodox writers who deny an OT revelation of the Trinity frequently acknowledge their dependence upon or appeal to Warfield on this point: q.v. Boettner, Lorraine, *Studies in Theology*, (Philipsburg: Presbyterian & Reformed, 1947), 96-106; Bray, Gerald, *The Doctrine of God: Contours of Christian Theology*, (Downers Grove: InterVarsity Press, 1993), 140; Reymond, Robert, *A New Systematic Theology of the Christian Faith*, (Nashville: Thomas Nelson Publishers, 1998), 207-211; White, James R., *The Forgotten Trinity: Recovering the Heart of Christian Belief*, (Minneapolis: Bethany House Publishers, 1998), 166; Kline, Meredith, *Images of the Spirit*, (Eugene: Wipf & Stock, 1999), 22-23; Letham, Robert, *The Holy Trinity in Scripture, History, Theology, and Worship*, (Philipsburg: Presbyterian & Reformed, 2004), 17-33; Sanders, Fred, *The Triune God*, (Grand Rapids: Zondervan, 2016), 22, 209-237; *et alia*.

back upon them. As Shedd observed, this is a modern trend that stands in stark contrast to the entire history of the Christian church:

> The trinitarianism of the Old Testament has been lost sight of to some extent in the modern construction of the doctrine. Patristic, medieval and reformation theologies worked this vein with thoroughness...[6]

---

[6] W. G. T. Shedd, in Augustine, *On the Holy Trinity*, NPNF Vol. 3, Schaff, Philip Ed., (Peabody: Hendrickson, 1995), 47, n3. With the exception of that line of theologians and commentators extending from Warfield, this has been the standard view of Protestants since the time of the Reformation: "Moses clearly teaches this [the Trinity] in the creation of the universe," John Calvin, *Institutes*, 1.13.7; "From the arguments adduced by us before...it might be satisfactorily inferred that it [the Trinity] was revealed and known under the Old Testament... It therefore becomes necessary to establish...the truth of this mystery not only from the New, but also from the Old Testament," Turretin, Francis *Institutes of Elenctic Theology, Vol. I: First Through Tenth Topics*, Ed. by James T. Dennison, Jr., (Philipsburg: Presbyterian & Reformed, 1992), 272; "...it evidently appears that the doctrine of the Trinity was revealed under the Old Testament," Boston, Thomas, *The Complete Works of Thomas Boston*, Vol. 1, (Wheaton: Richard Owen Roberts Pub., 1980 reprint), 144; "The doctrine of the Trinity is revealed in the Old Testament, in the same degree that the other truths of Christianity are; not with the clearness and fullness of the New Testament, yet really and plainly," Shedd, W. G. T., *Dogmatic Theology*, Vol. 1, (Minneapolis: Klock & Klock Christian Publishers, 1979), 261-266; "Thus the Old Testament contains a *clear* anticipation of the *fuller* revelation of the Trinity in the New Testament," Berkhof, Louis, *Systematic Theology*, (Grand Rapids: Eerdmans, 1991), 86; "We expect the doctrine of the Trinity to be taught in the Old Testament but to be much more clearly taught in the New Testament," Van Til, Cornelius, *Introduction to Systematic Theology*, (Phillipsburg: Presbyterian & Reformed, 1974), 220.

It is, therefore, with a view to defending what the church has held throughout the ages that the following chapter, through a protracted discussion of the historic trinitarian interpretation of Genesis 19:24, seeks to demonstrate that the Old Testament, while not as clear as the New, does speak to this issue with sufficient clarity, leaving those who deny that God is Triune in material breach of *both* Testaments. The view of the text herein defended is the same as Leupold's who, like Shedd, also noticed this downgrade trend:

> "We believe the view the church held on this problem from days of old is still the simplest and the best: *Pluit Deus filius a Deo patre* = 'God the Son brought down the rain from God the Father,' as the Council of Sirmium worded the statement. To devaluate the statement of the text to mean less necessitates a similar process of devaluation of a number of other texts like [Genesis] 1:26, and only by such a process can the claim be supported that there are no indications of the doctrine of the Trinity in Genesis. We believe the combined weight of these passages, including Gen 1:1, 2, makes the conclusion inevitable that the doctrine of the Holy Trinity is in a measure revealed in the Old Testament, and especially in Genesis. Why would not so fundamental a doctrine be made manifest from the beginning? We may see more of this truth than did the Old Testament saints, but the Church has through the ages always held one and the same truth."[7,8,9]

---

[7] The First Council of Sirmium in 351 further declared: "Whoever shall explain, 'The Lord rained fire from the Lord' (Gen xix. 24), not of the Father and the Son, and says that He rained from Himself, be he anathema. For the Son Who is Lord rained from the Father Who is Lord.'" Leupold's citation of the accuracy of this interpretation, which

In what follows it will first be shown that this is the correct interpretation of Genesis 19:24 in its Old Testament context, and then it will be shown that this interpretation is upheld and further illuminated by the New Testament.

The Old Testament Case for a Trinitarian Interpretation

A Prima Facie Distinction of Persons

On the face of it Genesis 19:24 appears to point up some kind of personal plurality or distinction within the Godhead, for it speaks of Yahweh doing something from Yahweh. To say the least, this would be an odd and unexpected way of saying that only one person is in view.

> This passage is remarkable regardless of how you deal with it. It simply states that there are two divine Persons. One on the earth and One in the heavens. Each Person is called יְהוָה (Yahweh).

> The first יְהוָה (Yahweh) who is on earth brings down brimstone and fire from the second יְהוָה (Yahweh) who is

---

indeed reflects "the view the church held on this problem from days of old," should not be construed as an endorsement of the entire creed put forth at this council.

[8] For a defense of the Trinity as a fundamental article of Christianity, as well as how this entails the necessity of an Old Testament revelation of the doctrine, see: Turretin, Francis, *Ibid.*, 261-265, 272-277; Gerhard, Johann, *On the Nature of God and On the Most Holy Mystery of the Trinity*, Trans. by Dinda, Richard J. Ed., with annotations by Mayes, Benjamin T. G., (Saint Louis: Concordia Publishing House, 2007), 267-270.

[9] Leupold, H. C., *Exposition of Genesis*, (Grand Rapids: Baker Book House, 1942), 570-571.

in the heavens. It is easy to see why this passage has irritated anti-Trinitarians for centuries.[10]

This *prima facie* reading may particularly be seen from the fact that some non-trinitarians, as well as others who are averse to seeing any indication of the Trinity in the Old Testament, find this text mystifying and insoluble as it stands and so either: 1) opt for charging the text with corruption at this point; or 2) resort to saying that the repetition of Yahweh in the verse is a result of bad editorial patchwork of two different sources.

An example of the first is seen in the words of John Skinner, who makes the following assertion:

"A distinction between Yahwe as present in the angels and Yahwe as seated in heaven...is improbable. We must either suppose that the original subject was 'the men'..., or that מֵאֵת יְהוָה is a doublet to מִן־הַשָּׁמָיִם: the latter phrase, however, is generally considered to be a gloss..."[11]

An example of the second is seen in Claus Westermann,[12] who argues that the plurality is the result of the poor editing of a composite text.[13]

---

[10] Morey, Robert, *The Trinity: Evidence and Issues*, (Grand Rapids: World Publishing, 1996), 97.

[11] Skinner, John, *The International Critical Commentary: A Critical and Exegetical Commentary on Genesis*, (Edinburgh: T & T Clark, 1910), 309. Skinner's *a priori* rejection of an OT revelation of the Trinity is already discernible from his comments on Genesis 1:26: "The difficulty of the 1st pers. pl. has always been felt.... The older Christian comm[entators] generally find in the expression an allusion to the Trinity (so even Calvin); but that doctrine is entirely unknown to the OT, and cannot be implied here," 30.

[12] In his commentary on Genesis 1:26, Westermann says of the

The fact that, on one hand, there is nothing problematic about the text for trinitarians who understand it to be referring to two divine persons, for that's exactly how one would expect it to read on such a supposition, and, on the other hand, that arbitrarily barring a trinitarian interpretation forces some to alter or find fault with the text rather than with their interpretation, constitutes tacit evidence that the trinitarian reading is the obvious reading.

Since this is the *prima facie* meaning, the one that first presents itself to the reader and most naturally accords with the way the text stands written, this interpretation ought to be taken seriously and the evidence offered for it should be carefully weighed and given a fair hearing.

An Exegetical Defense

When we move beyond a simple, surface-level observation of the text and look at the broader context and also analyze the grammar and syntax of the passage, we can see that the apparent

---

verse, "It was often explained in the early church as an expression of the Trinity, the threefold God...but that is a dogmatic judgment...." It appears to have escaped his notice that his dismissal of a trinitarian interpretation of the verse rests on his own dogmatic position that the doctrine of the Trinity is unknown to the Old Testament. However, the context mentions God creating all things by his Spirit (Genesis 1:2) and Word (Genesis 1:3, 6, 9, etc.), something that is also attested elsewhere (Job 33:4; Psalm 33:6, 104:30), and the original audience would have read or heard this verse in light of the threefold saving activity of the Lord, the Angel of his Presence, and his Holy Spirit (q.v. Isaiah 63:7-14). These facts are more than just anomalies that have no place in Westermann's theory, but realities that must forever remain antithetical to it.

[13] Claus Westermann, *Genesis 12-36: A Commentary*, Trans. by Scullion, John J., (Minneapolis: Augsburg Press, 1985), 306.

distinction it makes between two persons called Yahweh rests on solid exegetical ground.

To begin with, in the preceding chapter, which leads into the account of the destruction of the cities of the plain, Sodom and Gomorrah being given full mention as the most prominent among them,[14] we read of Yahweh's appearance to Abraham along with two others, at first identified as men (Genesis 18:1-2, 16, 22), but later as angels (19:1, 15). After supping with Abraham, Yahweh promises to give him a son and announces his intention to judge the cities of the plain for the outcry that has reached heaven. In the process we have the first contextual hints of a distinction of persons, both of whom are identified as Yahweh:

> *The LORD said* to Abraham, "Why did Sarah laugh and say, 'Shall I indeed bear a child, now that I am old?' Is anything too hard for *the LORD*? At the appointed time *I* will return to you, about this time next year, and Sarah shall have a son." (Genesis 18:13-14, emphasis mine)

> *The LORD said*, "Shall *I* hide from Abraham what *I* am about to do, since Abraham will surely become a great and mighty nation, and in him all the nations of the earth will be blessed? For *I* have chosen him, so that he may command his children and his household after him to keep the way of *the LORD* by doing righteousness and justice, so that *the LORD* may bring upon Abraham what *He* has spoken about him." (Genesis 18:17-19, emphasis mine)

---

[14] Sodom and Gomorrah were closely connected to other cities (Genesis 10:19, 14:2, 8), and we are later told that these cities were also involved in the conflagration (Deuteronomy 29:23; Hosea 11:8).

In these passages the Lord shifts from speaking of himself in the first person to speaking about the Lord in the third person. While some may desire to write this off as nothing more than a grammatical shift for rhetorical purposes,[15] it was just this sort of phenomena, so characteristic of divine speech in the OT, that ancient Jews believed was full of significance, especially since it often enough occurs in contexts that are rife with other indications of personal plurality within the Godhead. A foremost example of this is seen in Exodus 24:1-2, which records Yahweh's command to Moses to ascend Mount Sinai as follows:

> Then *he said* to Moses, "Come up *to the LORD*, you and Aaron, Nadab, and Abihu, and seventy of the elders of Israel, and worship from afar. Moses alone shall come near *to the LORD*, but the others shall not come near, and the people shall not come up with him."

Here again we see Yahweh speaking about Yahweh in the third person. Is this just a rhetorical device, or is there a more significant reason that accounts for why the Lord spoke this way, one that may even be discerned from the context? The answer to this question is close to hand: in the immediately preceding context we are told about the Angel/Messenger[16] that God is going to send

---

[15] See Malone, Andrew S. 2009. "God the Illeist: Third Person Self-References and Trinitarian Hints in the Old Testament," JETS, 52/3, 499-518; and Elledge, Rod, *Use of the Third Person for Self-Reference by Jesus and Yahweh: A Study of Illeism in the Bible and Ancient Near Eastern Texts and Its Implications for Christology*, (Bloomsbury: T&T Clark, 2017).

[16] As Burgos pointed out (see above pp. 5-6), the word for "angel" in both Hebrew and Greek is purely functional and simply means "messenger." It does not indicate what kind of being is in view. Depending on the context it can be used for God, one of the heavenly host, or a human being: "The root idea of מַלְאָךְ...is one sent, a

43

ahead of Moses and Israel to lead them into the promised land. This is no ordinary or created messenger, for his voice is to be obeyed and he has the prerogative of withholding forgiveness and punishing rebellion precisely because he bears the very name of God– Yahweh.

> Behold, I send an Angel before you to guard you on the
> way and to bring you to the place that I have
> prepared. Pay careful attention to him and obey his
> voice; do not rebel against him, for he will not pardon
> your transgression, for my name is in him. But if you
> carefully obey his voice and do all that I say, then I will
> be an enemy to your enemies and an adversary to your
> adversaries. (Exodus 23:20-22).

This name-bearing Angel or Messenger is undoubtedly the Angel of the Lord who had previously appeared to Moses at Mount Sinai, "the mountain of God" (Exodus 3:1), "in a flame of fire out of the midst of a bush" (Exodus 3:2; cf. Deuteronomy 33:16), first identifying himself as "the God of your father, the God of Abraham, the God of Isaac, and the God of Jacob" (Exodus 3:2, 6),[17] and then more specifically by his personal, covenant name:

---

messenger, or an envoy. Only in context does the term take on specificity," Battenfield, James, *An Exegetical Study of the [Malak Yahweh] In the Old Testament*, (Postgraduate Seminar: Old Testament Theology, Grace Theological Seminary, 1971), 3.

[17] The Angel of the Lord frequently appeared to the patriarchs and identified himself as their God. For this reason Jacob, when blessing the sons of Joseph, could say: "The God before whom my fathers Abraham and Isaac walked, the God who has been my shepherd all my life to this day, the Angel who has redeemed me from all evil, may he bless the boys…" (Genesis 48:15-16a, my translation). Since the verb, which is forestalled to the end of the verse, is singular (Heb. יְבָרֵךְ; "may

"God said to Moses, 'I Am Who I Am'. And he said, 'Say
this to the people of Israel: I Am has sent me to you.' God
also said to Moses, 'Say this to the people of Israel:
The LORD [Heb. יְהוָה, Yahweh], the God of your fathers,
the God of Abraham, the God of Isaac, and the God of
Jacob, has sent me to you. This is my name forever, and
thus I am to be remembered throughout all generations'"
(Exodus 3:14-15).

This is the same Angel who delivered Israel from Egypt, going
before and behind them in a pillar of cloud and fire (Exodus 13:21-
22, 14:19-20), the one who would later say the following, which
includes distinct echoes of the Lord's promise to the patriarchs, the
preface to the Ten Commandments, as well as Exodus 23:

Now the Angel of the LORD went up from Gilgal
to Bochim. And he said, "I brought you up from Egypt
and brought you into the land [Exodus 20:1-2] that I
swore to give to your fathers [Genesis 13:14-18, 15:1-20,
17:6-8]. I said, 'I will never break my covenant with you
[Genesis 17:7-8], and you shall make no covenant with
the inhabitants of this land [Exodus 23:32]; you shall

---

he bless"), the text identifies the Angel as the God of the patriarchs. The
comments of Gerhard von Rad are on point here: "Jacob's invocation
consists of three titles given to God, each one loftier than the preceding:
(1) 'God, before whom my fathers walked'; (2) 'God, who has been my
shepherd to this day'; (3) 'The angel who has redeemed me from all
evil.' The little hymn reaches the climax of its attempt to identify Jahweh
in descriptive terms in the third title. Any idea that the 'angel' means a
being subordinate to Jahweh is of course ruled out. This too is Jahweh –
but in contradistinction to the Jaweh of general providence, he is the
Jahweh of the specific saving action…," *Old Testament Theology*, Vol.
1, (New York: Harper & Row Publishers, 1962), 287.

break down their altars' [Exodus 34:12-13]. But you have not obeyed my voice [Exodus 23:20; cf. Genesis 22:18]. What is this you have done? So now I say, I will not drive them out before you, but they shall become thorns in your sides, and their gods shall be a snare to you." As soon as the Angel of the LORD spoke these words to all the people of Israel, the people lifted up their voices and wept. And they called the name of that place Bochim. And they sacrificed there to the LORD. (Judges 2:1-5)

Since the Angel of the Lord, about whom the Lord says, "My name is in him" (Exodus 23:20), is mentioned in the context immediately preceding Exodus 24, it answers the question of who the Lord was talking about when he said, "Come up the mountain to the LORD" (Exodus 24:1).[18] In light of this, it isn't surprising to see that ancient Jews came to the same conclusion, thus forcing later Rabbinic Jews to brand them as heretics and come up with clever ways to try and refute them. An example of this can be seen in the Talmud:

R. Nahman said: He who is as skilled in refuting the

---

[18] That the Angel of the Lord is "the Lord" whom Moses was told to come up to on Mount Sinai, where He is also referred to as "the God of Israel" (Exodus 24:9), is confirmed by Stephen in the New Testament: "This [Moses] is the one who was in the congregation in the wilderness together with the Angel who was speaking to him on Mount Sinai, and who was with our fathers; and he received living oracles to pass on to you" (Acts 7:38). It should be observed here that Stephen, a first century Jewish Christian, was speaking to first century non-Christian Jews, and in making this remark he was annunciating a non-controversial premise in order to enforce a particular conclusion. In other words, Stephen's non-Christian Jewish contemporaries shared with him the belief that it was "the Angel of the Lord" Moses ascended to and spoke with on Mount Sinai.

Minim as is R. Idi, let him do so; but not otherwise. Once a *Min* said to R. Idi: "It is written, 'And unto Moses He said, 'Come up to the Lord.' But surely it should have stated, Come up unto me!" — "It was Metatron," he replied, "whose name is similar to that of his Master, for it is written, 'For my name is in him.'" "But if so, we should worship him!" "The same passage, however," — replied R. Idi, "says: 'Be not rebellious against him, i.e., exchange Me not for him [*temireni*].'" "But if so, why is it stated: 'He will not pardon your transgression?'" He answered: "By our troth we would not accept him even as a messenger, for it is written, 'And he said unto him, If Thy presence go not etc.'"[19]

Several things are of note here:

1) While the "Min," a term that is roughly equivalent to heretic, in the above discussion is not explicitly identified, this portion of the Talmud is found in a larger section dealing with other passages used by so-called "Two Powers" advocates, i.e. those who believed the Old Testament spoke of more than one divine person,[20] and it is clear that at least some who were included in this category were non-Christian Jews. In fact, according to the Talmud, this view was even held at one point by the likes of Rabbi Akiva, one of the earliest and foremost sages of Rabbinic Judaism.[21] Moreover, as evidenced by the Memra/Logos theology of the Targums, this view was originally commonplace among Jews of the second temple period,[22] and it was only after the

---

[19] Babylonian Talmud: Tractate Sanhedrin, 38b.

[20] The seminal work on this subject is Segal, Alan, *Two Powers in Heaven: Early Rabbinic Reports About Christianity and Gnosticism*, (Waco, Texas: Baylor University Press, 2012).

[21] Babylonian Talmud, Hagiga 14a, 14b.

[22] Boyarin, Daniel, *Border Lines: The Partition of Judaeo-*

advent of Christianity that it was labeled a heresy and efforts like those found in the Talmud were made to suppress it.[23] Interestingly, there is copious evidence that this view—i.e. the view that the Angel/Messenger of the Biblical text, whether by that name or one of its many cognomens in Jewish thought (Memra, Logos, etc.), constituted a second divine person in the Godhead— even survived the Talmudic attempt to stamp it out and in one form or another continued to exert its influence in certain rabbinic and para-rabbinic Jewish circles up through the Middle Ages, which shows both the tenacity of this idea and just how firmly entrenched it was in ancient Jewish tradition.[24]

Christianity, (Philadelphia: Univ. of Pennsylvania Press, 2004), 89-150.

[23] "In the ancient church liturgy, adopted from the Synagogue, it is especially interesting to notice how often the term 'Logos'…was changed into 'Christ'…Possibly on account of the Christian dogma, rabbinic theology, outside of the Targum literature, made little use of the term 'Memra,'" Kohler, Kaufmann, *The Jewish Encyclopedia*, Vol. 8, (New York: Funk and Wagnalls Co., 1904), 465; "But in the Targumim we meet yet another expression, which, strange to say, never occurs in the Talmud. It is that of the Memra, Logos, or 'Word,' Alfred Edersheim, *The Life and Times of Jesus the Messiah* (Peabody: Hendrickson, 1993), 32; "In the pre-Christian Targums, there is a name for the Word of God, Memra, which recurs hundreds of times. But from the Talmud it has wholly disappeared. Evidently, to go on using it when Christians could point to its realization in a definite historical personage, would have been in the highest degree dangerous to Pharisaic orthodoxy," Eliakim and Little, Robert S., *The Living Age*, Vol. 197, (Boston: Littell and Co., 1893), 456.

[24] See Abrams, Daniel. 1994. "The Boundaries of Divine Ontology: The Inclusion and Exclusion of Metatron in the Godhead," *Harvard Theological Review*, 87:3, 291-321; Idel, Moshe, *Ben: Sonship and Jewish Mysticism*, Kogod Library of Judaic Studies, Vol. 5, (New York: Continuum, 2007); Wolfson, Eliot, *Through A Speculum That Shines: Vision and Imagination in Medieval Jewish Mysticism*, (Princeton: Princeton Univ. Press, 1994).

2) In Rav Idi's attempt to scuttle the Min's appeal to Exodus 24:1, he affirms rather than denies that the verse refers to two persons and that the second person is the Angel of the Lord, whom he calls Metatron, that had just been mentioned in the previous chapter. This, as was intimated above, shows that ancient Jews, even those who were reacting against the even earlier Jewish idea of a plurality of persons in the Godhead, did not understand Yahweh speaking about Yahweh in the third person as nothing more than a rhetorical device. Yahweh, according to Rav Idi, really was speaking about someone else.

3) Rav Idi's attempt to evade the implications of this by reducing "the Angel of the Lord" to a created angel called Metatron lacks cogency. The contention of the so-called "Min" is that Exodus 24:1 has two divine persons in view, i.e. Yahweh has told Moses to come up to Yahweh. Rav Idi's reply is that this refers to the Angel of the previous chapter who can be called Yahweh because the Lord said, "My name is in him" (Exodus 23:21). Since Yahweh is God's distinctive name, the name that is peculiar to him and denotes his eternal self-existence (Exodus 3:14-15), as the Talmud itself says in another place,[25] the Min rightly responds that if this Messenger bears the incommunicable name of God, then he must be God and ought to be worshipped. At this point Rav Idi engages in a game of verbal legerdemain. He points out that "be not rebellious [*Heb.* תמר] against him" can be interpreted as "do not exchange [*Heb.* תמירני] him for me," which is to say, "even though he is called by my name, do not worship him as God in place of me." In response, the Min then points out that such a reading destroys the logic of the text, for it goes on to say, "for he will not pardon your transgression." In other words, only if the text demands absolute obedience to the Angel and forbids any and all rebellion against him does the corresponding reason, i.e. "for he will not pardon your transgression," make any

---

[25] Babylonian Talmud: Tractate Sotah, Folio 38a.

sense. Indeed, this is the same point made elsewhere about the Lord: "Then Joshua said to the people, 'You will not be able to serve the LORD, for he is a holy God. He is a jealous God; he will not forgive your transgression or your sins'" (Joshua 24:19). In a colossal act of sidestepping this response, Rav Idi then points out that Moses rejected accepting an angelic guide in place of the Lord's own presence going before them, which is an allusion to Exodus 33. Conveniently, Rav Idi is given the last word.

While no further response from the Min is recorded, he very likely would have, or at least certainly could have, observed that the Angel spoken of in Exodus 23, whom God originally promised to send before Israel to lead them through the wilderness into Canaan, is not the same as the angel referred to in Exodus 33, whom Moses refused to receive in place of the Lord's presence. After the Lord promised in Exodus 23 that he was going to send before Israel the name-bearing Angel, the very one referred to elsewhere, and for this very reason, as "the Angel of his presence" (Isaiah 63:9), Israel violated the covenant by making and worshipping the Golden Calf (Exodus 32). In response to this new state of affairs the Lord said His presence would no longer go with Israel and He would send an ordinary angel instead: "I will send an angel before you…for I will not go up in your midst, because you are an obstinate people, and I might destroy you on the way" (Exodus 33:2-3). Unsatisfied with this, Moses interceded with the Lord for Israel and pleaded with Him to go before them as he formerly promised (Exodus 33:12-13), after which we read the following interchange between God and Moses:

> "And He said, 'My presence shall go with you, and I will give you rest.' Then he said to Him, 'If Your presence does not go with us, do not lead us up from here. For how then can it be known that I have found favor in Your sight, I and Your people? Is it not by Your going with us, so that we, I and Your people, may be distinguished from

all the other people who are upon the face of the earth? The LORD said to Moses, "I will also do this thing of which you have spoken; for you have found favor in My sight and I have known you by name'" (Exodus 33:14-17).[26]

Since it was in fact the Angel of the Lord who, following the renewal of God's promise that his presence would go with them, proceeded to lead Israel through the wilderness into the promise land (e.g. Joshua 5;[27] Judges 2:1-5), it is proof positive that he is not the same angel whom Moses refused to receive after Israel sinned by worshipping the golden calf. The former was the uncreated Angel/Messenger who bears God's very name and presence, the one whom the Lord promised to send when he established his covenant with Israel at Sinai; the latter was a created angel whom the Lord was going to send instead of his presence when Israel later violated the terms of the covenant,

---

[26] For a trenchant analysis of the inadequacy of Rav Idi's argument from a Jewish perspective, see Boyarin, 2010. "Beyond Judaisms: Metatron and the Divine Polymorphy of Ancient Judaism," *Journal of the Study of Judaism*, 41, 329-333.

[27] There are several reasons for equating the Captain of the Hosts with the Angel of the Lord: 1) He tells Joshua to take off his shoes for he is standing on holy ground (Joshua 5:15), the same thing the Angel of the Lord told Moses at the burning bush (Exodus 3:1ff); 2) he appears to Joshua with "a drawn sword" (Joshua 5:13), an identifying mark since it is exclusively used of the Angel of the Lord elsewhere (Numbers 22:23, 31; 1 Chronicles 21:16); 3) he is now poised, like a mighty warrior, to bring Israel into the land of promise (Joshua 5:13), the very thing God said the Angel of the Lord would do (Exodus 23:20-24) and Scripture later says he did do (Judges 2:1-5); and 4) after this appearance of the Captain of the Hosts to Joshua at Gilgal, the next time we hear of the Angel of the Lord is when it says, "He came up from Gilgal to Bochim" (Judges 2:1-5), which serves as a literary way of identifying the Captain of the Hosts as the Angel of the Lord.

something on which the Lord relented upon the intercession of Moses.

This long exercise shows that, just like the alternation in Exodus 24:1, the shift from first to third person found in Genesis 18:13-14 and 18:17-19 may, at the very least, be viewed as suggestive, even before getting to Genesis 19:24, of the fact that there is a distinction between Yahweh who appeared on earth to Abraham in the form of a man and the one he referred to in the third person as Yahweh.[28]

Second, whatever one makes of the above examples of shifting from first to third person speech in the context leading into Genesis 19, we are clearly told that the events about to unfold are "what I [Yahweh] am about to do (Genesis 18:17)."[29] In other words, as it says even more plainly in the verses that follow, Yahweh Himself is personally going to visit Sodom and Gomorrah and confirm the noxious report that has come up to heaven: "*I will go down now, and see* if they have done entirely according to its outcry, which has come to me; and if not, I will know" (Genesis 18:21). At this time the Lord dispatches the angels who accompanied him (Genesis 18:22), responds to Abraham's plea to save the righteous (Genesis 18:23-32), and finally departs from Abraham to go down to the cities (Genesis 18:33).

In keeping with these things chapter nineteen speaks first of the arrival of the two angels and their deliverance of Lot from the

---

[28] For an extensive treatment of what the Old Testament teaches about the deity and distinct personhood of the Angel of the Lord in the Godhead, see my article series, "The Malak Yahweh: Jesus, the Divine Messenger of the Old Testament," accessible here: https://www.answeringislam.org/authors/rogers/malak_yahweh1.html

[29] See also Genesis 19:14: "Lot went out and spoke to his sons-in-law, who were to marry his daughters, and said, 'Up, get out of this place, *for the LORD will destroy the city*.' But he appeared to his sons-in-law to be jesting..."

city (Genesis 19:1-22), which was then followed by the Lord destroying Sodom and Gomorrah. The point: the Lord, Yahweh, visited Sodom and executed his judgment, just as he previously announced to Abraham. Consequently, when Genesis 19:24 says, "the LORD rained fire on Sodom and Gomorrah from the LORD from the heavens," the distinction drawn is between someone on earth called "Yahweh," the same person who spoke to Abraham, and someone in heaven called "Yahweh," the one who poured out the fire. To state it simply: Yahweh on earth called down the fire from Yahweh in heaven.

Third, in agreement with the context, the grammar of Genesis 19:24, by means of a repetition of the divine name, the first of which is placed at the start of the verse to emphasize the divine cause of the disaster, וַיהֹוָה הִמְטִיר, the latter of which is the object in a prepositional phrase, מֵאֵת יְהוָה, clearly indicates a subject-object distinction and thus demarcates two persons.

In opposition to this some commentators maintain that the repetition of the divine name is simply to stress that the judgment was the Lord's doing and not a result of unguided natural causes. For example, Victor Hamilton states:

> "The repetition of the tetragrammaton at the end of the
> verse should not be dismissed as a doublet or a gloss. The
> twofold use of the tetragrammaton reinforces the fact that
> the disaster that struck Sodom and its environs was not a
> freak of nature. Rather, it was sent deliberately by
> Yahweh himself."[30]

---

[30] Hamilton, Victor P., *The New International Commentary on the Old Testament: The Book of Genesis, Chapters 18-50*, (Grand Rapids: Eerdmans, 1995), 46. Hamilton's aversion to finding the Trinity in the OT is apparent from his comments on Genesis 1:26, where he says: "Needless to say, earlier Christian commentators were prone to see here a reference to the Trinity. But even if one grants that Moses was in some way responsible for Gen 1, it is going too far to call Israel's hero a

If nothing else, Hamilton does not attempt to impugn the integrity of the written text in an effort to deny its trinitarian implications. Nevertheless, what he doesn't achieve by dismissing the repetition as "a doublet or a gloss" he seeks to make up for by reducing it to a redundancy. However, as previously mentioned, while the text does emphasize that Yahweh was the source of the disaster, something accomplished by placing the first occurrence of Yahweh at the head of the verse, to say the prepositional phrase, מֵאֵת יְהוָה, merely perpetuates this emphasis and does not indicate a distinct object is to assign a meaning to the construction that it does not have anywhere else.

Gordon Wenham also maintains that the repetition serves to emphasize Yahweh as the cause without also suggesting a two-fold source, i.e. Yahweh from Yahweh. In an effort that brings out the former and not the latter, Wenham proposes the following translation: Then the Lord rained fire and brimstone upon Sodom

---

trinitarian monotheist! Christian readers of the OT may indeed see a trinitarian context in Gen 1. The question remains whether that was the author's intention. The theological battle of Moses' day was not trinitarianism versus unitarianism," *The Book of Genesis, Chapters 1-17* (Grand Rapids: Eerdmans, 1990). Hamilton asserts without argument that it is going too far to say Moses knew that God is triune, and his comment that Moses was not combatting unitarianism in his day and so couldn't have made a statement with trinitarian import presupposes without argument that every statement in the Bible must have been made in order to oppose a contrary viewpoint. The latter is an erroneous assumption known as "mirror reading" and may just as easily be turned against Hamilton's preferred explanation. After all, the theological battle of Moses' day was not naturalism versus supernaturalism. For refutations of mirror reading, see Stein, Robert, *A Basic Guide to Interpreting the Bible: Playing by the Rules*, 2nd Ed., (Grand Rapids: Baker, 2011), 205-206; Douglas Moo, *NIV Application Commentary: 2 Peter, Jude,* (Grand Rapids: Zondervan, 1999), 129-130.

and Gomorrah: *it was from the Lord, from the heavens.*[31] However, the phrase "it was" does not occur in the Hebrew text and sufficient evidence is lacking to justify rendering מֵאֵת יְהוָה מִן־הַשָּׁמָיִם as a noun clause rather than as adverbial prepositional phrases that modify הִמְטִיר, which is the main verb.[32] In other words, contra Wenham, the text is best understood as saying: "Then Yahweh rained…from Yahweh out of heaven."

Several other attempts at a solution that seek to avoid seeing the Trinity here can be found in Genesis Rabbah, which says:

> Abba Hilfi, the son of Samkai, said in the name of R. Judah: Then the Lord caused to rain, etc. refers to Gabriel; From the Lord out of heaven, to the Holy One, blessed be He. R. Leazar said: Wherever 'And the Lord' occurs, it means, He and His heavenly Court. R. Isaac said: Both in the Torah, in the Prophets, and in the Writings we find a commoner mentioning his name twice in one verse. In the Torah: 'And Lamech said unto his wives: Adah and Zillah hear my voice;' this is not followed by, 'my wives,' but by 'Ye wives of Lamech' (Gen. IV, 23). In the prophets: 'And the king said unto them: Take with you the servants of your lord, and cause Solomon my son to ride upon mine own mule,' etc. (i Kings I, 33) — it does not say, 'Take my servants' but 'Take . . . the servants of your

---

[31] Wenham's presuppositional bias against finding the Trinity in the Old Testament is likewise apparent from his comments on Genesis 1:26, where he asserts: "Certainly the NT sees Christ as active in creation with the Father, and this provided the foundation for the early Church to develop a Trinitarian interpretation. But such insights were certainly beyond the horizon of the editor of Genesis," *Word Biblical Commentary: Genesis 1-15*, Vol. 1, (Grand Rapids: Zondervan, 1987), 28. Exactly where Wenham gets this "certainty" he does not say.

[32] See Barrick, William D. 2001. "The Integration of OT Theology with Bible Translation", *TMSJ*, 12/1, 28.

lord." In the Writings: For the writing which is written in the king's name, etc. (Est. vm, 8). Yet you wonder that the Holy One, blessed be He, mentions His name twice in one verse![33]

Three answers are given here by various rabbis, the first two of which affirm that the double occurrence of Yahweh in the text has two different referents, which, although they attempt to provide a gloss for the first occurrence of Yahweh that fails to fill up the full measure of the term, is a tacit admission that the text speaks of two that are called Yahweh. In addition, only the barest mention is made of Gabriel in the Old Testament, who is referred to only two times, both times in the book of Daniel (8:16, 9:21), and nothing is said on either occasion that would justify calling him by God's own name or that tells us how we may know when a text that mentions "the Lord" really means "Gabriel" instead of "the Lord." If this kind of thing takes place in the Old Testament, where a term can mean something else entirely, which is just to say, Scripture can be "broken,"[34] we can only wonder how often this sort of thing occurs and when the text means what it says. The same problems apply to the idea that "the Lord" sometimes means "his heavenly court."

As for the third answer, namely that it is a commonplace in the Old Testament for a person to speak about himself in the third person, John Owen's response to this view, particularly as taken up and employed by medieval rabbis, is decisive and deserves to be quoted at length:

Aben Ezra answers....that this is the elegancy of the tongue, and the sense of it is, "from himself;" and this

---

https://archive.org/stream/RabbaGenesis/midrashrabbahgen027557mbp_djvu.txt

[34] John 10:35.

gloss some of our late critics embrace. And there are instances collected by Solomon Jarchi to confirm this sense—namely, the words of Lamech, Gen. iv. 23, "Hear my voice, ye wives of Lamech," not "my wives;" and of David, 1 Kings i. 33, "Take with you the servants of your lord," not "my servants;" and of Ahasuerus unto Mordecai, Esther viii. 8, "Write ye for the Jews in the King's name," not "in my name." But the difference of these from the words under consideration is wide and evident. In all these places the persons are introduced speaking of themselves, and describe themselves either by their names or offices, suitably unto the occasion and subject spoken of: but in this place [Genesis 19:24—AR] it is Moses that speaketh of the Lord, and he had no occasion to repeat מֵאֵת יְהֹוָה, were it not to intimate the distinct persons unto whom that name, denoting the nature and self-existence of God, was proper; one whereof then appeared on the earth, the other manifesting his glorious presence in heaven….There is therefore in this place an appearance of God in human shape, and that of one distinct person in the Godhead, who now represented himself unto Abraham in the form and shape wherein he would dwell amongst men, when of his seed he would be 'made flesh.' This was one signal means whereby Abraham saw his day and rejoiced; which himself lays upon his *preexistence* unto his incarnation, and not upon the promise of his coming, John viii 56, 58. A solemn preludium it was unto his taking flesh, a revelation of his divine nature and person, and a pledge of his coming in human nature to converse with men.[35]

---

[35] Owen, John, *An Exposition of the Epistle to the Hebrews with Preliminary Exercitations*, The Works of John Owen, Vol. XVII (Carlisle: The Banner of Truth Trust, 1991), 222, Italics Original.

As Owen correctly points out, none of the examples provided of self-reference in the third person are to the point, for Genesis 19:24 is not an instance of Yahweh speaking, third person or otherwise, but an inspired description of Yahweh acting, and that "from" Yahweh.

Consequently, the trinitarian reading of Genesis 19:24 rests on solid exegetical ground. Non-trinitarian attempts to assert a different meaning are out of accord with the context, contrary to the grammar, and in some cases even require turning Scripture into a book of indiscernible codes where a word actually means something else entirely.

Old Testament Reinforcement

This exegetical conclusion is reinforced elsewhere in the Old Testament. On this score one may especially observe that the distinction drawn in Genesis 19:24 is not a unique phenomenon; neither is it something that is limited to the Spirit-inspired editorial comments of the biblical writers, for it can be found on the lips of the Lord himself. Although it is possible to cite instances in the Bible of passages unrelated to the destruction of Sodom and Gomorrah that draw a distinction between more than one divine

---

Luther's remarks are also worth noting here: "Since the [unbelieving – AR] Jews are audacious, yes, even rash, they explain the particle as a pronoun, so that the sense is: 'The Lord rained from Himself, the Lord.' But who ordered them to have the audacity to do this in the case of God's Book? For if one were at liberty to trifle in this way with Holy Scripture, no article of faith would remain intact. Hence it is characteristic of the unbelieving Jews and of the godless papists to be teachers of the Holy Spirit and to teach Him what or how to write. But let us be and remain pupils, and let us not change the Word of God; for we ourselves should be changed through the Word," *Lectures on Genesis: Chapters 15-20*, as it appears in Luther's Works, Vol. III, Ed. by Jaroslav Pelikan, (Saint Louis: Concordia Publishing House, 1958), 297.

person (e.g. Psalm 45; 110:1; Hosea 1:7; Jeremiah 14:10; Zechariah 2:8-11; 13:7; Malachi 3:1; etc.), it is just as possible, and, therefore, all the more striking, to see that the Lord repeatedly and consistently perpetuates this distinction every time he refers back to this event and mentions the agency of Sodom's destruction.

> "Behold, *I* am going to stir up the Medes against them [i.e. Babylon], who will not value silver or take pleasure in gold. And their bows will mow down the young men, they will not even have compassion on the fruit of the womb, nor will their eye pity children. And Babylon, the beauty of kingdoms, the glory of the Chaldeans' pride, will be as when *God* overthrew Sodom and Gomorrah." (Isaiah 13:17-19, emphasis mine)

> "As when *God* overthrew Sodom and Gomorrah with its neighbors," declares *the LORD*, "No man will live there, nor will any son of man reside in it." (Jeremiah 50:40, emphasis mine)

> "*I* sent a plague among you after the manner of Egypt; *I* slew your young men by the sword along with your captured horses, and *I* made the stench of your camp rise up in your nostrils; yet you have not returned to *Me*," declares *the LORD*. "*I* overthrew you, as *God* overthrew Sodom and Gomorrah, and you were like a firebrand snatched from a blaze; yet you have not returned to *Me*," declares *the LORD*. (Amos 4:10-11, emphasis mine)

These passages complement Moses' description of the agency of Sodom's downfall, thereby providing inspired prophetic commentary on Genesis 19:24. Were someone tempted to say that the way Sodom's destruction is described in Genesis 19:24 is an isolated phenomena, as if for that reason it could be dismissed, or were they to say that these are Moses' words and not the Lord's, as if this objection is any better, the passages just cited would be their undoing, for they provide repeated testimony from God himself that a distinction is in view.

This complementary relationship works the other way as well. Since it is grammatically possible to refer to oneself in the third person—though, as was pointed out above in the discussion of Exodus 24:1, this can't be automatically assumed in every case, and the consistency and frequency of the Lord speaking this way in the prophets of Sodom's destruction is arresting and surely cries out for a more robust explanation—it has been suggested that this is all that is going on in the passages just cited from Isaiah, Jeremiah, and Amos. But this objection is self-defeating as it only serves to underscore the distinction drawn in Genesis 19:24. After all, as just mentioned, it is Moses and not Yahweh who there speaks.

The Nature and Proper Divinity of These Two Persons

The surest proof that both of these persons are truly divine stems from the fact that the name *Yahweh* is applied to both. Contrary to some cultic,[36] occultic,[37] and otherwise sectarian groups of the past and present, Jews[38] and Christians[39] have always

---

[36] For example, this view was held by the Socinians in the past and is held by the Christadelphians in the present.

[37] An example of this can be seen in Barrett, Francis, *The Magus, or Celestial Intelligencer; Being a Complete System of Occult Philosophy* (London: Lackington, Allen, & Co., 1801), bk. 2, ch. 14.

[38] See the Babylonian Talmud, Tractate Sotah, 38a; and Cohen, Abraham, *Everyman's Talmud: The Major Teachings of the Rabbinic Sages*, (New York: Shocken Books, [1949], 1995), 24. The fact that this is the Jewish view makes it all the more disquisitive that some Jews, as evidenced above in the quotes from the Talmud and Genesis Rabbah, would momentarily part with it when attempting to explain away passages like Genesis 19:24, Exodus 24:1, *et alia*.

[39] "But we say that this name is so peculiar to God as to be

taken the biblical view that the name Yahweh, here applied to two persons, is incommunicable; it does not properly apply to creatures.

This is easily inferred from the answer God gave to Moses on their first encounter at the burning bush, when Moses asked God

---

altogether incommunicable to creatures," Turretin, Francis, *Institutes of Elenctic Theology, Volume One: First Through Tenth Topics*, (Philipsburg: Presbyterian & Reformed, 1992), 184; "...Jehovah is the proper and peculiar name of the only true God of Israel;— a name as far significant of his nature and being as possibly we are enabled to understand...," Owen, John, *Vindiciae Evangelicae; Or, the Mystery of the Gospel Vindicated and Socinianism Examined*, The Works of John Owen, Vol. XII, (Carlisle: The Banner of Truth Trust, 1991), 249; "In the name 'Jehovah' the O.T. revelation of God reaches its culmination: no new names are added. God's 'proper name par excellence' is Jehovah ... This name is, therefore, not used of any other than Israel's God, and never occurs in the construct state, in the plural or with suffixes," Bavinck, Herman, *The Doctrine of God*, (Carlisle: The Banner of Truth Trust, 1991), 107; "Hence, from the nature of the case this name cannot be analogically transferred to any creature, however eminent or exalted," Thornwell, J. H., *The Collected Writings of James H. Thornwell: Lectures on the Doctrine of God and Divine Government*, Vol. 1, (Carlisle: The Banner of Truth Trust, 1974), 154; "Jehovah ... has ever been esteemed by the Church the most distinctive and sacred, because [it is] the incommunicable name of God," Dabney, R. L., *Systematic Theology*, (Carlisle: The Banner of Truth Trust, 1985), 145; "[Jehovah], the Name of God, the Name par excellence, in which God's nature is revealed in the highest sense of the word, and by which He is distinguished forever even from the deities of the heathen," Hoeksema, Herman, *Reformed Dogmatics* (Grand Rapids: Reformed Free Publishing Association, 1966), 66; "It [Jehovah] has always been regarded as the most sacred and the most distinctive name of God, the incommunicable name... It stresses the covenant faithfulness of God, is His proper name par excellence ... and is therefore used of no one but Israel's God," Berkhof, *Systematic Theology*, 49.

for his name (i.e., his distinctive or personal name), in answer to which the Lord said:

> "'I Am Who I Am'; and he said, 'Thus you shall say to the sons of Israel, I Am has sent me to you.' God, furthermore, said to Moses, 'Thus you shall say to the sons of Israel, The LORD [Yahweh], the God of your fathers, the God of Abraham, the God of Isaac, and the God of Jacob, has sent me to you. *This is my name forever, and this is my memorial-name to all generations*" (Exodus 3:14-15, emphasis mine).

It can also be gleaned from that other famous passage where Moses asks the Lord for a greater revelation of his glory, a request that is answered by God hiding Moses in the cleft of a rock and declaring his name as he passed by: "The LORD descended in the cloud and stood there with him as he called upon the name of the LORD. Then the LORD passed by in front of him and proclaimed, 'The LORD, the LORD God, compassionate and gracious, slow to anger, and abounding in lovingkindness and truth...'" (Exodus 34:5-6).[40] The following passages also speak to this point:

---

[40] The apostles (and the original recipients of their letters) knew there was an especially sanctified and personal name for God, a name that was exclusive to him and above all other names, for they could simply refer to "the name" without further explanation and expect it to be understood: "For they went out for the sake of *the Name*, accepting nothing from the Gentiles" (3 John 1:7). In addition, when Jesus returned to the glorified position he shared with the Father before the world was created (Jn. 1:1-3; 17:1-5), he received "the name" that is above all names (Eph. 1:20-21), a name that was already his by virtue of his divinity (q.v. John 8:24, 28, 58) but which was also conferred on him as the incarnate Word and victorious Messiah at his exaltation (Phil. 2:5-10). A comparison of the OT verse cited by Paul in this text makes it clear that it was the name Yahweh/Lord (Isaiah 45:23-25).

"I am the LORD, that is my name; I will not give my glory to another, nor my praise to graven images..." (Isaiah 42:8)

"For my own sake, for my own sake, I will act; for how can my name be profaned? And my glory I will not give to another." (Isaiah 48:11)

"Let them be ashamed and dismayed forever, and let them be humiliated and perish, that they may know that You alone, whose name is the LORD, are the Most High over all the earth." (Psalm 83:18)

When confronted with the implications of this for the Trinity or the deity of Christ, many non-trinitarians have been motivated to jettison the incommunicable nature of the divine name and have sought out many devices by which to get around it. None of these efforts have ever been able to successfully withstand refutation, for the name Yahweh, in its strict and proper sense, used without a trope, is never applied to false gods or pagan deities, which are everywhere treated as lies and vanity, and it is never, as such, given to any created individual, place, or thing. The name belongs to the true God alone.[41]

The Personal Identity of the "Earthly" Yahweh

At this point the relevant issue becomes whether or not we can further identify these two persons from the Old Testament. Toward this end it is significant to observe not only the equal divinity of the two as betokened by the use of the name Yahweh, but also the different roles that these persons assume. Whereas in the first instance Yahweh condescends to enter into the world, appears in the form of a man, and holds converse with sinful men, in the second instance Yahweh remains exalted in the heavens, apparently holds converse only with Yahweh on earth, and is not

---

[41] In defense of this, see Turretin, *ibid.*,183-187.

seen directly at any time. Furthermore, though the former, the "earthly" Yahweh, is undoubtedly Lord and sets about to determine the propriety of the impending judgment, he does not exercise his divine prerogative to do so apart from the will of Yahweh in heaven, for he rains down the fire not of or by himself but from the Lord out of heaven. The two act in perfect agreement.

1. The Angel of the Lord

The above consideration strongly suggests that the one who appeared to Abraham and rained fire and brimstone from Yahweh was the Angel of the Lord who is frequently mentioned in the Old Testament.[42]

> Three persons in human form appeared to Abraham. Two of them passed on to Sodom on a mission of righteous judgment; and they are called angels. The third had remained with Abraham; and he repeatedly receives and assumes the name Jehovah. Though he is not expressly denominated the Angel, yet the attendant circumstances are such as agree with other manifestations in which that appellation is used. Upon this passage [Genesis 18:1— AR], the Jerusalem Targum says; 'the Word of Jehovah appeared to him in the valley of vision.' Other Jewish writings have the following explications: 'The Shekinah was associated with them, and detained Abraham until the angels departed.—he said not who he was: but, in all

---

[42] The following are those passages that mention the Angel of the Lord/God by name: Gen 16:7-14; 21:14-20; 22:1-18; 28:10-22, 32:22-32 (cf. Hos 12:2-6); 48:15-16; Exod 3:1-22; 13:21-22 (cf. 14:19); 23:20-33; 32:34; Num 20:16; 22:22-35; Judg 2:1-3 (cf. Exod 34:10-14); 6:11-24, 13:1-25; 2 Sam 14:15-20; 19:26-28; 24:15-17; 1 Kings 19:4-8; 2 Kings 1:1-4, 19:35; 1 Chron 21:1-30; 2 Chron 32:20-23; Ecc 5:6; Isa 9:5 (LXX), 37:36; 63:7-14; Zec 1:7-17, 3:1-10, 12:8; Mal 3:1; and Psa 34:7; 35:5-6.

these [appearances—AR], it was the 'Angel of the covenant.'[43]

Although Genesis 18-19 does not explicitly refer to the one who appeared to Abraham and subsequently overturned Sodom and Gomorrah as the Angel of Yahweh, it is indeed the case, as the following points further demonstrate, that the attendant circumstances perfectly comport with this identification:

First, the distinct possibility that the one who "rained down fire and brimstone…from Yahweh from heaven" is the Angel of the Lord arises from the fact that he is identified as (e.g., Exodus 3:2, 14-15; Hosea 12:2-5) and distinguished from Yahweh (e.g., 2 Samuel 24:16; Zechariah 1:12-13), the very thing we see in Genesis 19:24.

Second, some passages that originally refer to an appearance of God in an unspecified way, that is, they do not further specify that it was the divine, name-bearing Angel, are explained this way elsewhere in Scripture. For example, Genesis 28:10-22 says that Yahweh appeared to Jacob in a dream at Bethel (vv. 13, 16-17), and later in Genesis 31:10-13 we are told that the one who appeared to him was "the Angel of God" (v. 11) and "the God of Bethel" (v. 13); Genesis 32:24-30 tells us that God (v. 30) appeared to Jacob in the form of a man (vv. 24, 25), and speaking of this event sometime later the prophet Hosea tells us it was "the Angel" (12:4-5). The same thing can be seen moving in the other direction. For instance 1 Chronicles 21:14-20 says that David saw the Angel of the Lord who told him to erect an altar, but later in 2 Chronicles 3:1-2 we are told that it was Yahweh who appeared to David on that occasion. These examples create a precedent for viewing other instances of Yahweh appearing, such as Genesis

---

[43] Smith, John Pye, *The Scripture Testimony to the Messiah: An Enquiry with a View to a Satisfactory Determination of the Doctrine Taught in the Holy Scriptures Concerning the Person of Christ*, Vol. 1, (Edinburgh: William Oliphant & Company, 1859), 297.

19:24, along the same lines.

Third, the Angel of Yahweh frequently condescends and appears on earth as a man (Genesis 16:13, 32:24-30; Numbers 22:22-35; Joshua 5:13-6:5; Judges 6:11-23, 13:3-23, *et alia*), just like Yahweh appeared to Abraham as a man in Genesis 18-19.

Fourth, the same thing the Lord said he would accomplish through Abraham, "in him all the nations of the earth will be blessed (Genesis 18:18), the Angel of the Lord said he would do for Abraham: "Then the Angel of the LORD called to Abraham a second time from heaven, and said,…'In your seed all the nations of the earth shall be blessed, because you have obeyed my voice'" (Genesis 22:18).

Fifth, the Angel of the Lord is often the one by whom the Lord executes his judgment (2 Samuel 24:15-17; 1 Chronicles 21:14-17; 2 Kings 19:32-35; Isaiah 37:33-38; Psalm 35:1-2, 6-7), which is what Yahweh does from Yahweh in Genesis 19:24.

Sixth, the narrative flow found in Genesis 17-19, at the center of which is God's appearance to Abraham in human form, is recapitulated in Joshua 5-6, at the center of which is the Angel of the Lord's appearance to Joshua in human form. In both cases the theophany is preceded by an act of corporate circumcision (Genesis 171-27; Joshua 5:1-9) and is followed by the Lord overthrowing evil cities (Genesis 19; Joshua 6). Along with this there are a number of verbal as well as conceptual and factual parallels between these two appearances: even as it says of Abraham, "He lifted up his eyes and looked, and behold…" (Genesis 18:2a), so it says of Joshua, "He lifted up his eyes and looked, and behold…" (Joshua 5:13a); as in the case of Abraham, who saw that "three men were standing before him" (Genesis 18:2b), one of whom was the Lord, so Joshua saw that "a man was standing before him" (Joshua 5:13b), namely the Prince or Captain of the Hosts; as Abraham is said to have "bowed himself to the earth" (Genesis 18:2c), so Joshua "fell on his face to the earth" (Joshua 5:14b). These parallels strongly point to identifying the figure that appeared to Abraham with the figure that appeared to Joshua.

Seventh, in the blessing Jacob invoked upon Ephraim and Manasseh, the Angel of the Lord is denominated "the God before whom my fathers Abraham and Isaac walked" (Genesis 48:15), which echoes what the Lord said of Abraham in Genesis 18:16-21.

Everything said in Scripture about the Angel of the Lord perfectly comports with and strongly supports the conclusion that the one who appeared to Abraham in Genesis 18 and rained down fire from Yahweh in Genesis 19 is, in fact, the Angel of the Lord.

2. The Coming Messiah

Having more specifically identified the "earthly Yahweh" who rained down judgment on Sodom as the Angel of the Lord, we may advance still further in identifying him by observing that the Angel of the Lord is assimilated to and even identified as the coming Messiah.

Before coming to more explicit testimonies, it is well to observe that the possibility and even likelihood that the Angel of the Lord is the coming Messiah arises from several facts:

First, like the Angel of the Lord, the coming Messiah is both identified as God and distinguished from God, sometimes in the same passage (Psalm 2, 45, 110:1; Isaiah 7:14; Daniel 7:13-14). Indeed, the Messiah bears God's memorial name (Isaiah 40:3; Jeremiah 23:6).

Second, because the coming Messiah is God, which entails his preexistence, he certainly could have been active during the Old Covenant period. To say otherwise is to say he sat idly by as God and his Spirit ran the show. The only other divine figure who was active during the Old Covenant period, under the name of which the Messiah could have been active, is the Angel of the Lord.

Third, since the Old Testament predicts that the Messiah would be born as a human being (Isaiah 7:14, 11:1, 52:13-53:1-12), it is not inconsistent to believe that he temporarily appeared on occasion in human form as a kind of foretaste and foreshadowing of what he would do in the fullness of time.

Fourth, it is said of the Messiah, even as it is said of the Angel (Genesis 48:16; Isaiah 63:1-6, 9), that he is the redeemer of God's people (Job 19:25; Psalm 72:12-15; Isaiah 59:20).

Fifth, even as the Angel of the Lord is said to execute God's fiery wrath in Genesis 19:24, so it is said of the Messiah (Psalm 2:10-12; Isaiah 63:1-6).

The above observations provide a strong cumulative basis for believing that the Angel of the Lord is the coming Messiah. But there are even more explicit testimonies that clinch this conclusion:

1) In Micah 5:2 it is written of the Messiah: "But you, O Bethlehem Ephrathah, who are too little to be among the clans of Judah, from you shall come forth for me one who is to be ruler in Israel, whose coming forth is from of old, from ancient days." This passage, which says the Messiah "shall come forth" [Heb. יֵצֵא; literally: "he shall go forth,"] from Bethlehem, and that for the purpose of being the "ruler in Israel," points to the birthplace and therefore the humanity of the coming Davidic ruler. At the same time, in as much as it also says, "whose coming forth is from of old" [Heb. וּמוֹצָאֹתָיו מִקֶּדֶם; literally: "whose goings forth are from of old"], from ancient days [Heb. מִימֵי עוֹלָם; literally: "the days of eternity"]," it also points to the eternal preexistence and past activity of the Messiah. In other words, the Messiah, who will be born and go forth from Bethlehem, has existed from eternity and gone forth on numerous other occasions in the past. Although what

he will accomplish in the future will be more glorious, his going forth at Bethlehem will not be the first time he has appeared on the scene of history. It has been anticipated or preceded many times. Nothing else answers to this accept the numerous goings forth of the Angel of the Lord during and after patriarchal times.[44]

2) Isaiah 9:6 contains the following description of the Messiah: "For to us a child is born, to us a son is given; and the government shall be upon his shoulder, and his name shall be called Wonderful Counselor, Mighty God, Everlasting Father, Prince of Peace." Here again we have the expectation of the birth and humanity of the coming Messiah ("For to us a child is born"), a clear statement of his deity ("his name shall be called…Mighty God"), and an indication that he is eternal ("Everlasting Father").[45] But what is of special relevance in this text is the fact that one of Messiah's titles is "Wonderful," a term that is only used in the Old Testament for God or divine works of redemption and judgment (Exodus 15:11; Psalm 77:11, 14, 78:12, 88:10, 12, 89:5, 119:129; Isaiah 25:1, 29:14), and the Angel of the Lord: "And Manoah said to the Angel of the LORD, 'What is your name, so that, when your words come true, we may honor you?' And the Angel of the LORD said to him, 'Why do you ask my name, seeing it is Wonderful?'" (Judges 13:17-18; cf. LXX, Genesis 32:39). This is no doubt the reason why the pre-Christian Jewish translation of this verse into Greek, which is really more of a paraphrase at this point, reads this way: "For a child is born to us, and a son is given to us, whose government is upon his shoulder: and his name is called the Angel of great counsel."

---

[44] For further treatment of this passage, see Reymond, Robert L., *Jesus, Divine Messiah: The Old Testament Witness*, (Great Britain: Christian Focus Publications, 1990), 56-63.

[45] Regarding the phrase "Eternal Father" see Burgos Jr., Michael R., *Against Oneness Pentecostalism*, 2nd Ed., (Winchester: Church Militant, 2017), 98-101.

3) Isaiah 63:7-14 speaks of the threefold saving activity of "the Lord," "the Angel of his Presence" or "his glorious arm," and "his Holy Spirit" or "the Spirit of the Lord." The text is both retrospective, looking back to what God, the Angel, and the Spirit did in the past in saving and liberating the people of Israel from Egypt (vv. 7-9), after which they rebelled against him (v. 10), and prospective, crying out for the Lord to return and do the same for them in the future (vv. 11-14). Only two chapters earlier, in a text that is clearly Messianic, Isaiah had already predicted that God would do this very thing: "The Spirit of the LORD God is upon me, because the LORD has anointed me to bring good news to the poor; he has sent me to bind up the brokenhearted, to proclaim liberty to the captives, and the opening of the prison to those who are bound; and to proclaim the year of the LORD'S favor" (Isaiah 61:1-2a). If Isaiah's cry for the Lord, the Angel, and the Spirit to come and save his people is to be fulfilled by the Lord, the Messiah, and the Spirit, then the Messiah is the Angel of the Lord.

4) In Malachi 3:1, the Lord through the prophet declared: "Behold, I send my messenger, and he will prepare the way before me. And the Lord whom you seek will suddenly come to his temple; and the messenger of the covenant in whom you delight, behold, he is coming, says the Lord of hosts." Here the Messiah is referred to as הָאָדוֹן, "the Lord," a rare form only used five other times, always for God (Isaiah 1:24, 3:1, 10:16, 33, 19:4), and the temple is referred to as "his temple," two clear indicators of his deity. In addition, he is also referred to as "the Messenger/Angel of the Covenant," which harkens back to passages like Judges 2, where the Angel/Messenger of the Lord referred to the covenant as "My covenant." This prophecy is also verbally and thematically related to Exodus 23:20, where the Lord promised to send the Angel of the Lord to prepare the way before Israel. This prophecy in Malachi is a reversal upon that one: whereas the Angel of the Lord was the Messenger the Lord previously sent before Israel,

now the Lord is going to send an Israelite messenger to prepare the way for the Angel.

In all of these ways the Lord who appeared to Abraham and rained down fire from the Lord is further identified by the Old Testament as the Angel of the Lord and the coming Messiah.

Confirmation from Early Jewish Sources

In light of all that has been said, it isn't surprising, as noted above by John Pye Smith with reference to the Targums, that ancient Jews prior to and contemporaneous with the Talmudic Rabbis also interpreted Genesis 19:24 as a reference to two divine persons. This may first of all be seen in the Targum of Onkelos, which accentuates the distinction found in the Hebrew text when it paraphrases the verse as follows:

"And the Lord rained upon Sedom and upon Amorah sulphur and fire from *before* the Lord from the heavens, and destroyed those cities and all the plain, and all the dwellers in the cities and the herbage of the earth."

More tellingly, the Fragmentary Targum makes the same point by speaking of the first person called Yahweh as "the Memra/Word of the Lord," and the second person simply as "the Lord":

And *the Word of the Lord Himself* had made to descend upon the people of Sedom and Amorah showers of favour, that they might work repentance from their wicked works. But when they saw showers of favour, they said, So, our wicked works are not manifest before Him. He [i.e. the Word] turned (then), and caused to descend upon them bitumen and fire from before the Lord from the heavens.[46]

This paraphrase, where the first occurrence of Yahweh is understood to be referring to "the Word of the Lord," represents a phenomena found through the Targums, where the Word, just like the Angel of the Lord, is both distinguished from and identified as God. So frequently and clearly is this the case that one could not be faulted if he, in an effort to summarize what the Targums say about the Word, said: "In the beginning was the Word, and the Word was with God, and the Word was God." The following citations from the Targums, among the hundreds that could be given, are sufficient to demonstrate the point:

> And I will appoint *My Word* with thee there, and will speak with thee from above the mercy-seat, between the two kerubaia that are over the ark of the testament, concerning all that I may command thee for the sons of Israel. (Tg. Ps. J., Exodus 25:22)

> It was when the ark went forward. Mosheh stood, with hands (outstretched) in prayer, and said, *Arise now, O Word of the Lord, in the power of Thy might, and let the adversaries of Thy people be scattered, and make Thine enemies flee before Thee.* But when the ark rested, Mosheh lifted his hands in prayer, and said, *O Word of the Lord, turn from the strength of Thy anger, and return unto us in the goodness of Thy mercy, and bless the myriads and multiply the thousands of the children of Israel.* (Frag. Tg., Numbers 10:35)

> Be strong and of good courage, fear not, nor be broken before them; *for the Word of the Lord thy God will be the*

---

[46] See also the Tg. Ps. J.

leader before thee, He will not forsake thee, nor be far off from thee. And Mosheh called Jehoshua, and said to him before the eyes of all Israel, Be strong and of good courage; for thou art to go in with this people to the land which the Lord hath sworn to their fathers to give it to them, and thou shalt cause them to inherit. But the Lord, He is the leader before thee; *His Word shall be thy helper,* for He will not forsake thee, nor be far from thee; fear not, nor be dismayed. (Tg. Onq., Deuteronomy 31)

And Jacob vowed a vow, saying, "If the Word of the Lord will be my support, and will keep me in the way that I go, and will give me bread to eat, and raiment to put on, so that I come again to my father's house in peace; *then shall the Word of the Lord be my God.* (Tg. Neof., Genesis 28)

And *the Word of the Lord said* to Mosheh, He who spake to the world, Be, and it was; and who will speak to it, Be, and it will be. And he said, Thus shalt thou speak to the sons of Israel, *EHEYEH hath sent me unto you.* (Frag. Tg., Exodus 3)

And I will set the Shekinah of My Glory among you, *and my Word shall not abhor you,* but the Glory of My Shekinah shall dwell among you, *and My Word shall be to you for a redeeming God,* and you shall be unto My Name for a holy people. (Tg. Ps. J., Leviticus 26)

But the custom of (other) nations is to carry their gods upon their shoulders, that they may seem to be nigh them; but they cannot hear with their ears, (be they nigh or) be they afar off; but *the Word of the Lord sitteth upon His throne high and lifted up, and heareth our prayer what time we pray before Him and make our petitions*. (Tg. Ps. J., Deuteronomy 4)

This day you have made *the Word of the LORD your God to be King over you so that he may be for you a savior God*, [promising] to walk in ways that are right before him." (Tg. Neof., Deuteronomy 26)

There is no God like the God of Israel, whose Shekinah in the skies is thy help, and whose power is in the heaven of heavens. The habitation of Eloha is from eternity, *and the world was made by His Word*; and He will drive out thy enemies from before thee, and will say, Destroy. (Tg. Onq., Deuteronomy 33)

It was this belief, here set forth by way of a distinction between the Lord and his Word, held by second temple Jews before and during the time of Christ, which was part of the background to the "Two Powers" controversy among the later Talmudic Rabbis. In the Babylonian Talmud, right after discussing Exodus 23-24, elaborated upon earlier, we find the following:

A Min once said to R. Ishmael b. Jose: "It is written, 'Then the Lord caused to rain upon Sodom and Gomorrah brimstone and fire from the Lord:' but 'from him' should have been written!" A certain fuller said, "Leave him to me, I will answer him. "It is written, 'And Lamech said to his wives, Ada and Zillah, Hear my voice, ye wives of Lamech;' but he should have said, 'my wives!' But such is the Scriptural idiom — so here too, it is the Scriptural idiom.

The inadequacy of this reply was already pointed out in the above quote from Owen. The relevant observations being made here are simply that this portion of the Talmud constitutes further evidence that belief in more than one divine person was still current during the time of the Talmud's composition, and it shows that one of the passages used by those who continued to hold onto this view of earlier Jews was Genesis 19:24.

While more evidence that Jews before, during, and even after the time of Christ interpreted Genesis 19:24 as a reference to two divine persons could easily be marshaled, what has been presented is sufficient to overturn the overused and wrongheaded appeal anti-trinitarians often make to "the Jews." While it is certainly true that many later Jews, especially those responsible for constructing the Talmud, opposed this view in favor of a unitarian understanding of God; it is also the case, and all the more telling, that this view was the dominant one among Jews before the advent of Christianity, and that even after post-Christian rabbis attempted to stamp it out, no doubt because of its obvious consanguinity with Christian teaching, some Jews still continued to cling tenaciously to it. Consequently, when non-trinitarians appeal to "the Jewish" view of God or "the Jewish interpretation" of a passage in an effort to dismiss a trinitarian understanding, they are really only selectively appealing to a particular group of post-Christian reactionary Jews who are just as certainly opposed to the Christian doctrine of the Trinity as they are to the view that flourished among Jews of the second temple period.

Conclusion

Given what we have found so far, we may at this point confidently conclude that Genesis 19:24, based on an analysis of the context and grammar of the passage and the reinforcement it receives elsewhere in the prophets, all of which was recognized by the vast majority of Jews prior to and at the time of Christ, and not a few afterwards when efforts were being made by many to suppress it, clearly refers to two divine persons. Those who would argue against this thesis must either show that no distinction is in view in Genesis 19:24 between two persons, or provide a defensible reason not to identify both persons as deity. In light of the foregoing, neither of the above projects would seem possible, for a distinction is clearly drawn in Genesis 19:24, and it is drawn precisely between one person on earth called Yahweh and another person in heaven who is also called Yahweh.

THE "HEAVENLY" & "EARTHLY" YAHWEH: A PROTO-TRINITARIAN INTERPRETATION OF GENESIS 19:24

Anthony Rogers

Part II

Introduction

The New Testament never quotes Genesis 19:24. It does, however, say many things about Jesus that are relevant to identifying him as the one who appeared to Abraham and called down fire and brimstone on Sodom and Gomorrah from the Lord from heaven.

The New Testament Witness

In the first place, the New Testament identifies Jesus as God (Matt 1:21; John 1:1, 18, 20:28; Acts 20:28; Rom 9:5; Titus 2:13; 2 Peter 1:1; Heb 1:8)[1] and distinguishes him from God (1 Cor

---

[1] On the accuracy of the text, translation, and interpretation of these passages as references to Christ as God, see "Jesus as Θεὸς: A Textual Examination," in Wallace, Daniel B. Ed., *Revisiting the*

1:3; 2 Cor 1:2; Gal 1:3; Eph 1:2; Phil 1:2; 1 Thess 1:1; 2 Thess 1:2; 1 Tim 1:2; 2 Tim 1:2; Titus 1:4; Phile 1:3).[2] Indeed, Jesus, although distinguished from God the Father, is identified as the Lord of glory (1 Cor 2:8; Jas 2:1), which is just to say, Yahweh (Mark 1:2-3; Matt 3:2; Luke 3:4; John 1:23; Heb 1:10-12),[3] the "I Am" of the Old Testament (Mark 6:50, 13:6, 14:62; Matt 14:27; Luke 21:8, 22:70; John 4:26, 6:20, 8:24, 28, 58, 13:19, 18:5-8).[4]

Corruption of the New Testament: Manuscript, Patristic, and Apocryphal Evidence, (Grand Rapids: Kregel Academic, 2011), 229-266. For comprehensive treatments of the deity of Christ in the New Testament, see: Warfield, B. B., *The Lord of Glory: A Classic Defense of the Deity of Christ*, (Birmingham, Alabama: Solid Ground Christian Books, 2003); Reymond, Robert, *Jesus, Divine Messiah: The New Testament Witness* (Philipsburg: Presbyterian & Reformed, 1990); and Bowman Jr., Robert M., Komoszewski, J. Ed, *Putting Jesus in His Place: The Case for the Deity of Christ*, (Grand Rapids: Kregel Publications, 2007).

[2] While these passages make a clear distinction between God the Father and the Lord Jesus Christ, they simultaneously point to His deity. See "God Our Father and the Lord Jesus Christ," in Warfield, B. B., *Biblical Doctrines*, The Works of B.B. Warfield, Vol. II (Grand Rapids: Baker Books, 1932), 213-234.

[3] It is a remarkable fact that many call into question whether Jesus is Yahweh according to the New Testament, for in the writings of Paul alone, thirty three of the forty-five times an Old Testament passage containing the tetragrammaton is cited or echoed, it is applied to Jesus. This contrasts the twelve times Yahweh texts in Paul are applied to the Father, and yet the identity of the Father as Yahweh is never called into question. See Fee, Gordon, *Pauline Christology: An Exegetical-Theological Study*, (Grand Rapids: Baker Academic, 2007), 631-638. See also, Capes, David B., *Old Testament Yahweh Texts in Paul's Christology*, Library of Early Christology, (Baylor Univ. Press, 2017).

[4] See Rogers, Anthony, 2015. "Mark My Words: The Deity of the Son in the Gospel of Mark," *Puritan Reformed Journal*, Vol. 7.1, 15-30; and "A Word that Bridges the Gap: The Old Testament and Jewish Background for the 'I Am' Sayings of the Logos—the Lord Jesus

As God from God, the second person of the Trinity, Jesus is clearly the New Testament counterpart to the one who appeared on earth in human form to Abraham and other Old Testament saints.

In fact, not only does the New Testament identify the Son as fully God while personally distinguishing him from God the Father, the same reality that comes to the fore in Genesis 19:24, but the relationship between the "heavenly" and "earthly" Yahweh of Genesis 18-19 and the distinct role that each one assumes in that account are equivalent to the relationship and roles assumed and sustained by the Father and the Son according to the New Testament. Occasion has already been given to note certain features of this in relation to Yahweh causing it to rain sulfur and fire from Yahweh, such as how one person remained unseen in heaven and carried out all activities in and through the person who came to earth in the appearance of a man, but this becomes all the more poignant when brought into contact with the New Testament. As Luther observed as he reflected on Genesis 19:24:

> "But we know from the gospel that Christ keeps this mode of speaking [and acting – AR] everywhere; for he relates everything, both his sayings and his deeds, to the Father (John 7:16). He says: 'Philip, he who sees me sees my Father;' (John 14:10): 'The Father abides in me, and I in the Father'; and (John 5:19), 'Whatever the Father does, the Son does the same.' What else is this than what Moses says: Christ teaches, Christ works, but from the Father or out of the Father."[5]

Christ," at the following url:
http://www.answeringislam.org/authors/rogers/i_am_sayings.html#fn_2.
[5] Pelikan, Jaroslav Ed., *Luther's Works: Lectures on Genesis*, Vol. 3, (St. Louis: Concordia, 1986), 297.

Related to the above is the fact that just as Yahweh in the Old Testament came to earth and called down the fire from Yahweh in heaven, so the Lord Jesus according to the New Testament will, in the same manner, come from the bosom of God the Father to judge the world by fire on the last day. The divine prerogative exercised by Yahweh in the Old Testament account of the destruction of Sodom, which itself sets an Old Testament precedent of what God says he does and will do when he comes in his wrath, finds a direct correspondence in the work of Jesus according to the New Testament.

Does the Old Testament speak of the Lord Yahweh as one who will "come in fire and his chariots like the whirlwind, to render his anger with fury, and his rebukes with flames of fire" (Isa 66:14-16)? Then so does the New Testament say of the Lord Jesus that he "will be revealed from heaven with his mighty angels in flaming fire, dealing out retribution to those who do not know God and to those who do not obey the gospel of our Lord Jesus" (2. Thess 1:7). Does the Old Testament speak of God when he comes forth to judge as one whose "apparel is red ... like the one who treads in the wine press" (Isa 63:2)? Then so does the New Testament say of Jesus: "He is clothed with a robe dipped in blood, and his name is called the Word of God ... he treads the wine press of the fierce wrath of God, the Almighty" (Rev 19:11-15). And does the Old Testament speak of "the breath of Yahweh, like a stream of burning sulfur" setting a wicked land ablaze (Isa 30:33)? Even so the New Testament says that the Lord Jesus will "overthrow with the breath of his mouth and destroy by the splendor of his coming" (2 Thess 2:8), ultimately casting the wicked into the lake that burns with fire and brimstone (Matt 25:41-46; Rev 14:9-11, 19:20-21, 20:11-15).

The New Testament speaks of the Lord Jesus exercising this divine prerogative in a way that exactly corresponds to what Yahweh is said to do according to the Old Testament, and it also does so in a way that could hardly be passed over in its specific relevance to the destruction of Sodom and Gomorrah.

> "For the Son of Man in his day will be like the lightning
> which flashes and lights up the sky from one end to the
> other. But first he must suffer many things and be rejected
> by this generation … It was the same in the days of Lot.
> People were eating and drinking, buying and selling,
> planting and building. *But the day Lot left Sodom, fire and
> sulfur rained down from heaven and destroyed them all. It
> will be just like this on the day the Son of Man is
> revealed."* (Luke 17:24-25, 28-30)

In comparing the destruction of Sodom and Gomorrah by fire to
the conflagration that the apostles predicted Christ would carry out
on a much larger scale in the future, the New Testament
unmistakably casts Jesus in the same role as the "Earthly" Yahweh
of Genesis 18-19.

Second, through various lines of evidence it may be
determined from the New Testament that Jesus is the Angel of the
Lord. As shown previously, it was specifically that member of the
Godhead known in the Old Testament as the Angel of the Lord
who appeared to Abraham, and in certain places he was referred to
by the Jewish Targumim as the Word of the Lord. The apostle
John was certainly familiar with the teachings of the Targums,[6]
and he explicitly ascribed this cognomen to Christ (John 1:1, 14; 1
John 1:1-5; Rev 19:13). It was also shown that the promised
Messiah spoken of in Isaiah 9 is the Angel of the Lord, for his
name is Wonderful, a title only otherwise given to the Angel of the
Lord (Judges 13:17-18), a fact recognized by the Jewish translators

---

[6] See Ronning, John, *The Jewish Targums and John's Logos
Theology*, (Peabody, Hendrickson, 2010); and 2007. "The Targum of
Isaiah and the Johannine Literature," *Westminster Theological Journal*,
Vol. 69, No. 2, 247-278.

of the Septuagint when they referred to the Messiah as "the Angel of Great Counsel" (Isa 9:5, LXX). The New Testament quotes from the larger context of this passage and locates its fulfillment in Jesus (e.g. Matt 4:15-16; Luke 1:79; cf. Isa 9:1-2), for he is the Son who was given (John 3:16; cf. Isa 9:6) and is the One who was destined to fulfill the ancient promises made to David that one of his descendants would be raised up and seated on the throne (Luke 1:32-33; cf. Isa 9:7). As well, the Angel of the Covenant (q.v. Gen 16:7, LXX), whose coming was predicted by the prophet Malachi (Mal 3:1), is identified in the New Testament as Jesus (Mark 1:2-11; Matt 11:10).[7]

---

[7] Although the meaning is debated, potential support for this may also be found in what Paul said to the Galatians: "...you did not scorn or despise me, but received me as an angel of God, as Christ Jesus" (Gal 4:14). The Greek reads as follows: ἀλλὰ ὡς ἄγγελον θεοῦ ἐδέξασθέ με, ὡς Χριστὸν Ἰησοῦν. If this is a reference to the Angel of the Lord, the anarthrous ἄγγελον θεοῦ may be understood as definite, which is also how the definite construction in the Hebrew text is rendered in the LXX, and ὡς Χριστὸν Ἰησοῦν may be understood appositionally. On this understanding, Paul should then be understood as saying, "you.... received me as the Angel of God, namely Christ Jesus." Interestingly, there is precedent for this way of speaking in the Old Testament: "On that day the LORD will protect the inhabitants of Jerusalem, so that the feeblest among them on that day shall be like David, and the house of David shall be like God, like the Angel of the LORD, going before them" (Zec 12:8; cf. 2 Sam 19:27). As in the passage in 2 Samuel, where "like the Angel of the LORD" further explains "like God," if this reading of Paul's statement in Galatians 4 is correct it would indicate that "as Christ Jesus" further explains "as the Angel of God." As such it would not be an indication that Jesus is a created angel, an idea Paul repudiates elsewhere (Col 1:15-17, 2:8-10, 18; cf. Heb 1-2), but the uncreated divine messenger of the Old Testament. As is evident from 1 Corinthians 10, where Christ is identified by Paul as the one who guided Israel in the wilderness, which is certainly a reference to the Angel of the Lord (Exod 3:1-22, 14:19, 23:20-25, 33:14-15; Judg 2:1-5; Isa 63:7-14), this

In addition to the above, there are a number of times in the gospels where Old Testament events featuring the Angel of the Lord are conspicuously reenacted by Jesus in the New Testament. Most worthy of note here in light of the previous discussion of Exodus 23-24 is how the Sinai theophany is mirrored at the transfiguration. While it may easily be discerned that the transfiguration, in fulfillment of what was shadowed forth at Sinai and predicted in Deuteronomy 18:15-22, presents Jesus as a new Moses,[8] nevertheless, it also presents Jesus as the Angel of the Lord.

In Exodus 24:1 Yahweh told Moses to come up to Yahweh on Sinai, which means that there were at least two divine persons involved in the Sinai theophany, one of whom, as previously demonstrated, was the name-bearing Angel whose voice Moses and Israel were told to listen to in Exodus 23. This was confirmed by Stephen in the New Testament when he said, "This [Moses] is the one who was in the congregation in the wilderness with the Angel who spoke to him at Mount Sinai, and with our fathers. He received living oracles to give to us" (Acts 7:38). Similarly on the mount of transfiguration, we again meet with two divine persons on a mountain, namely the Father and the Son. On this occasion, the Father said, "This is my beloved Son, listen to him" (Mark 9:7; par. Matt 17:5; Luke 9:35). Just as God told Israel in the Old

---

grammatically possible interpretation is in keeping with his theology.

[8] For example, just as Moses took three people with him, Aaron, Nadab, and Abihu (Exod 24:1, 9), and after six days entered into the cloud (Exod 24:15-18), as a result of which "the skin of his [Moses'] face shone because of his speaking with him [Yahweh]" on the mountain (Exod 34:29), so Jesus, after six days, took three people with him, Peter, James, and John (Matt 17:1), and "was transfigured before them; and his face shone like the sun, and his garments became as white as light" (Matt 17:2).

Testament to render absolute obedience to the Angel, so God the
Father in the New Testament says absolute obedience is to be
rendered unto the Son.[9]

Accordingly the transfiguration shows Jesus to be both the
New Moses/Messiah and the Angel of the Lord. Moreover this is
exactly what the Old Testament itself was pointing to as may be
seen by carefully attending to the words of Exodus 23:21 and
Deuteronomy 18:15:

> A[n]…indicator of the oneness of Yahweh and his 'angel'
> is the way the angel's authority is commended: "Pay
> attention to him and listen to what he says [שְׁמַע בְּקֹלוֹ]"
> (23:21). The Hebrew idiom (שָׁמַע בְּקֹל) usually translated
> "listen to" is actually a *terminus technicus* of covenantal
> literature. It means in effect "to obey" and is used
> routinely vis-à-vis Yahweh in his covenant dealing with
> Israel. In other words, it is normally Yahweh's "voice"
> that Israel must "obey"-but now it is the voice of
> Yahweh's "angel." The covenantal background of the
> phrase thus implies an identity of Yahweh and the angel.
> The same phraseology is echoed later, when Moses
> describes the prophet to come: "Yahweh your God will
> raise up for you a prophet like me from among your own
> brothers. You must listen to him [אֵלָיו תִּשְׁמָעוּן]" (Dt 18:15).
> The prophet to come is identified as Christ in Acts 3:22-
> 23. The Horeb/Sinai theophany shows the need for such a
> prophet, who must be God himself (and as such, must be
> obeyed).[10]

---

[9] It is also of interest that David's description of the Lord
ascending from Sinai in Psalm 68 is applied to the ascension Christ in
Ephesians 4:7-16.

[10] Niehaus, Jeffrey J., *God at Sinai: Covenant & Theophany in*

Since the Angel of the Lord is identified elsewhere as the coming Messiah, this shouldn't be surprising. Indeed, one of the prophecies already looked at that equates the Angel with the coming Messiah even does so by echoing the words of Exodus 23:20:

"Behold, I am going to send an Angel before you to guard you along the way

[הִנֵּה אָנֹכִי שֹׁלֵחַ מַלְאָךְ לְפָנֶיךָ לִשְׁמָרְךָ בַּדָּרֶךְ] and to bring you into the place which I have prepared." (Exodus 23:20)

"Behold, I am going to send My messenger, and he will clear the way before Me

[הִנְנִי שֹׁלֵחַ מַלְאָכִי וּפִנָּה־דֶרֶךְ לְפָנָי]. And the Lord, whom you seek, will suddenly come to His temple; and the Angel of the covenant, in whom you delight, behold, He is coming," says the Lord of hosts. (Malachi 3:1)

A marked difference between these two passages is that it was the Angel in Exodus 23 whom God was sending before Israel, while in Malachi 3:1 it is a representative Israelite whom God is going to send as a messenger or herald before the Angel, the latter of whom is also referred to as "the Lord" who will come to "His temple."[11] Significantly Malachi associates the messenger who will prepare the way with Elijah (Mal 4:5-6), who also encountered the Lord on Mount Sinai (1 Kings 19), and who appeared together with Moses on the mount of transfiguration to speak once again with Jesus. For Moses and Elijah, encountering the Son on a mountain would have been an all too familiar experience.

---

the Bible and Ancient Near East, Studies in Old Testament Biblical Theology, (Grand Rapids: Zondervan, 1995), 194-195.

[11] See Robertson, O. Palmer, The Christ of the Prophets, (Philipsburg: Presbyterian & Reformed, 2004), 401.

Since the New Moses/Messiah is the divine Angel of the Lord by whom God spoke to the fathers through prophets like Moses and Elijah the Lord Jesus Christ, having now come in the flesh to speak directly to his people in these last days, is superior to all other prophets and the revelation brought by him is complete and final. As the author of Hebrews said:

> Long ago, at many times and in many ways, God spoke to our fathers through the prophets, but in these last days he has spoken to us by his Son, whom he appointed the heir of all things, through whom also he created the world. He is the radiance of the glory of God and the exact imprint of his nature, and he upholds the universe by the word of his power. After making purification for sins, he sat at the right hand of the Majesty on high… (Hebrews 1:1-3).

While Moses reflected the glory of God because he spoke face to face with the Angel of the Lord on Mount Sinai, the glory of Christ seen on the mount of transfiguration was the radiance, outshining, or effulgence of the glory that properly belongs to him as the exact imprint of the Father's nature.

Third, from the fact that Jesus in the New Testament is identified as God and as the distinct divine figure known previously under the title "the Angel of the Lord," it follows from the apostolic testimony that Jesus is both preexistent and the subject of earlier theophanies to the patriarchs and Israel, including Abraham. The soundness of this inference requires no further support and yet the New Testament is rife with explicit statements that Jesus, as a fully divine person, the eternal creator of everything (John 1:1-3, 10; 1 Cor 8:6; Rev 3:14), including the ages (Heb 1:2), is before all things (Col 1:15-17; Heb 7:3; Rev 1:8, 17, 3:14, 22:13, 16), and that he was sent out or came down from the Father from heaven into the world at the time of his incarnation (Matthew 5:17, 8:29, 9:13 [par. Mark 2:17; Luke 5:32], 10:34 [par.

Luke 12:51, v. 35; 20:28 [par. Mark 10:45]; Mark 1:24 [par. Luke
4:34], 1:38 [par. Luke 4:43]; Luke 12:49; 19:10; John 3:13, vv. 17;
4:34; 5:24, vv. 30, 36, 37, 38; 6:29, vv. 32-33, 41, 42, 44, 50-51,
57-58, 62; 7:16, vv. 18, 28-29, 33; 9:4, v. 39; 10:36; 12:44-50;
13:3, vv. 16, 20; 15:21, v. 22; 16:5, vv. 27-28; 17:3, vv. 5, 8, 18,
21, 23, 25; 18:37; 20:21; Rom 8:3-4; Gal 4:4; 1 Tim 1:5; Heb 7:3;
1 Pet 1:20).[12]

Since Jesus is the eternal God and preexistent Angel of the
Lord: the author of Hebrews could say that Moses, in choosing to
identify with the Lord and his people rather than Pharaoh and the
Egyptians, "considered the reproach of Christ greater wealth than
the treasures of Egypt" (Heb 11:26); Jude could say that it was the
Lord Jesus who rescued the people out of Egypt and later
destroyed those who did not believe (Jude 1:5); the apostle Paul
could say that Jesus was the spiritual Rock that followed the
people of Israel (1 Cor 10:4, v. 9; cf. Exod 14; Deut 32:1-43); and
John could say that it was the Lord Jesus who appeared to Isaiah in
his vision of Yahweh seated on his throne (Isa 6; cf. John 12).
Most pointedly, and also comprehensively, this is why John could
conclude the prologue to his gospel by saying: "No one has ever
seen God; the only God, who is at the Father's side, he has made
him known" (John 1:18). In other words, while Jesus did not
become flesh until the first century, he was always the one who
temporarily assumed a human form and revealed God to men in
past ages. This also entails that all previous appearances of
Yahweh in a human form in the Old Testament, which was a

---

[12] For a full treatment of the import of the passages cited from
the synoptic Gospels as they pertain to Christ's preexistence, see
Gathercole, Simon, *The Preexistent Son: Recovering the Christologies of
Matthew, Mark, and Luke,* (Grand Rapids: Eerdmans, 2006). On the New
Testament witness as a whole, see McCready, Douglas, *He Came Down
From Heaven: The Preexistence of Christ and the Christian Faith*
(Downers Grove: InterVarsity Press, 2005).

schoolmaster to lead men to Christ (Gal 3:24), may therefore be viewed as a foretaste and anticipation of what happened in the fullness of time when "God sent forth his Son, born of a woman, born under the law, to redeem those who were under the law, that we might receive the adoption as sons" (Gal 4:4).

In keeping with all of the above, a final section of Scripture of special relevance to identifying the divine persons denominated Yahweh in Genesis is found in John 8:12-59. In the midst of a lengthy debate with the religious leaders Jesus makes several statements about his divine identity, preexistence, and personal familiarity with Abraham, all of which lead inexorably to the conclusion that the theophany in Genesis 18-19 was an appearance of the preincarnate Lord Jesus.[13]

There are at least two ways in John 8 that Jesus identifies himself as a divine person. He does this first of all by referring to God as his Father and to himself as the Son (John 8:16, vv. 18, 19, 28, 36, 38, 49, 54). This is clearly an indication of deity in John's gospel, for while others may become the children of God, they receive this right through Jesus (John 1:12), who is the only begotten or unique Son of the Father (John 1:14; 3:16, v. 18; cf. 1 John 4:9). As God's unique Son Jesus is equal to the Father, one with him in his essential nature, and can do all that the Father does (John 5:1-47, esp. vv. 17-8; John 1:1; 10:22-42).[14]

A second way John 8 evinces the deity of Christ is found in Jesus' "I Am" statements, a divine self-asseveration or identification formula used by Yahweh several times in the Old Testament. Jesus self-referentially uses this formula three times in

---

[13] For more on this, see Hiram Diaz's essay, "Yahweh: A Man Who Told Abraham the Truth," in this volume.

[14] An especially profitable treatment of Christ's Sonship in John's gospel may be found in Murray, John, "Jesus the Son of God," in *Collected Writings of John Murray*, (Carlisle: The Banner of Truth Trust, 1982), 4:58–81. See also Morris, Leon, *Jesus is the Christ: Studies in the Theology of John*, (Grand Rapids: Eerdmans, 1989), 89–106.

John 8: "I told you that you would die in your sins, for unless you believe that I Am, you will die in your sins" (v. 24, author's trans.); "So Jesus said to them, 'When you have lifted up the Son of Man, then you will know that I Am...'" (v. 28, author's trans.); "Jesus said to them, 'Truly, truly, I say to you, before Abraham became, I Am'" (v. 58, author's trans.).

Although this self-identification formula has traditionally been related directly back to Exodus 3:14, where God referred to Himself as "I Am Who I Am" and told Moses to tell the Israelites "I Am" was sending him to them (Exod 3:14), it has become more and more apparent to commentators that the Old Testament background of direct relevance is found in the seven *ani hu* declarations of Yahweh that occur in Deuteronomy and Isaiah.[15] In part, this is because the "I Am" sayings of Christ in the New Testament are not identical to the Septuagintal rendering of Exodus 3:14 (*egō eimi ho ōn*), which contains a predicate,[16] but

---

[15] "...by their formulation, the 'I am' sayings without an image [i.e. absolute, without a predicate—AR] appeal to the ani hu of Second Isaiah so that Jesus is identified with the words, acts and nature of God," Ball, David M., 1993. "'I Am' In Context," *Tyndale Bulletin*, 44:1, 180; "The Hebrew expression אֲנִי הוּא has long been regarded as providing the key to a proper understanding of the absolute use of ἐγώ εἰμι in the Fourth Gospel," Williams, Catrin H., *I Am He: The Interpretation of Ani Hu in Early Jewish and Early Christian Literature*, (Tübingen: Mohr Siebeck, 2000), 1; "Although this view has fallen into disfavor in some circles in recent times, it is still nonetheless almost certainly correct, and continues to be supported by the majority of scholars," McGrath, James, *John's Apologetic Christology: Legitimation and Development in Johannine Christology*, (New York: Cambridge University Press, 2001), p. 104.

[16] While the Septuagint rendering of Exodus 3:14 may be challenged, for which reason its background relevance to Christ's sayings ought not to be completely dismissed, the fact remains that it is the Greek rendering of the *ani hu* declarations that are most directly

they are identical to the way the Septuagint ordinarily renders the *ani hu* declarations of Yahweh that are found in Deuteronomy 32:39 and Isaiah 41:4; 43:10, v. 13; 46:4; 48:12; 52:6. Unlike the Greek translation of Exodus 3:14 the latter are both emphatic and absolute.[17]

As the eternal I Am, Jesus also speaks of his preexistence in John 8. He does this by telling his opponents that he is "going away" and that they will not be able to go where he is going (8:21-22) precisely because he is "from above" and they are "from below" (8:23). Since he is from above, he also tells them that he "came from God" (8:42) and was "sent" by the Father (8:16, vv. 18, 26, 29, 42) to teach what he saw and heard in the Father's presence (8:26, vv. 28, 38, 40).

---

relevant to Christ's "I Am" sayings. In addition to the fact that the Greek translation of this Hebrew identification formula is identical to the sayings of Christ in the New Testament, note the further similarities between the Greek of: Isaiah 52:6 and John 4:26, both of which have: *ego eimi, ho lalon*; Isaiah 43:10 and John 8:58, both of which feature a contrast between *ego eimi* and *egeneto* (cf. Psalm 90:1-2); and Isaiah 43:10 and John 13:19, both of which have: *hina pisteusete...hoti ego eimi*. For more on this, see Ball, David M., 1996. "'I Am' in John's Gospel: Literary Function, Background and Theological Implications," *JSNTS*, (Sheffield: Sheffield Academic Press), 124.

[17] Isaiah 43:13 and 48:12 are exceptions to the rule. However, while the LXX does not stick to its own pattern of translating הוּא אֲנִי as ἐγώ εἰμι in these two cases, it does add an additional "I Am" in its translation of Isaiah 46:4, another in Isaiah 45:18 as a translation of יְהוָה אֲנִי, and the same Hebrew expression in the following verse, 45:19, is translated ἐγώ εἰμι ἐγώ εἰμι κύριος. Finally, it also translates a related Hebrew expression, אָנֹכִי אָנֹכִי הוּא, as ἐγώ εἰμι ἐγώ εἰμι in Isaiah 43:25 and 51:12. The LXX translation of Isaiah 52:6 is not an exception here when it translates it ἐγώ εἰμι αὐτός, for this is to make what is already emphatic even more so. In any case, the same expression is found on the lips of Jesus in Luke 24:39.

It is in the context of these remarks that Jesus speaks of knowing and being known by Abraham. After telling the Jews that his Word can set them free, to which they object that they are Abraham's descendants and have never been in slavery to anyone (8:31-33), we read:

> "Jesus answered them, 'Truly, truly, I say to you, everyone who commits sin is the slave of sin. The slave does not remain in the house forever; the son does remain forever. So if the Son makes you free, you will be free indeed. I know that you are Abraham's descendants; yet you seek to kill Me, because My word has no place in you. I speak the things which I have seen with My Father; therefore you also do the things which you heard from your father'" (8:34-38)

While Jesus explicitly acknowledges that the Jews are descendants of Abraham in one sense, he implies that in a more important sense they are not. After all, while the Jews are descendants of Abraham, they are showing by their actions that God's word has no place in them, something that could not be said of Abraham. In effect, Jesus is intimating a distinction between the biological and spiritual lineage of his detractors: they are sons of Abraham after the flesh, but their works indicate that they are not of faith along with Abraham, and so they are not children of the promise or Abraham's spiritual heirs (Romans 4:1-25, 9:6-13; Galatians 3:1-29). Here it is significant to note that the work that calls their Abrahamic sonship into question is the fact that they are seeking to kill Jesus ("I know that you are Abraham's descendants, yet you seek to kill me").

This is followed by the Jews insisting all the more stridently that Abraham is their father, and the point that Jesus originally made is now stated more forcefully: "They answered and said to him, 'Abraham is our father.' Jesus said to them, 'If you are Abraham's children, do the deeds of Abraham. But as it is,

you are seeking to kill me, a man who has told you the truth, which
I heard from God; this Abraham did not do'" (8:39-40). According
to Jesus the Jews are not Abraham's children because they are not
doing the deeds of Abraham, and this is especially evidenced by
the fact that they are seeking to kill him. "You are seeking to kill
me" is the antecedent of the phrase "this Abraham did not do." In
other words, Abraham did not seek to kill Jesus like those who
now claim to be his children. This presupposes an occasion when
Abraham, like the Jews in John 8, knew Jesus face to face.

That Jesus is claiming to have face to face knowledge of
Abraham, a fact the Jews in their dullness at first seem to overlook,
becomes all the more apparent from what follows later in the
context. After Jesus goes on to say, "Truly, truly, I say to you, if
anyone keeps my word, he will never see death" (8:51), the Jews
recognize that Jesus is claiming to be superior to Abraham and all
the prophets and so question him about his identity:

> "The Jews said to him, "Now we know that you have a
> demon! Abraham died, as did the prophets, yet you
> say, 'If anyone keeps my word, he will never taste death.'
> Are you greater than our father Abraham, who died? And
> the prophets died! Who do you make yourself out to be?"
> (8:52-53)

In response, Jesus once again claims to be the divine Son of God
and asserts his personal familiarity with Abraham, for Abraham
rejoiced at the prospect of seeing Jesus' day, meaning the day of
his visitation, and instead of trying to kill him was full of gladness:

> Jesus answered, "If I glorify myself, my glory is nothing.
> It is my Father who glorifies me, of whom you say, 'He is
> our God.' But you have not known him. I know him. If I
> were to say that I do not know him, I would be a liar like
> you, but I do know him and I keep his word. Your father

Abraham rejoiced that he would see my day. He saw it
and was glad.'" (8:54-56).

Finally getting the point, the Jews give voice to what they take to
be an incongruity between Jesus' statement and their belief that he
is not old enough to have seen Abraham, who lived millennia
before Jesus was born: "So the Jews said to him, 'You are not yet
fifty years old, and have you seen Abraham" (8:57)?

In this section Jesus claims that Abraham never tried to kill
him but instead received his word, looked forward to the day of his
visitation, and rejoiced and was glad when it came to pass. This
can refer to no other occasion than Genesis 18 when the Angel of
the Lord appeared to Abraham to announce the destruction of
Sodom and Gomorrah (18:16-33) and to announce the coming
birth of a son (18:9-15). On that occasion, rather than try to kill
him, Abraham received the Lord in all hospitality (18:1-8), and the
Lord said to him: "I will surely return to you about this time next
year, and Sarah your wife shall have a son" (18:10). According to
this promise, not only would a son be born to Abraham and Sarah
next year but his birth would coincide with the return of Yahweh.
Significantly, the name Abraham gave to the child was Isaac,
whose name means laughter, a reminder not only of Sarah's initial
incredulity in the face of the promise (18:12-15), but also of how
the Lord turned laughter into rejoicing (21:6). No wonder Jesus
said that Abraham rejoiced that he would see his day, and that he
was glad when he saw it.

Conclusion

The New Testament confirms the distinction drawn in Genesis
19:24 between the "earthly" Yahweh, i.e. the one who appeared to
Abraham in Genesis 18, and the "heavenly" Yahweh, i.e. the one
from whom he called down the fire from heaven. It does this by
identifying the Lord Jesus Christ as God from God, the Angel of
the Lord, and the coming Messiah, as well as in its teaching that

Jesus is eternally preexistent and that he was active during the Old Testament period, even appearing to Old Testament saints like Abraham. The doctrine of the Trinity is a biblical doctrine, and it is supported by the whole of Scripture, the Old Testament as well as the New Testament. As stated at the beginning, those who deny the Trinity are in material breach of both Testaments. The God of the Bible is Triune. There is no other.

PROTO-TRINITARIANISM IN THE BOOK OF DANIEL

by Hiram R. Diaz III[1]

Blessed be the God of Shadrach, Meshach, and Abednego, who has sent his angel and delivered his servant. (Dan 3:28)

Introduction

Although the Old Testament (hereafter, OT) does not explicitly lay out the relationships between the Father and the Son and the Holy Spirit, as John in his upper room discourse does,[2] it nevertheless contains the same doctrine in seminal form. We find

---

[1] Hiram R. Diaz III is a lay-apologist, husband of one, father of four, writer, and musician, whose academic background is in literature, literary theory, philosophy, and systematic theology. He is a member of Port Cities Reformed Baptist Church in Lewiston, ID where he occasionally preaches. Hiram is the author of *Soul Sleep: An Unbibilcal Doctrine, Non-Neutrality: A Personal Testimony*, and the forthcoming *Reclaiming Hell: A Scripturalist Defense of Eternal Torment*. He also writes for and maintains the apologetics blogs Invospec.org and BiblicalTrinitarian.com.

[2] Cf. John 14-16.

the three persons of the Trinity in their distinct relations to one another in the historical books of the OT. For example, Moses' writings contain numerous references to God sending his Angel to speak, execute justice, and save God's people. This Angel is distinct from all others, is called Yahweh, and is worshiped by God's people. Likewise, many of the prophets rather clearly declare that God will send his Angel and his Spirit to accomplish his will, also using the divine name of Yahweh in reference to the one sent by Yahweh to judge and save.[3]

The abundance of evidence pointing to the Triunity of God in the OT flies in the face of claims that the OT knows nothing of a personally-plural monotheism. In actuality, the OT hints at this doctrine as early as Genesis 1, where the One True God declares: "Let *Us* make man in *Our* image, after *Our* likeness."[4] Not only this, but in the next chapter it is revealed that God "formed man out of the dust of the earth," suggesting either an anthropomorphism or an actual shaping, molding, forming performed by actual hands.[5] That it is less likely that Gen 2:7 is an anthropomorphism can be inferred from Gen 3:8, wherein it is revealed that Adam and Eve heard the sound of the Lord God—who is Spirit[6]—walking in the garden of Eden.

Many more examples can be pulled from the OT, but in the following article we will limit our attention to the book of Daniel. It will be demonstrated that upon close examination the book of Daniel reveals the intratrinitarian relationships later articulated in the New Testament (hereafter, NT). The purpose of this is to establish that the doctrine of the Trinity is not derived from pagan philosophy but the Scriptures.

---

[3] Cf. Isa 6:8, 42:1, 48:16; Zec 2:7-11; *et al.*
[4] Gen 1:26a.
[5] Cf. Gen 2:7.
[6] John 4:24.

§ 1. *God the Father: Sending his Angel/Son to Save His Elect,*
Rewarding the Son of Man With Glory and Honor and Dominion

In Daniel 3 we have the first differentiation of divine persons in the book. Shadrach, Meshach, and Abednego fall under the judgment of Nebuchadnezzar, and are cast into a fiery furnace. They are saved by a fourth man whose appearance is like "the Son of God." The ESV translation renders this as "a son of the gods," but in keeping with Scripture it is difficult to maintain that view since Nebuchadnezzar goes on to proclaim:

> Blessed be the God of Shadrach, Meshach, and Abednego, who has sent his angel and delivered his servants, who trusted in him, and yielded up their bodies rather than serve and worship any god except their own.[7]

As he did in the Exodus,[8] God sends his Angel to save his covenant people. The Angel is identified explicitly as the Son of God, indicating his sharing in the nature of God while simultaneously remaining personally distinct from God who sent him. This appears to occur again in Dan 6:22, where the prophet's life is saved by God's Angel. Daniel declares:

> "My God sent his angel and shut the lions' mouths, and they have not harmed me, because I was found blameless before him; and also before you, O king, I have done no harm."

Thus God, once more, saves his covenant people/person by means of his Angel.

The act of sending is spoken of repeatedly in our Lord's trinitarian discourse in the upper room just prior to his arrest and

---

[7] Dan 3:28.
[8] Cf. Ex 3:2; Num 20:16; Judg 2:1.

crucifixion.[9] Christ was sent to save those whom have been given to him by the Father (i.e. the elect covenant people of God). Once the Lord Christ had completed his atoning work, God the Father

> ...highly exalted him and bestowed on him the name that is above every name, so that at the name of Jesus every knee should bow, in heaven and on earth and under the earth, and every tongue confess that Jesus Christ is Lord, to the glory of God the Father.[10]

This *giving* of glory to the Son is also found in the book of Daniel. After the Angel of the Lord is twice revealed to be the savior of God's covenant people, sent down from heaven, descended into the fire of judgment and the pit of lions to deliver Daniel, he is then shown to be the one to whom God gives

> Dominion and glory and a kingdom, that all peoples, nations, and languages should serve him...an everlasting dominion, which shall not pass away, [and his] kingdom... shall not be destroyed.[11]

Thus, Daniel reveals God the Father as saving his elect people through the sending of his Angel, his Son, who descends into the fire and pit of judgment. The book also reveals the Father as rewarding the Son of Man (i.e., the Son) with glory and honor and dominion, as Paul reveals in his epistle to the Philippians and, likewise, in 1 Cor 15:22-28.

---

[9] Cf. John 14:26; 15:26; 17:3, vv. 8, 18, 20-23, 25.
[10] Phil 2:9-10.
[11] Dan 7:14.

§ 2. *God the Son: Son of God, Son of Man, and the Anointed One*

As has already been touched upon above, Daniel reveals the Son of God as descending from heaven to save God's people. The prophet also reveals the Son of Man, upon finishing his salvific work, as ascending to heaven to receive his kingdom from God the Father. Thus, the Son of God is also the Son of Man, the Angel of the Lord who shares equally the divinity of the Father and the humanity of those who will occupy his eternal kingdom. That the Holy Spirit, through the prophet's writing, intends to present Christ in his two natures as divine and human, moreover, is evident when consideration is given to the pattern of descending to save and ascending to receive glory from the Father found repeatedly in the NT.

On the road to Emmaus, the Lord Jesus rebukes the spiritual blindness and unbelief of his forlorn disciples. He exclaims:

> "O foolish ones, and slow of heart to believe all that the prophets have spoken! Was it not necessary that the Christ should suffer these things and enter into his glory?"[12]

The apostle Peter later repeats that this structure is found throughout the OT, stating that:

> Concerning this salvation, the prophets who prophesied about the grace that was to be yours searched and inquired carefully, inquiring what person or time the Spirit of Christ in them was indicating when he predicted *the sufferings of Christ and the subsequent glories.*[13]

---

[12] Luke 24:25-26.
[13] 1 Pet 1:10-11. (emphasis added)

"The sufferings" is a reference to Christ's atoning work, the task for which he came down from heaven to perform. As he tells his disciples:

> "I have come down from heaven, not to do my own will but the will of him who sent me."[14]

That will was to *die*, to suffer for God's elect people in order to redeem them from the fires of hell, and the pit of eternal destruction.

This teaching is elaborated upon in Daniel 9:24-26a, where the ministry of "the Anointed One" is given in dense, but very exact, details. The Anointed One will,

> finish transgression, put an end to sin, atone for iniquity, bring in everlasting righteousness, seal both the vision and prophet, and anoint a most holy place.

In his descent, foretold in the above prophecy, the Lord Jesus will save his people from their sins. Whereas Daniel 3 portrays this typologically in the descent of the Angel who enters the fires of judgment to save his elect, Daniel 9 reveals propositionally that the Lord will save his people from not only the consequences of their sins but their sins as well, by bringing in everlasting righteousness. And if this is not clear enough, the prophet Daniel is later told that these prophecies were not intended for him but for those in the end time, thus following Peter's declaration in precise detail. As we read in Daniel 12:8-10:

> I heard, but I did not understand. Then I said, "O my lord, what shall be the outcome of these things?" He said, "Go

---

[14] John 6:38.

your way, Daniel, for *the words are shut up and sealed until the time of the end.* Many shall purify themselves and make themselves white and be refined, but the wicked shall act wickedly. And none of the wicked shall understand, but those who are wise shall understand."[15]

This descent/ascent language is used, moreover, by the Lord himself when he rebukes Nicodemus for not knowing the Scriptural teaching regarding the Son of God, saying:

"Are you the teacher of Israel and yet you do not understand these things? Truly, truly, I say to you, we speak of what we know, and bear witness to what we have seen, but you do not receive our testimony. If I have told you earthly things and you do not believe, how can you believe if I tell you heavenly things? *No one has ascended*

---

[15] Note that the apostle Paul, referring specifically to the knowledge of Christ revealed by the Spirit to the righteous, explains:

...the word of the cross is folly to those who are perishing, but to us who are being saved it is the power of God. For it is written,

"I will destroy the wisdom of the wise,
and the discernment of the discerning I will thwart."

Where is the one who is wise? Where is the scribe? Where is the debater of this age? Has not God made foolish the wisdom of the world? For since, in the wisdom of God, the world did not know God through wisdom, it pleased God through the folly of what we preach to save those who believe. For Jews demand signs and Greeks seek wisdom, but we preach Christ crucified, a stumbling block to Jews and folly to Gentiles, but to those who are called, both Jews and Greeks, Christ the power of God and the wisdom of God. For the foolishness of God is wiser than men, and the weakness of God is stronger than men. (1 Cor 1:18-25)

> *into heaven except he who descended from heaven, the Son
> of Man.*"[16]

Paul the apostle repeats that Christ is he who descended from heaven, as well as ascended to heaven from whence he came, writing:

> ...the righteousness based on faith says, "Do not say in your heart, 'Who will *ascend* into heaven?'" (that is, to bring Christ down) "or 'Who will *descend* into the abyss?'" (that is, to bring Christ up from the dead). But what does it say? "The word is near you, in your mouth and in your heart" (that is, the word of faith that we proclaim); because, if you confess with your mouth that Jesus is Lord and believe in your heart that God raised him from the dead, you will be saved.[17]

Christ is the Son of God who "was manifested in the flesh," Paul says elsewhere, and "taken up in glory."[18] Once again, he repeats the descending to save/ascending to receive glory that is present in the book of Daniel.

§ 3. *God the Holy Spirit: Giver of Wisdom & Understanding*

Daniel does not make much mention of the Holy Spirit, but what he does mention is significant. Translations, perhaps under the assumption that pagans would not speak of the Spirit of the Holy God typically translate the Hebrew phrase as "the spirit of the

---

[16] John 3:10-13. (emphasis added). The shorter reading of v. 13 (here represented by the ESV) has excellent support among early MSS esp. p^{66} and p^{75}. However, Black has made a good case for "who is in heaven." See Black, David A., 1985. "The Text of John 3:13," *Grace Theological Journal*, 6.1, 49-66.

[17] Rom 10:6-9. (emphasis added)

[18] 1 Tim 3:16.

holy gods." Thus, the phrase, appearing in Dan 4:8, 9, 18 & 5:11, is understood to be a reference to the spirit (sing.) of the pagan deities (pl.), and not the Holy Spirit. Given that those who are speaking this way of Daniel are pagans, it seems likely that they were looking at Daniel through their overriding religious presupposition (*viz.* polytheism).

However, it could also be the case that, as Gill suggests, they were "speaking in the dialect of the Jews, [meaning] the one true God who is holy, and from whom alone is the spirit of prophecy or of foretelling things to come."[19] Evidence that Gill's suggestion is very likely the case, moreover, can be gathered from the instances in which the word *holy* appears in Daniel. The word is elsewhere used with reference to Yahweh's angels and saints,[20] making its application to foreign deities, in this text, an anomaly. Additionally, while Yahweh is understood to be one deity among many, the pagans in Daniel recognize that he is distinct from them all. Thus, king Nebuchadnezzar tells Daniel:

> "Truly, your God is *God of gods* and Lord of kings, and a revealer of mysteries, for you have been able to reveal this mystery."[21]

Likewise, upon seeing that God rescued Daniel from the fiery furnace, Nebuchadnezzar even more clearly identifies Yahweh as the "*Most High* God,"[22] and declares:

> "Blessed be the God of Shadrach, Meshach, and Abednego, who has sent his angel and delivered his servants, who trusted in him, and set aside the king's command, and

---

[19] *Gill's Exposition of the Entire Bible*, Daniel 4:8.
[20] Angels: 4:13, vv. 17, 23.
Saints: 7:18, vv. 21, 22, 25, 27.
[21] Dan 2:47. (emphasis added)
[22] Dan 3:26. (emphasis added)

yielded up their bodies rather than serve and worship any god except their own God. Therefore I make a decree: Any people, nation, or language that speaks anything against the God of Shadrach, Meshach, and Abednego shall be torn limb from limb, and their houses laid in ruins, for *there is no other god who is able to rescue in this way.*"[23]

Yahweh had already been identified as absolutely distinct from all of the other deities for being "a revealer of mysteries."[24] He now is identified as absolutely distinct for his unique ability to rescue his people.

Consequently, given that the Lord is recognized as being unique among the gods (i.e. as holy) for his ability to reveal mysteries and exercise sovereign control over creation, it seems much more likely that the phrase "spirit of the holy gods" is incorrect. Grammatically, such a translation is possible; however, the context of Daniel—in which holiness is solely ascribed to God, his angels, and his people—the Spirit of the Holy God is much more fitting.

This, in conjunction with the aforementioned implicit Christology of the book of Daniel, then, reveals the Holy Spirit's relationship to the Father and the Son. The Spirit of the holy God takes up residence in Daniel, illuminating his understanding in general, granting him wisdom in general, revealing the person and work of the Son of God/Son of Man, as well as revealing the relationship between the Father (as sender of the Son) and the Son (as Savior, exalted King, and Judge). Not only this, but by means of the law of transitivity we can deduce the deity of the Spirit of God from the book of Daniel.

---

[23] Dan 3:28-29. (emphasis added)
[24] Dan 2:47.

1. The God of heaven is the revealer of mysteries.[25]
2. The revealer of mysteries is the Spirit of the Holy God.[26]
3. Therefore, the Spirit of the Holy God is the God of heaven.

Conclusion

The book of Daniel contains a proto-trinitarianism whose exact details are later fleshed out by the Lord Jesus Christ in his upper room discourse. In Daniel, God sends his Son/Angel to enter the fire of judgment and save the elect. He later rewards the Son of Man, who is equally divine,[27] after the Son has fulfilled his role and ascended to the heavenly throne. The Son of God/Son of Man is fully God and fully man, the anointed One who comes down from heaven to save God's people by entering into the fires of judgment and the stone-enclosed pit,[28] and who ascends back to the throne of God to receive honor, glory, power, and majesty to the glory of him who sent him. These truths, finally, are revealed by the Spirit of the Holy God who indwells God's elect (spec. Daniel), setting him apart from the world, gifting him with true wisdom and not the falsehoods of the world.[29]

---

[25] Dan 2:28.

[26] Dan 4:8-9.

[27] Cf. Dan 7:13-14 & 6:25-26.

[28] See Dan 6:17.

[29] Cf. 1 Cor 3:16-22.

JEWISH PROTO-TRINITARIANISM

Michael R. Burgos Jr.

The fact that there existed a contingent of devout Jews who affirmed a form of proto-trinitarianism prior to the birth of Christ, and that this belief subsisted within the purview of orthodox Israelite religion, is good evidence that the above OT interpretations are not in contradiction with Moses' intent. Segal, a late devout Jew and Semitic studies scholar, has documented the existence of a pre-Christian Jewish tradition in which there existed a belief in a second divine figure who is at the same time Yahweh. Segal has argued that "The early biblical theophonies which picture God as a man or confuse YHWH with an angel are the basis of the tradition."[1] Segal notes that this Jewish tradition, known pejoratively by its rabbinic detractors as "two powers in heaven," "grew through differing exegeses of a variety of theophany texts," and was present "among of groups and was later canonized by the rabbinic community."[2] This tradition posited both a distinction of person in God and monotheism. Rightly, Segal

---

[1] Segal, Alan F., *Two Powers in Heaven: Early Rabbinic Reports about Christianity and Gnosticism*, (Waco: Baylor Univ. Press, 2012), 261.

[2] Ibid.

goes far enough to say that this two powers tradition "seems to be one of the basic issues over which Judaism and Christianity separated."[3] However, assumed in that statement is the existence of a form of Judaism which naturally flowed into orthodox Christianity. Barker has similarly argued, "The roots of Christian trinitarian theology lie in pre-Christian Palestinian beliefs about the angels."[4] Additionally, there is good evidence to suppose that the prominence of the unitarian stream of rabbinic theology was, in part, a reaction against Jewish proto-trinitarianism. Boyarin has observed:

> Two different strands of the religious imagination, one in which the ancient binitarianness of Israel's God is essentially preserved and transformed and one in which that duality has been more thoroughly suppressed, live side by side in the Jewish thought world of the Second Temple and beyond, being mixed in different ways but also contesting each other and sometimes seeking to oust the other completely.[5]

Hence, when subordinationists, modalists, and theological liberals appeal to the unitarian theology of Judaism, they are appealing to a theology that is, in part, predicated upon a rejection of Jesus Christ.[6]

---

[3] Ibid., 262.

[4] Barker, *The Great Angel: A Study of Israel's Second God*, (Louisville: Westminster John Knox, 1992), 3.

[5] Boyarin, Daniel, *The Jewish Gospels: The Story of the Jewish Christ*, (New York: The New Press, 2012), Kindle, loc. 1455. See also Boyarin, *Border Lines*, 90,

[6] Should this sentiment be correctly understood, the Christological establishment represented by Dunn would cease to exist. Dunn has argued that the fourth gospel uniquely presents "claims on the lips of Jesus which could be understood as subversive of the unity of God."

Jewish proto-trinitarianism is heartily portrayed in the Targumim (i.e., the second temple era Jewish translation-commentaries of the Hebrew Bible into Aramaic).[7] Admittedly, the predominant view among scholars today is that the Memra of the Targums is not a distinct divine person from Yahweh.[8] For instance, McNamara wrote, "The Memra of the Lord is merely a reverent circumlocution for 'the Lord.'"[9] McNamara went further to cite Wolfson who stated, "No scholar nowadays will entertain the view that it is either a real being or an intermediary."[10] Even so, there is substantial basis to reject this consensus. The typical

---

Since John's gospel is a progressive continuation of a theology that belonged to Israelite biblical monotheists to begin with, Dunn's argumentation has become, at least in part, an anachronistic appeal to a unitarian presupposition. Dunn, James D. G., *The Parting of the Ways Between Christianity and Judaism and Their Significance for the Character of Christianity*, (London: Trinity Press Intl., 1991), 135.

[7] Although dating the Targumic literature is a difficult proposition, most all scholars agree that the Targums reflect the traditions of second temple Judaism. See Shepherd, Michael B., 2008. "Targums, the New Testament, and Biblical Theology of the Messiah," *JETS*, 51/1, 45, 46-48. McNamara, Martin, *Targum and the Testament Revisited*, 2nd Ed., (Grand Rapids: Eerdmans, 2010), 92-100. McNamara, Martin, *The Aramaic Bible: Targum Neofiti 1: Genesis*, Vol. 1A, (Collegeville: Liturgical Press, 1992), 43-45.

[8] E.g., Barrett, C. K., *The Gospel According to St. John*, 2nd Ed., (Louisville: Westminster John Knox Press, 1978), 128. See also Ronning, *The Jewish Targums and John's Logos Theology*, 263. Ronning wrote, "The old argument that the Targumic Word is a 'hypostasis,' meaning a being distinct from God, certainly overstretched the evidence." While Ronning did an admirable job demonstrating the Targumic influence in John, he did not make an adequate assessment of the Angel of Yahweh texts. If the Angel of Yahweh is a distinct person from Yahweh, then *so is the Memra*.

[9] McNamara, *Targum and Testament Revisited*, 162.

[10] Ibid.

rationale for the rejection of the Memra as a hypostasis is that the term serves as a literary device which distances God from anthropomorphic description of him in the Hebrew Bible. Flesher and Chilton go as far as to call the Memra an "anti-anthropomorphism."[11] The difficulty with this view is that is basically makes the utilization of Memra a monolith and it relies upon poor logic. Boyarin has argued,

> Surely, however, this position collapses logically. If the Memra is just a name that allows one to avoid asserting that God himself has created, appeared, supported, and saved, and thus preserves his absolute transcendence, then who, after all, did the actual creating, appearing, supporting, saving? Either God himself—in which case one has hardly "protected" him from contact with the material word—or there is some other divine entity, in which case Memra is not just a name. Indeed, as Burton Mack has pointed out, Sophia/Logos developed within Judaism precisely to enable a "theology of the transcendence of God." The currently accepted and dominant view ascribes the use of the Memra only to the counterfeit coinage of a linguistic simulation of a theology of transcendence of God without the theology itself. Rather than assuming that the usage is meaningless, it seems superior on general hermeneutic grounds to assume that it means something. It follows, then, that the strongest reading of the Memra is that it is not a mere name, but an actual divine entity, or mediator.[12]

If the Memra were an attempt at distancing God, it was used

---

11 Flesher, Paul V. M., Chilton, Bruce, *The Targums: A Critical Introduction*, (Leiden: Brill, 2011), 45.

12 Boyarin, *Border Lines*, 117, see also 291 n. 40. See 2001. "The Gospel of the Memra: Jewish Binitarianism and the Gospel of John," *Harvard Theological Review*, 94.3, 255.

horribly since there are many places in the Targumim wherein anthropomorphisms are used of God. *Neofiti I* identifies the Memra as the one who spoke creation into existence (Gen 1:3ff), but interspersed within the creation account Tg. Neof. simply states "the Lord created..."[13] Additionally, there exists an important set of considerations that these those who hold the predominant view neglect. Etheridge summarized:

> We admit that the term Memra, like that of *Logos*, does not etymologically necessitate the idea of personal subsistence. Each term—the former in the New Testament, where, along with nearly thirty aspects of meaning, there is one in which the Λóγος shines resplendent as a title of Him who was in the beginning, who was with God, who was God, and by whom all things were made; so in the Targums, among several applications there are some about which it is impossible, with any show of truth, to deny that they set forth a personal subsistence, and one personal subsistence as distinguished from another in the Divine nature.[14]

Etheridge has gone on to identify three general ways the Targums uses Memra:

> We admit, also, that the Targumists sometimes use this form *Memra da Yeya* to denote the energy of God in action; as when the Word is said to give forth the snow and the floods; (Job 37:10) or when the Lord sends forth his Word as arrows for the destruction of the wicked; (Ps 18:15); or by his Word he founds the earth and builds up the heavens. (Is 45:12). It is

---

[13] E.g., Tg. Neof. Gen 1:6, v. 14.

[14] Etheridge, J. W., *The Targums of Onkelos and Jonathan Ben Uzziel on the Pentateuch with Fragments from the Jerusalem Targum*, (London: Longman, 1862), 17-18.

employed, too, we allow, as an exponent for the dispositions of the Divine mind, and as such is an equivalent for the Hebraistic idiom, "the heart of God;" as, where in Hebrew we have, "God said in his heart," the Targum gives it, "God said in his Word;" (Gen 8:21); or chap, 6:6, Hebrew, "It grieved Him in His heart;" Chaldee, "in his Word." In other places, moreover, it signifies, the Divine wisdom displayed in the dispensations of Providence; as when the Word of the Lord is said to deliver the law, to punish the guilty, and to be the helper of the good. But though he who considers even these examples will find it difficult to divest them of the idea of substantial personality, he will meet with a variety of other passages in which the phrase in question is only used to express the presence and agency of a real Person.[15]

Edersheim noted, "Rabbinic theology has not preserved to us the doctrine of Personal distinctions in the Godhead. And yet, if words have any meaning, the Memra is a hypostasis."[16] Howell has observed,

In Genesis, the Targums interpret the Memra as God's creative agent similarly to how John describes Jesus. In *Neofiti* Genesis 1, Memra occurs nineteen times related to creation. At times, the Memra only speaks and yet his speech effects creation (Tg.Neof Gen 1:16...). The Memra also authoritatively named the created order, calling dry land "earth" and the waters "seas"... Furthermore, when the Hebrew Bible's says, "and it was so" (Gen 1:10...) *Neofiti* and *Fragmentary Targum P*

---

[15] Ibid., 18.

[16] Edersheim, Alfred, *The Life and Times of Jesus the Messiah*, (Whitefish: Kessinger Pub., 2010), 214. See also Schwöbel, Christoph. 2009. "The Trinity Between Athens and Jerusalem," *Journal of Reformed Theology*, 3.22-41, 24.

interpret this to mean "it was according to his Memra" (Gen 1:7...). In each of these verses, the Memra was active in creation as the agent of God.[17]

In many places the Targums identify the *mal'āk* Yahweh as the Memra. The *Jerusalem Targum* and *Targum Neofiti* translate Genesis 16:13 "And Hagar gave thanks, and prayed in the name of the Word of the Lord who had been manifested to her." One of the angels in Genesis 18 is identified as "Memra of God" in *Targum Onkelos*. Whereas the Hebrew account of the sacrifice of Isaac states that it was the Angel of Yahweh who called to Abraham to stop the sacrifice (Gen 22:11), *Targum Pseudo-Jonathan* tells us it was the "Memra of the Lord." It also tells us that the Angel in the burning bush (Exodus 3:4-5) is the Memra of the LORD *who appeared* to Moses. The Angel of the LORD who appeared to Balaam is interpreted to be the Memra (Num 22:22) by *Targum Onkelos*. So too, *Onkelos* identifies the Angel who wrestled with Jacob and said, "I am the God of Bethel" as the Memra. When the Angel of Yahweh appears to Gideon, the Targum says it was the Memra (Judges 6:12).

Isaiah 63:7-10 states,

I will recount the steadfast love of the Lord, the praises of the Lord...For he said, "Surely they are my people, children who will not deal falsely. And he became their Savior. In all their affliction he was afflicted, and the angel of his presence saved them; in his love and in his pity he redeemed them; he lifted them up and carried them all the days of old. But they rebelled and grieved his Holy Spirit; therefore he turned to be their enemy, and himself fought against them.

---

[17] Howell, A. J., *Finding Christ in the Old Testament Through the Aramaic Memra, Shekinah, and Yeqara*, PhD Diss., 2015, The Southern Baptist Theological Seminary, 61.

Targum Pseudo-Jonathan translates this passage:

> I will remember the kindness of the Lord, and the praise of the
> Lord…For they are my people said the Lord, children who do
> not lie; and his Memra was their redeemer. Every time they
> sinned before him, so that they might have brought tribulation
> upon them, he did not afflict them, and the angel sent from his
> presence redeemed them. In his love and pity, behold, he
> liberated them, and bare them, and carried them all the days of
> old…But they would not obey, so his Memra became their
> enemy, and fought against them.

Gieschen has cited the following examples:

> "The Destroyer" or "Angel of YHWH" in the Exodus
> Passover is substituted with "My Memra" in the Targumim:
> "And I, in My Memra will pass by over the land of Egypt
> on this Passover night" (Tg. Neof. Exod 12.12; cf. Tg.
> Neof. Exod 11.4; 12.13). The Angel of YHWH who guided
> Israel in the desert is also reinterpreted: "And the Shekinah
> of the Memra of YHWH will go before you" (Tg. Ps-J.
> Deut 31.6. The "Angel of the Covenant" in Mal 3.1
> becomes "My Memra" (Tg. NEB. Mal 3:1).[18]

Gieschen rightly concludes that "This substitution demonstrates
the possibility that the Memra could have been interpreted as a
divine hypostasis by some Jewish exegetes."[19]

Both the coming "Angel of the covenant" (Mal 3:1) and the
Son of Man in Daniel 7:13 are interpreted as the Memra in Targum

---

[18] Gieschen, Charles A., *Angelomorphic Christology: Antecedents &
Early Evidence*, (Leiden: Brill, 1998), 113.

[19] Ibid., 113-114.

Pseudo-Jonathan. Clearly, there exists a strong messianic flavor to the Memra that is writ large in the prologue of John and the prologue of Hebrews.

If one supposes, as most unitarians do, that the Angel of Yahweh and(or) the Son of Man is a distinct person from Yahweh (i.e., a created agent), then consistency demands that the Memra ought to be similarly understood. As it turns out, consistency is not a feature of unitarian exegesis. A case in point is the study offered by Chang. He identifies the angel of Yahweh as either a theophany or as "ordinary angels,"[20] and yet argues extensively that the Memra of the Targums is non-personal. Chang wrote, "Memra is absolutely *never* referred to another person distinct from Yahweh."[21] Such a position is self-contradictory. On the one hand, many subordinationists relegate the Angel of Yahweh to creaturely finitude or they insist he is God the Father himself, while on the other, they insist that the Memra, the Targumic translation/interpretation of the Angel of Yahweh, is non-personal.[22]

Targum Neofiti's rendering of Genesis 1:1 is of much interest here:

מלקדמין בחכמה ברא דייי שכלל ית שמיא וית ארעא:

In the beginning, with wisdom, the Son of Yahweh created the heavens and the earth.[23]

---

[20] Chang, Eric H. H., *The Only True God: A Study of Biblical Monotheism*, (Bloomington: Xlibris, 2013), 377.

[21] Ibid., 464.

[22] This is further compounded since the Memra is said to have received prayer and regularly speaks with his people (e.g., Exod 14:10ff in Tg. PsJ. and the Frag. Tg).

[23] Shepherd, "Targums, the New Testament, and Biblical Theology of the Messiah," 51. Driscoll and Breshears have translated Gen 1:1 in

Shepherd, who has furnished the above translation, has observed the following:

> In the Hebrew text of Gen 1:1, ברא clearly means "he created." But in Aramaic ברא can also be בר ("son") plus the suffixed definite article א ("the"). The Targum features this Aramaic option and adds שמיא for "he created" (or "he finished/decorated").[24]

The critical edition of Neofiti rejects the above reading, stating, "The text, however, in MS itself is corrected after an erasure; "and" of the original is visible before "perfected.""[25] Similarly, Alexander identifies the reading as "startling," and claims that it is the result of tampering.[26] The critical edition has as its primary reading:

> From the beginning with wisdom the Memra of the Lord created and perfected the heavens and the earth.[27]

Tg. Neof.: "In the beginning, by the firstborn, God created the heavens and the earth." Admittedly, I do not understand the basis of translating ברא as "firstborn." Unfortunately, these authors provided no further discussion. See Driscoll, Mark, Breshears, Gerry, *Doctrine: What Christians Should Believe*, (Wheaton: Crossway, 2010), 19.

[24] Shepherd, "Targums, the New Testament, and Biblical Theology of the Messiah," 51.

[25] McNamara, *Neofiti 1: Genesis*, 52. Cf. Macho, Diez Alejandro, *MS Neophyti 1 IV Numeros*, (Madrid: de la Biblioteca Vaticana, 1968), 2-3.

[26] Alexander also rejects the critical reading calling it "unparalleled." Alexander, Philip in Grypeou, E., Spurling, H. Eds., *The Exegetical Encounter Between Jews and Christians in Late Antiquity*, (Leiden: Brill, 2009), 11.

[27] McNamara, *Neofiti 1: Genesis*, 52. Cf. Anderson, Gary. 1990.

Cargill has issued the most extensive argumentation against the reading "Son of the Lord." Citing his "Rule of Creative Completion," Cargill has claimed that scribes never used שכלל "as the sole verb of a creating process."[28] He has based this rule upon the ten examples in the entirety of the Pentateuch. Ultimately however, what determines whether Cargill's rule is actually a rule at all is the authentic reading of Tg. Neof. at Gen 1:1. Cargill has theorized the following:

This redactor appears to have altered the text in such a way as to introduce a 'son of The Lord' as creative agent. The introduction of a 'son of The Lord' may have been an attempt by a Christian editor to introduce a pre-existent 'Son' with the hope of harmonizing Tg. Neof.'s translation of Gen. 1.1 with the later Christian doctrine of the Trinity. Alternatively, it may have been an attempt by later Jewish redactor to introduce the increasingly discussed concept of the 'Memra of The Lord' or *Logos* as creative or co-creative agent with YHWH into Gen 1.1.[29]

It is fascinating that Cargill, who is no friend of orthodox Christianity,[30] thinks that the introduction of the Son is consistent

---

"The Interpretation of Genesis 1:1 in the Targums," *The Catholic Bible Quarterly*, 52.1, 27-28.

[28] Cargill, Robert R. 2012. "The Rule of Creative Completion: Neofiti's Use of שכלל," *Aramaic Studies*, 10, 175.

[29] Ibid., 188-189. Cargill has presupposed a rejection of proto-trinitarianism in the OT. If the OT does teach proto-trinitarianism, Cargill's suggestion is invalid.

[30] Cargill identifies "trinitarian apologists" as "ignorant or dismissive" upon the basis of their alleged rejection of the plural of majesty at Gen 1:26. Since the plural of majesty is not a feature of verbs, it would seem that Cargill is either ignorant or dismissive. Cargill,

with a Jewish conception of the Memra and *Logos*. Gurtner and Perrin have observed that "Such Christian tampering is not characteristic of the manuscript elsewhere."[31] Regarding the textual variation, Sailhamer has noted,

> A marginal note in the critical edition of Neofiti I suggests that the [previously cited] translation is a secondary Christian reworking of the original, which read, "In the beginning with Wisdom, Yahweh created and completed the heavens and the earth." The question revolves ultimately into that of the originality of the conjunction "waw" (and) in the translation "and completed" above. It is clear from the photographs of the manuscript that the "waw" has been erased by a second hand. In the absence of the "waw" the Aramaic Targum ברא would mean "the son" rather than "he created," hence "The Son of Yahweh created…" The photographs of the manuscripts also show, however, that though the "waw has been erased, it still appears to have been secondary because there is not enough room between the two words for the "waw" and space dividing the words…The earliest text did not have a "waw." The "waw" was written into the text and subsequently erased.[32]

Robert R. 2010. "How Not to Read Targum Neofiti," *RobertCargill.com*, https://robertcargill.com/2010/12/17/how-not-to-read-the-targums/.

[31] Green, Joel B. Ed., *Dictionary of Jesus and the Gospels*, 2nd Ed., (Downers Grove: Intervarsity Press, 2013), 933.

[32] Sailhamer, John H., *Introduction to Old Testament Theology: A Canonical Approach*, (Grand Rapids: Zondervan, 1995), 222, n. 61.

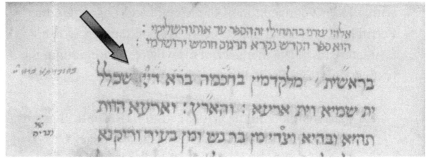

Fig. 1: Neofiti 1: Genesis 1:1. Courtesy of the Vatican Digital Library

It is possible that Sailhamer is correct given that the line spacing tends to be the most consistent on the first line of the first leaf.[33] Even if we were to accept the critical reading, "the Memra of the Lord created…," agency is not out of the question. In any event, the reading shouldn't be dismissed out of hand since the Hebrew Bible itself recognizes the existence of God's Son within the context of creation:

> Who has ascended to heaven and come down? Who has gathered the wind in his fists? Who has wrapped up the waters in a garment? Who has established all the ends of the earth? What is his name, and what is his son's name? Surely you know! (Proverbs 30:4)

Jewish Proto-Trinitarianism & Philo

According to Josephus, Philo of Alexandria was a skilled philosopher and "a man eminent on all accounts."[34] That Philo wrote to "Jews devoted to the Bible" is indisputable.[35] What we see in Philo is the presence of a second temple Jewish (read: monotheistic) theology that is comfortable with a divine Word who

---

[33] See the spacing on the similar construction on the bottom of 4r on Tg. Neof. at Gen 2:22.

[34] Josephus, Antiquities XVIII. 8.1.

[35] Boyarin, *Border Lines*, 113.

is God's firstborn Son, even δεύτερος θεός.[36] Whereas the New Testament's Word is the divine Creator and Exegete of the Father and the "Image of the invisible God,"[37] Philo's Word is the "image of God...by which all the world was made."[38] Segal notes that the phrase "second God" is "a synonym for 'two powers' in rabbinic thought." [39]

The existence of this theology in Philo implies "that this way of thinking about God was a vital inheritance of at least Alexandrian Jewish thought," and "that for one branch of pre-Christian Judaism there was nothing strange about a doctrine of a *dueteros theos*, a 'second' God."[40] Lest one write-off Philo as a singular anomaly, Boyarin indicates that "Notions of the second god as the personified Word or Wisdom of God were present among Semitic-speaking Jews."[41] He cites the *Apocalypse of Abraham* and the character named Yahoel. This character is said to be "an angel sent in the likeness of man" to Abraham, who has, like the Angel of Yahweh in Exodus 23:21, the name of God in him.[42] Hannah notes, "The author of this apocalypse seeks to re-enforce the close association between this angel and the divine name."[43] Further, judging by the presence of a Jew in Justin's *Dialogue* who accompanied Trypho and who admitted "that one of the two angels who had gone to Sodom was called 'God' by Abraham," Segal has suggested that "Justin Martyr also knew of Jews who allowed one name of God to refer to something like a

---

[36] *On Husbandry*, 51, and *On Dreams*, 39.1.228.

[37] John 1:3; v. 18; Col 1:15 resp.

[38] *The Special Laws I*, XVI. 81.

[39] Segal, *Two Powers in Heaven*, 159.

[40] Boyarin, *Border Lines*, 113.

[41] Ibid., 116.

[42] *Apocalypse of Abraham*, 10:3; v. 8.

[43] Hannah, Darrell D., *Michael and Christ: Michael Traditions and Angel Christology in Early Christianity*, (Tübingen: Mohr Siebeck, 1999), 53.

logos but refused to identify the *logos* with Jesus as he had done."[44]

AN EXEGESIS & SYNTHESIS OF JOHN 1:1-3

Michael R. Burgos Jr.

A Speaking God

It is noteworthy that God's image bearers are, like God, users of language. Henry observed, "Revelation is personal communication. Its personal originator is God, and persons are its recipients."[1] God spoke creation into existence saying, "Let there be" and "Let us make." Who exactly was God speaking to? Given the above evidence, the only tenable answer to that question is that God was speaking to God. That is not to say that God was soliloquizing. Rather, since the Bible, both Old and New Testament, teaches that one divine person speaks to the other two divine persons, it is apparent that God's language in creation does not fall upon deaf ears. The Father, Son, and Spirit communicate to each other. The Angel of Yahweh (i.e., God the Son) and Yahweh (i.e., the Father) speak with each other (1 Sam 24:16; Zec1:12; John 12:28), and the Spirit communicates with the Father and Son (John 16:13-15; Rom 8:26-27; Rev 22:17). Poythress has noted,

This speaking on the part of God is significant for our thinking

---

[1] Henry, *God, Revelation, & Authority Vol. II*, 151.

about language. Not only is God a member of a language communist that includes human beings, but the persons of the Trinity function as members of a language community among themselves. Language does not have as its sole purpose human-human communication, or even divine-human communication, but also divine-divine communication. Approaches that conceive of language *only* with reference to human beings are accordingly reductionistic.[2]

The communication of God is not merely a convention of creation. God spoke *before* creation existed. "By the word of the LORD the heavens were made" (Psalm 33:6), and therefore divine language pre-existed creation. The earth was formed "by the word of God"—it was divine language that effected the creation of all created things. God's communication presupposes another party, and in the case of Genesis 1:26, another party who is also God.[3]

Interpreters sometimes conflate the word that God spoke in the creation account with that of John's λόγος. In its plainest sense, conflating actual divine language with John's λόγος results in a view of the λόγος John clearly did not intend. Subordinationist and modalist interpreters compound this error by defining the λόγος in terms of "God's plan," "power," "self-expression," or a variation

---

[2] Poythress, Vern Sheridan, *In the Beginning was the Word: Language—A God Centered Approach*, (Wheaton: Crossway, 2009), 18.

[3] The supreme form of divine communication is that of love, for "God is love" (1 John 4:8; v. 16). John's assertion is a characterization of God's nature, and therefore in the same manner that "God is holy" (Ps 99:9), God is love. Thus, since God's essential attributes are independent of his creation, and since love is necessarily communication, the unitarian God is either dependent upon his creation for his nature, or he is a God who engages in vanity (i.e., self-love). For example, the Islamic god is said to have ninety-nine eternal names of which *Al-Wadud* (the All Loving) is one in Surah 85:14.

thereof.[4] John makes it entirely clear that the λόγος is neither a plan nor language, but a person, indeed God the Word. To demonstrate this, an exegesis of John 1:1-13 is in order. In another sense, there is a legitimate association between the λόγος of the prologue and God's spoken word. Jesus is identified as the λόγος since he is the one who is the revealer of God. He is the μονογενὴς θεὸς who makes the Father known (John 1:18). Or in Pauline terms, "He is the image of the invisible God" (Col 1:15). Jesus is akin to the spoken word of God in the sense that he also functions as revelation. The difference however, is that the λόγος is personal, indeed God the Son. John has shown an affinity for using metaphor to characterize Jesus, and "Word" is one of those metaphors. In the fourth gospel Jesus is identified as "the light" (1:7-9), "the lamb of God" (1:29), "the bridegroom" (3:29), "bread" (6:51), "the door" (10:7), and "the true vine" (15:1). Consistency would demand therefore, that any interpretation of John's gospel which understands λόγος in wooden sense so as to mean God's literal speech or a plan, reason, etc., then one ought to understand the other metaphorical language used for Jesus accordingly.

An Exegesis of John 1:1-3

Below, Dalcour has provided his own exegesis of John 1:1-3, particularly focusing upon the preexistent, personal, and divine nature of John's λόγος. Here, I will provide a complement Dalcour's work, giving a brief exegesis that will demonstrate the continuity of apostolic theology with Old Testament proto-trinitarianism, especially that of the Targumic Memra.

---

[4] E.g., Buzzard, Anthony, "John 1:1 *Caveat Lector* (Reader Beware)," http://focusonthekingdom.org/articles/john1.htm, Bernard, David K., *Pentecostal Theology Volume 1: The Oneness of God*, (Hazelwood: Word Aflame Press, 2007), Kindle, loc. 525, Graeser, Lynn,, Schoenheit, *One God & One Lord*, 212, Gill, *The One*, 129.

In the beginning was the Word, and the Word was with God, and the Word was God. He was in the beginning with God. All things were made through him, and without him was not anything made that was made. (John 1:1-3)

Ἐν ἀρχῇ ἦν ὁ λόγος, καὶ ὁ λόγος ἦν πρὸς τὸν θεόν, καὶ θεὸς ἦν ὁ λόγος. οὗτος ἦν ἐν ἀρχῇ πρὸς τὸν θεόν. πάντα δι᾽ αὐτοῦ ἐγένετο, καὶ χωρὶς αὐτοῦ ἐγένετο οὐδὲ ἕν. ὃ γέγονεν (John 1:1-3, NA28)[5]

The above text begins with the familiar words, "In the beginning" (Ἐν ἀρχῇ) which are certainly intended to invoke Genesis 1:1.[6] John, by placing the Word in the place where we might expect God, has already identified the Word with Yahweh. Throughout vv. 1 and 2, John utilized the imperfect verb of 'to be' (ἦν) thereby indicating that the Word was in existence *before* the beginning. The use of ἦν is distinguished from vv. 3, 6, and 14 wherein the verb ἐγένετο is employed to communicate something coming to exist or coming to a place. Therefore, given the placement of the Word within John 1:1a, in the same way that the personhood and eternality of God is assumed in Genesis 1:1, the personhood and eternality of the Word ought to be assumed.

Like the first and third clauses, the apostle has placed the Word in the nominative case in the second clause, indicating that his intention is to tell his audience about the Word. The preposition

---

[5] In this volume, unless otherwise indicated, all GNT citations are from *Novum Testamentum Graece: Nestle-Aland* (NA28), 28th Rev. Ed., (Stuttgart: Deutsche Bibelgesellschaft, 2012).

[6] Cf. Tg. Neof.; Gen 1:1 LXX; Heb 1:10. The unitarian contention that "In the beginning" is a reference to "the new creation of which Jesus Christ is the prototype" does not accord either with the grammar of the prologue or its chronology. Graeser, Lynn,, Schoenheit, *One God & One Lord*, 214.

used to distinguish the Word and God is πρὸς, and it used as "a marker of association, often with the implication of interrelationships."[7] Morris has noted that if one were to take a wooden translation of the term the clause would be rendered, "the Word was toward God,"[8] as πρὸς generally indicates movement toward an object.[9] However, Wallace has identified that in phrase ὁ λόγος ἦν πρὸς τὸν θεόν "the preposition and the verb do not match: The verb is stative and the preposition is transitive."[10] Thus, the context dictates that the preposition be translated "with." Carson has observed,

> In all but one or two peculiar constructions (e.g., 1 Pet 3:15), *pros* may mean 'with' only when a person is with a person, usually in some fairly intimate relationship. And that suggests that John may be pointing out, rather subtly, that the 'Word' he is talking about is a person, with God and therefore distinguished from God, and enjoying personal relationship with him.[11]

The Word was in a relationship with God. He was in close communion; indeed he was in fellowship with God. This however, ought not to be surprising since John's gospel goes on to tell us that the Father and Son were glorious together (17:5), in a loving relationship "before the foundation of the world" (17:24).

The last clause "and the Word was God," features θεὸς as an

---

[7] *Louw-Nida*, 89.112.

[8] Morris, Leon, *New International Commentary on the New Testament: The Gospel According to John*, Rev. Ed., (Grand Rapids: Eerdmans, 1995), Kindle, loc. 2053.

[9] See Wallace, *GGBB*, 358.

[10] Ibid., 359.

[11] Carson, D. A., *The Pillar New Testament Commentary: The Gospel According to John*, (Grand Rapids: Eerdmans, 1991), 216-217.

anarthrous predicate nominative. Θεὸς is here functioning qualitatively, providing a description about the λόγος. Because θεὸς resides in the place of emphasis, it cannot be that John is communicating the ontological subordination of the λόγος.[12] Rather, all that God is, his Word is.[13] The implication of the construction of John 1:1c is that any attempt to interpret the λόγος in terms of an impersonal plan, idea, or otherwise necessarily requires that the God of John 1:1b is impersonal. Thus, if God is personal, the Word is personal.

For sake of emphasizing the eternal personal distinction between God the Word and God, John repeated himself in v. 2, "He was in the beginning with God." God the Word, who was with God in the beginning was also the one through whom all things were made (v. 3). Unlike Paul who used the articular "all things" (τὰ πάντα) in his description of the Son as Creator in 1 Corinthians 8:6 and Colossians 1:16, John has placed simply "all" (πάντα) at the feet of God the Word. Of the clause, "all through him came into being," Morris has stated,

> John is saying that everything owes its existence to the Word. He does not say that all was made "by" him, but "through" him. This way of putting it safeguards the truth that the Father is the source of all that is. The relation of the first two Persons of the Trinity in the work of creation is of interest. There is a careful differentiation of the parts played by the Father and the Son (1 Cor. 8:6). Creation was not the solitary act of either. Both were

---

[12] For a comprehensive evaluation of the *New World Translation's* rendering "And the Word was a god," see Bowman Jr., Robert M., *Jehovah's Witnesses, Jesus Christ, and the Gospel of John*, (Grand Rapids: Baker, 1989), 25-63, esp. 39-63.

[13] This is the teaching of the writer to the Hebrews, who identifies the Son in 1:3 as the exact imprint (χαρακτὴρ) of the Father's nature (τῆς ὑποστάσεως).

at work (and, for that matter, still are; cf. 5:17, 19). The Father created, but he did it "through" the Word.[14]

Unlike the explicit complementarity present in 1 Corinthians 8:6, John 1:3 implies the agency of the Word in the economy of creation by means of the surrounding context. The construction πάντα δι' αὐτοῦ ἐγένετο identifies the Word's activity in creation as the Father's personal and active instrument. The preposition, διά when used with a genitive as it here, is defined as "a marker of personal agency."[15] The second clause emphasizes the assertion of the first clause— "Apart from him nothing came into being that has come into being" (χωρὶς αὐτοῦ ἐγένετο οὐδὲ ἕν ὃ γέγονεν).

Analogia Scriptura: Hebrews as Intertextual Commentary on John 1:1-3

The epistle to the Hebrews serves as something of a commentary upon the Johannine λόγος:

> Long ago, at many times and in many ways, God spoke to our fathers by the prophets, but in these last days he has spoken to us by his Son, whom he appointed the heir of all things, through whom also he created the world. (Heb 1:1-2)

Above, the writer to the Hebrews characterizes the Son as the Word of God that is superior to that which was mediated by the prophets.[16] The Son is also identified as the one through whom all

---

[14] Morris, *The Gospel According to John*, loc. 2098.

[15] Bauer, W. F. W, Danker, W. F., Arndt, and F. W. Gingrich., *A Greek-English Lexicon of the New Testament and Other Early Christian Literature* [*BDAG*], 3rd Ed. (Chicago: Univ. of Chicago Press, 2000), 225. See *TDNT*, Vol. 2, 66. Wallace, *GGBB*, 164.

[16] Buzzard's claim, "It is a common but patent misreading of the opening of John's Gospel to read it as if it said: "In the beginning was

things were made using the same kind of construction (διά + the genitive pronoun) used in John 1:3. Further in Hebrews 1, the writer presents a series of proof-texts intended to identify the supremacy and superiority of the Son as compared to other messengers of God's Word. Of particular relevance is Hebrews 1:8-12:

> But of the Son he says, 'Your throne, O God, is forever and ever, the scepter of uprightness is the scepter of your kingdom. You have loved righteousness and hated wickedness; therefore God, your God, has anointed you with the oil of gladness beyond your companions.' And, 'You, Lord, laid the foundation of the earth in the beginning, and the heavens are the work of your hands; they will perish, but you remain; they will all wear out like a garment, like a robe you will roll them up, like a garment they will be changed. But you are the same, and your years will have no end.' (Hebrews 1:8-12)

πρὸς δὲ τὸν υἱόν· ὁ θρόνος σου ὁ θεὸς εἰς τὸν αἰῶνα τοῦ αἰῶνος, καὶ ἡ ῥάβδος τῆς εὐθύτητος ῥάβδος τῆς βασιλείας σου. ἠγάπησας δικαιοσύνην καὶ ἐμίσησας ἀνομίαν· διὰ τοῦτο ἔχρισέν σε ὁ θεὸς ὁ θεός σου ἔλαιον ἀγαλλιάσεως παρὰ τοὺς μετόχους σου. καί· σὺ κατ' ἀρχάς, κύριε, τὴν γῆν ἐθεμελίωσας, καὶ ἔργα τῶν χειρῶν σού εἰσιν οἱ οὐρανοί· αὐτοὶ ἀπολοῦνται, σὺ δὲ διαμένεις, καὶ πάντες ὡς ἱμάτιον παλαιωθήσονται, καὶ ὡσεὶ περιβόλαιον ἑλίξεις αὐτούς, ὡς ἱμάτιον καὶ ἀλλαγήσονται· σὺ δὲ ὁ αὐτὸς εἶ καὶ τὰ ἔτη σου οὐκ ἐκλείψουσιν. (Hebrews 1:8-12, NA28)

The above pericope begins with the phrase "But to the Son"

---

the Son," neglects both actual exegesis and the analogy of Scripture via Hebrews 1:1-2; 1:10-12. Buzzard, *Caveat Lector*.

(πρὸς δὲ τὸν υἱόν), and in so doing implies the verb λέγει from v. 6 (And again, when he brings the firstborn into the world, he says...). Ellingworth has noted that "πρὸς means 'to,' not 'about, with reference to,' as in v. 7."[17] That the Father is identified as the subject is implied and indeed contextually demanded by the repetitive identification of the Son. The application of Psalm 45[18] is quite simply the recording of a dialogue between the Father and Son wherein the Father addresses the Son as "God," in vv. 8 and 9. Any suggestion that the Psalmist is indicated as the speaker ignores the authoritative application of the Psalm by the writer as it is found within the context of the argument. The argument of the prologue finds its weight in the identification of things said by the Father of and to the Son of God.

It is in vv. 10-12 that the Son's active role in creation is explicitly identified. It is here that we see what is meant by "through whom also he created the world." The writer has applied Psalm 101:26-28 LXX and in so doing he has explicitly attributed creation to the work of the Son "in the beginning" (κατ᾽ ἀρχάς). The conjunction καί and vocative κύριε demonstrate continuity with vv. 8-9. The Son is directly addressed using the Septuagintal translation of the tetragrammaton, and the one addressing him is the Father. Like v. 5 which uses the second person to identify the Father addressing the Son, the writer applies the quotation in vv. 10-12 in like manner.

The Christology articulated in Hebrews 1:2 and 1:10-12 is in many ways identical to that articulated in John 1:1-3. However, the explicit articulation of the Son's personal pre-incarnational existence in vv. 10-12 is unrivaled— the Son is the LORD who "laid the foundation of the earth in the beginning," and this *according to the Father.*

---

[17] Ellingworth, *Hebrews*, 122.
[18] Ps 44:6-7 LXX is quoted.

Further Consideration of the Targumic Memra

It is the position of this author that the atypical use of "Word" in the Hebrew Bible, the Septuagint, Targumim, and his personal involvement with Jesus, serve as the basis for John's λόγος. The prologue speaks in the currency of the Targums especially. Aside from the aforementioned texts wherein the Angel of Yahweh is translated Memra, consider the following examples wherein the Hebrew Bible is compared with the Targumim:

Text	Hebrew Bible	Targum
Gen 1:26	So God created man in his own image, in the image of God he created him.	And the Word of the LORD created man in his likeness, in the. likeness of the presence of the Lord he created him. Tg. Jer.
Gen 1:3	And God said, "Let there be light," and there was light.	And the Word of the Lord said, "Let there be light," and there was light according to the decree of his Word. Tg. Neof.
Gen 2:8	And the LORD God planted a garden in Eden, in the east, and there he put the man whom he had formed.	And a garden from the Eden of the just was planted by the Word of the LORD God before the creation of the world, and he made there to dwell the man when he had created him. Tg. P.

Gen 3:8, 10	And they heard the sound of the LORD God walking in the garden in the cool of the day…And he said, "I heard the sound of you in the garden.	And they heard the voice of the Word of the LORD God walking in the garden in the evening of the day… And they heard the voice of the Word of the LORD God walking in the garden in the evening of the day.[19] Tg. Onq.
Gen 5:2	Male and female he created them, and he blessed them and named them Man when they were created.	Male and female he created them, and blessed them in the name of his Word. Tg. P.
Gen 7:16	And the LORD shut him in.	And they coming entered, male and female, of all flesh unto him, as the LORD had instructed him; and the Word of the LORD covered over the door of the ark upon the face thereof. Tg. P.
Gen 9:13	I have set my bow in the cloud, and it shall be a sign of the	I have set my bow in the cloud and it shall be for a sign of the

---

[19] Cf. Tg. Neof.: "And they heard the sound of the *Memra* of the Lord God walking within the garden at the breeze of the day." In v. 10 Adam says to the Lord, "I heard the sound of your *Memra*."

	covenant between me and the earth.	covenant between my Word and between the earth. Tg. Onq.
Gen 9:17	This is the sign of the covenant that I have established between me and all flesh that is on the earth.	And the LORD said, This is the sign of the covenant which I have established between my Word and between all flesh which is upon the earth. Tg. Onq.
Gen 12:17	But the LORD afflicted Pharaoh and his house with great plagues because of Sarai, Abram's wife	And the Word of the LORD sent great plagues against Pharaoh and the men of his house, on account of Sara, Abram's wife. Tg. P.
Gen 15:1	Fear not, Abram, I am your shield.	Fear not... My Word will be your shield. Tg. P.
Gen 15:6	And he believed the LORD, and he counted it to him as righteousness.	And he believed in the LORD, and had faith in the Word of the LORD, and he reckoned it to him for righteousness. Tg. Onq.
Gen 18:1	And the Lord appeared to him by the oaks of Mamre,	And the Word of the LORD was revealed to Abraham in the plain of the vision... Tg. Neof.

Gen 19:24	Then the LORD rained on Sodom and Gomorrah sulfur and fire from the LORD out of heaven.	And the Word of the LORD Himself had made to descend upon the people of Sodom and Gomorrah showers of favor, that they might work repentance from their wicked works. But when they saw the showers of favor, they said, So, our wicked works are not manifest before Him. He turned [the Word], and caused to descend upon them bitumen and fire from before the LORD from the heavens. Tg. P.
Gen 20:3	And God came to Abimelech.	And the Word from before the LORD came to Abimelech. Tg. Onq.
Gen 21:22	God is with you in all that you do.	The Word of the LORD is your helper in everything you do. Tg. Onq.
Gen 22:8	Abraham said, "God will provide for himself the lamb for a burnt offering, my son."	And Abraham said, The Word of the LORD will prepare for me a lamb; and if not, then thou art the offering, my son! Tg.

		Jer.
Gen 40:23	Yet the chief cupbearer did not remember Joseph, but forgot him.	Blessed be the man who trusts in the name of the Word of the LORD. Tg. Jer.
Exodus 1:20-21	So God dealt well with the midwives. And the people multiplied and grew very strong. And because the midwives feared God, he gave them families.	And the LORD did good to the midwives… and the Word of the LORD built for them a royal house, even the house of the high priesthood. Tg. Pal.
Exodus 4:31	And the people believed; and when they heard that the LORD had visited the people of Israel and that he had seen their affliction, they bowed their heads and worshiped.	And Israel saw the mighty hand which the LORD performed on the Egyptians, and the people were afraid from before the LORD and believed in the name of the Word of the LORD, and the prophecy of Moses his servant. Tg. Pal.
Exodus 6:2-3	God spoke to Moses and said to him, "I am the LORD. I appeared to Abraham, to Isaac, and to Jacob, as God Almighty, but by my name the LORD I did not make myself known to them.	And the LORD was revealed in His Word unto Abraham, to Isaac, and to Jacob, as the God of Heaven; but the Name of the Word of the LORD was not known to them. Tg. Jer.

Exodus 13:21	And the Lord went before them by day in a pillar of cloud.	And the Word of the LORD was leading them during the day in a pillar of cloud. Tg. Neof.
Exodus 19:17	Then Moses brought the people out of the camp to meet God, and they took their stand at the foot of the mountain.	And Moses led forth the people out of the camp to meet the Word of the LORD; and they stood at the lower parts of the mount. Tg. Onq.
Exodus 25:22	There I will meet with you, and from above the mercy seat, from between the two cherubim that are on the ark of the testimony, I will speak with you about all that I will give you in commandment for the people of Israel.	And I will appoint My Word with you there; and I will speak with you. Tg. Onq.
Exodus 29:42-43	It shall be a regular burnt offering throughout your generations at the entrance of the tent of meeting before the LORD, where I will meet with you, to speak to you there. There I will meet with the people of Israel,	At the door of the tabernacle of ordinance before the LORD, where I have appointed my Word with you, to speak with you there. And I will appoint my Word there unto the sons of Israel, and my glory will I sanctify it. Tg.

	and it shall be sanctified by my glory.	Onq.
Exodus 33:21-22	And the LORD said, "Behold, there is a place by me where you shall stand on the rock, and while my glory passes by I will put you in a cleft of the rock, and I will cover you with my hand until I have passed by."	And the LORD said, "Behold, there is a place prepared before me, and you shall stand upon the rock, and it shall be, when my glory passed, I will put you in a cavern of the rock, and my Word shall overshadow you until I have passed." Tg. P.
Lev 20:23	You shall not walk in the customs of the nation that I am driving out before you, for they did all these things, and therefore I detested them.	You shall not walk in the laws of the peoples whom I drive away from before you; for they have committed all these things, and my Word hath abhorred them. Tg. Onq.
Lev 27:34	These are the commandments that the LORD commanded Moses for the people of Israel on Mount Sinai.	These are the statutes and judgments and laws which the LORD appointed between his Word and the sons of Israel, in the mountain of Sinai, by the hand of Moses. Tg. Onq.
Num 4:28	This is the service of the clans of the sons	These are the numbered of the Ben-

	of the Gershonites in the tent of meeting, and their guard duty is to be under the direction of Ithamar the son of Aaron the priest.	Gershon, everyone who did service in the tabernacle of ordinance, whom Moses and Aaron numbered by the mouth of the Word of the LORD. Tg. Onq.
Num 9:18-19	At the command of the LORD the people of Israel set out, and at the command of the LORD they camped. As long as the cloud rested over the tabernacle, they remained in camp. Even when the cloud continued over the tabernacle many days, the people of Israel kept the charge of the Lord and did not set out.	By the Word of the LORD the sons of Israel journeyed, and by the Word of the LORD they encamped; all the days that the Cloud rested, they remained. However long the time the Cloud was upon the Tabernacle, many the days, the sons of Israel kept the watch of the Word of the LORD, and journeyed not. Tg. Onq.
Num 10:35-36	Arise, O LORD, and let your enemies be scattered…Return, O LORD, to the ten thousand thousands of Israel.	Let the Word of the LORD be now revealed…Return now, Word of the LORD, in the goodness of your mercy and lead your people Israel. Tg. Ps-J.
Num 14:9	Only do not rebel against the LORD. And	Only be not rebellious against the Word of

	do not fear the people of the land, for they are bread for us. Their protection is removed from them, and the LORD is with us; do not fear them.	the LORD, nor be afraid of the people of the land, for they are delivered into our hand; their strength is departed from them, and the Word of the LORD is our helper. Tg. Onq.
Num 14:41	Why now are you transgressing the command of the LORD, when that will not succeed?	Wherefore do you transgress against the decree of the Word of the LORD? Tg. Onq.
Num 21:5	And the people spoke against God and against Moses, "Why have you brought us up out of Egypt to die in the wilderness?"	And the people murmured against the Word of the LORD, and contended with Moses, "Why have you brought us up out of Egypt to die in the desert?"[20] Tg. Onq.
Num 23:16	And the LORD met Balaam and put a word in his mouth and said, "Return to Balak, and thus shall you speak..."	And the Word from before the LORD met Balaam, and put a word in his mouth, and said, "Return to Balak, and thus speak..." Tg. Onq.

---

[20] Cf. 1 Cor 10:1-10. Paul's interpretation is the same; the one the Israelites grumbled against was God the Word, namely the Son.

Deut 2:7	For the LORD your God has blessed you in all the work of your hands. He knows you're going through this great wilderness. These forty years the LORD your God has been with you. You have lacked nothing.	He has given you sufficient for your need in your going about in this great wilderness; these forty years the Word of the LORD your God hath been your helper. Tg. Onq.
Deut 3:22	You shall not fear them, for it is the LORD your God who fights for you.	Fear them not, for the Word of the LORD your God will fight for you. Tg. Onq.
Deut 4:7	For what great nation is there that has a god so near to it as the LORD our God is to us, whenever we call upon him?	The Word of the LORD sits upon his throne high and lifted up, hearing our prayer what time we pray before him and make our petitions. Tg. Ps-J.
Deut 4:24	For the LORD your God is a consuming fire, a jealous God.	For the Word of the LORD thy God is a consuming fire: He is a jealous God. Tg. Onq.
Deut 18:16	Just as you desired of the LORD your God at Horeb on the day of the assembly, when you said, 'Let me not hear again the voice of the LORD my God or see this great fire any	According to all that you ask before the L your God at Horeb on the day of the assembly, saying: Let me not again hear the voice of the Word of the LORD my God,

	more, lest I die.'	and let me not see the great fire any more, lest I die. Tg. Onq.
Deut 20:1	When you go out to war against your enemies, and see horses and chariots and an army larger than your own, you shall not be afraid of them, for the LORD your God is with you, who brought you up out of the land of Egypt.	When you go out to war with your adversaries, and you see horses, and chariots, and more people than you, be not afraid of them; for your helper is the Word of the LORD thy God, who brought you up from the land of Egypt.[21] Tg. Onq.
Deut 33:7	Hear, O LORD, the voice of Judah, and bring him in to his people.	Hear, O Word, the voice of the prayer of Judah and bring him back safely from the battle lines to his people in peace. Tg. Neof.
Deut 33:27	The eternal God is your dwelling place, and underneath are the everlasting arms.	And the world was made by his Word. Tg. Onq.
Isaiah 43:2	When you pass through the waters, I will be with you; and through the rivers, they shall not	The Word was a guardian…When you passed through the Red Sea my Word was your support. Tg.

---

[21] Cf. Judges 2:1.

	overwhelm you; when you walk through fire you shall not be burned, and the flame shall not consume you.	Is.
Isaiah 44:24	Thus says the LORD, your Redeemer, who formed you from the womb: "I am the LORD, who made all things, who alone stretched out the heavens, who spread out the earth by myself,	I am the LORD who made all things; I stretched out the heavens by my Word. Tg. Is.
Isaiah 45:12	I made the earth and created man on it; it was my hands that stretched out the heavens, and I commanded all their host.	By my Word I made the earth, and created man upon it. Tg. Is.
Isaiah 48:13	My hand laid the foundation of the earth.	Indeed, by my Word I founded the earth. Tg. Is.
Amos 4:11	I overthrew some of you, as when God overthrew Sodom and Gomorrah.	My Word loathed you just as the LORD loathed Sodom and Gomorrah. Tg.

		Amos

John says of the divine Word, "the world was made through him" (1:10), just as *Onkelos* states, "And the world was made by his Word." Whereas John's prologue identifies the Word with light (vv. 4-5, 9), *Neofiti* states,

> The earth was void and empty and darkness was spread over the face of the abyss. And the Word of the Lord was the light and it shone; and he called it the first night.

The Hebrew Bible also speaks of a divine Word who is personal:

> After these things the word of the LORD came to Abram in a vision: "Fear not, Abram, I am your shield; your reward shall be very great." (Gen 15:1).

Here, the Word is a *visible* manifestation of God; the Word appeared to Abram "in a vision." Similarly, in 1 Samuel 3:1-21, the Word of the LORD appeared to Samuel in a vision. Were the "Word of the Lord" merely a circumlocution for God's audible speech, it would be incongruous for the Word to appear. It is the perspective of this author, given the above evidence, that the Targumic Memra often reflects the theology the non-unitarian stream of Jewish orthodoxy, indeed, it reflects Jewish belief in a divine person who is distinct from the Lord, and at the same time, God himself. So too, it is that stream of Jewish thought which has found a home in the fourth gospel.

Unitarians & Their "10,000 Pronouns"

Subordinationists and Oneness Pentecostals have attempted to marshal evidence for unitarianism based upon the use of the singular personal pronouns used of Yahweh in the Old Testament. Yates, a Oneness Pentecostal, has argued,

> If singular pronouns designating The One God, along with

the consistent and overwhelming witness of Scripture, cannot persuade the reader that God is a single individual, then sadly, there is little else in language that can. [22]

Buzzard has argued similarly:

Jews for the whole of their history had no problem with the cardinal tenet of the national faith. God was a single, undivided Divine Person, designated in their holy writings by thousands of singular personal pronouns and designating Himself as the one, single Lord of the universe, the one Divine Person who alone is God. This One God used every device known to language to convey the concept that He and no one else is God, that there is no other God. Singular personal pronouns define a single person. Christians claim to be rooted in the grammatical method where the standard laws of grammar are decisive.[23]

---

[22] Yates, Larry L., *The Divided God: Apostolic Theology and the Biblical Challenge to Contemporary Trinitarianism*, (Raleigh: Lulu, 2013), 44.

[23] Buzzard, Anthony, *Jesus Was Not a Trinitarian*, 39-40. See also Deuble, Greg S., *They Never Told Me This in Church*, (Atlanta: Restoration Fellowship, 2006), 88, and the comments of Dale Tuggy. Tuggy has asserted that trinitarians "Generally disregard the thousands of singular pronouns and verbs applied to Yahweh all over the Old Testament." 2016. "10 steps towards getting less confused about the Trinity – #1 Who's to say? – Part 1," *Trinities: Theories About the Father, Son, and Holy Spirit*, http://trinities.org/blog/10-steps-towards-getting-less-confused-trinity-1-whos-say/. Accessed 05/31/2016. Cf. Anderson, citing Tuggy's interpretation of both singular pronouns and the *Shema*, asserts "There is remarkably strong support" for unitarianism. Anderson, James, *Paradox in Christian Theology: An Analysis of Its Presence, Character, and Epistemic Status*, (Eugene: Wipf & Stock, 2007), 269f.

The fundamental assertion underlying the countless unitarian arguments based upon these singular pronouns was summarized by Buzzard: "Singular personal pronouns define a single person." However, if this assertion can be shown to be unbiblical, the unitarian contention will be shown to hang in the proverbial air.

There are many places within the Old Testament wherein singular personal pronouns are used of more than one personal subject. For instance, there is a covenantal use of singular personal pronouns that occurs with frequency in the major prophets. Consider the following underlined examples which are but a fraction of that contained in the Old Testament:[24]

So God created man in his own image, in the image of God he created him; male and female he created them. (Gen 1:27)

Fallen, fallen is Babylon; and all the carved images of her gods he has shattered to the ground. (Isaiah 21:9)

Speak tenderly to Jerusalem, and cry to her that her warfare is ended, that her iniquity is pardoned, that she has received from the Lord's hand double for all her sins. (Isaiah 40:2)

But now thus says the Lord, he who created you, O Jacob, he who formed you, O Israel: "Fear not, for I have redeemed you; I have called you by name, you are mine." (Isaiah 43:1)

Is Israel a slave? Is he a homeborn servant? Why then has he

---

[24] I am here, for the benefit of the uninitiated reader, appealing to the ESV, where the underlying Hebrew may have either a singular verb or noun with an implied singular pronoun. Cf. the fascinating discussion in Hasker, William, *Metaphysics & the Tri-Personal God*, (New York: Oxford Univ. Press, 2013), 228-231.

become a prey? (Jer 2:14)

Your evil will chastise you [i.e., the people of Israel], and your apostasy will reprove you. Know and see that it is evil and bitter for you to forsake the LORD your God; the fear of me is not in you. (Jer 2:19)

Hear the word of the Lord, O nations, and declare it in the coastlands far away; say, "He who scattered Israel will gather him, and will keep him as a shepherd keeps his flock." (Jer 31:10)

Fear not, O Jacob my servant, declares the Lord, for I am with you. I will make a full end of all the nations to which I have driven you, but of you I will not make a full end. I will discipline you in just measure, and I will by no means leave you unpunished. (Jer 46:28)

For Israel has forgotten his Maker and built palaces, and Judah has multiplied fortified cities; so I will send a fire upon his cities, and it shall devour her strongholds. (Hos 8:14)

When Israel was a child, I loved him, and out of Egypt I called my son. (Hos 11:1)

On the day I punish Israel for his transgressions… (Amos 3:14)

Then I said, "O Lord GOD, please cease! How can Jacob stand? He is so small!" (Amos 7:5)

But as for me, I am filled with power, with the Spirit of the LORD, and with justice and might, to declare to Jacob his transgression and to Israel his sin. (Mic 3:8)

A related consideration is the consistent interpretation of John's use of singular personal pronouns in his description of the Word, not to mention the Holy Spirit.[25] In John 1:2-4 and the topically connected clause in v. 10 ("the world was made through him"), there are no less than four personal pronouns used to describe the pre-incarnate Word. Hence, it is contradictory to adopt the unitarian contention regarding pronouns (i.e., "Singular personal pronouns define a single person") and the unitarian reading of the prologue (i.e., λόγος = a non-person).

Unitarians who make the aforementioned argument from pronouns engage in at least two very significant interpretive errors. First, they refuse to allow Scripture to buck conventional language. There are places where the Bible defines its own terms such that our conventional assumptions must be altered. Consider the following: Both redeemed men and women are "sons" in the kingdom of God.[26] A husband and his wife, while clearly being two distinct beings, are actually "one flesh."[27] Men or women, Christians constitute the "bride" of Christ.[28] A singular pronoun used of God in the Old Testament may refer to one of the divine persons individually,[29] or may refer to God generically and so incorporate all of the divine persons,[30] akin to the singular pronouns used of the nation of Israel. Because unitarian interpreters have imbibed a wooden rationalistic (i.e., anthropocentric) hermeneutic, they neglect to see such nuances.[31]

---

[25] Esp. John 14:16-17; 15:26; 16:4-15.

[26] Gal 4:6-7.

[27] Gen 2:24.

[28] Rev 19:7.

[29] E.g., Psalm 2:7.

[30] Psalm 100:3.

[31] This is also visible in the marriage between subordinationism and anthropological monism (i.e., an anthropology which rejects orthodox

Second, unitarians neglect the interpretive repercussions of the progressive nature of Scripture. This is most evident in the refusal of Christological Socinians to come to grips with the New Testament's teaching on the preexistence of Christ and the personhood of the Spirit, and the implications of these doctrines in Old Testament interpretation.

---

body/soul dualism) and annihilationism. For a refutation of both see Morey, Robert, *Death and the Afterlife*, (Minneapolis: Bethany House, 1984). See also Diaz III, Hiram R., *Soul Sleep: An Unbiblical Doctrine*, (Lewiston: Scripturalist Publications, 2017), and Peterson, Robert A., *Hell On Trial: The Case for Eternal Punishment*, (Phillipsburg: P&R, 1995), esp. 161-202.

YAHWEH: THE MAN WHO TOLD ABRAHAM THE TRUTH

Hiram R. Diaz III

Sound Doctrine Permeates the Totality of Scripture

The Gospel of John is nearly universally recognized as the Gospel which most clearly teaches the preexistence and deity of the Son of God.[1] From its opening declaration that "the Word was God,"[2] to its final declaration that Jesus Christ is "God" and "Lord,"[3] the text unambiguously teaches that the Savior Christ was, is, and will always be the co-equal, co-eternal divine second person of the Trinity.[4] Due to their clarity, these "deity passages"

---

[1] This is the consensus among Christian and non-Christian scholars. Non-Christian scholars postulate a progressive deification of Jesus that reaches its pinnacle in the so-called "high Christology" of the Gospel of John and the Pauline epistles. For example, see Bart D. Ehrman's *How Jesus Became God: The Exaltation Of A Jewish Preacher From Galilee* (New York: HarperOne, 2014). Christian scholars find the doctrine throughout the Scriptures, demonstrating this via exegesis and biblical and systematic theological analysis. E.g., Robert M. Bowman and J. Ed Komoszewski's *Putting Jesus In His Place: The Case For The Deity Of Christ*, (Grand Rapids: Kregel Publications, 2007).

[2] John 1:1; cf. 1:18.

[3] John 20:28.

[4] Ed L. Miller succinctly relays the nearly universal consensus

are useful proof-texts for the doctrine among scholars and non-scholars alike.

In response, anti-trinitarians attack either the interpretation, translation, or both, of each proof-text, as if the doctrines of Christ's deity and preexistence were entirely dependent on these fragments of the Scriptures. Biblical theological and systematic theological concerns are largely, if not completely, ignored; a method contrary to the interpretive practices of the Son of God and his apostles. God the Son reveals that the Scripture cannot be broken.[5] His Word is a divinely unified and, therefore, unbreakable set of true propositions.[6]

The "deity passages" in John 1:1 and 1:18, for example, find corroboration in passages of the same book which are not directly, although they are perhaps laterally, concerned with teaching the personal preexistence and deity of Christ. This is due to the fact that these doctrines are the foundational presuppositions upon which the text of John's Gospel has been built,[7] clearly evidencing

---

among scholars regarding the unequivocal "deity-passages" in the New Testament:

> Out of these eight [unequivocal] passages, three are found in John. Of these three, everyone acknowledges John 20:28 to be an unequivocal 'deity-passage,' even the otherwise skeptical Taylor who calls it the 'one clear ascription of Deity to Christ.' John 1:18 has always been clouded by a textual problem, but most scholars now correctly take *monogenes theos* ('only God') rather than *monogenes huios* ('only Son') to be the original reading. In addition to being the *lectio difficilior*, it is supported by a long list of MSS., Fathers, and Versions, including Vaticanus, Sinaiticus, and now also p^{66} and p^{75}. When the textual problem is thus decided, this verse too becomes an unambiguous proof-text for the deity of Jesus.

1981. "'The Logos Was God'," in *The Evangelical Quarterly* 53: 65–77.
   [5] John 10:35.
   [6] See Ps 19:9; 119:142, vv. 151, 160; Prov 30:5; Rom 3:4.
   [7] Similarly, the Synoptic Gospels and John were composed by men

this in several places.[8] The most striking text in this category is John 8:40, where Christ implies his deity and personal preexistence in the short sentence: "This is not what Abraham did."

---

who already believed that Jesus Christ had fulfilled the Messianic prophecies regarding his life and death and resurrection. Their texts, therefore, explicitly and implicitly reflect their beliefs. The Gospel writers often retroactively assess their previous bafflement at Jesus' teaching (e.g. Mark 6:52; 9:32; Luke 2:50; 9:45; John 8:27; 10:6; 12:16; 20:9), indicating that their texts were composed with a more mature understanding of what they had experienced and what they were taught.

[8] Briefly, we may consider a curious explanatory remark made in John 6:6. The people following Jesus are hungry and without any bread. They had seen him exercise power over sicknesses and demons, thereby establishing his credentials as a man from God, blessed by God, and sent to lead and save God's elect people. Parallels between this scenario of God's hungry people following God's miracle working deliverer Moses are clearly intentional. The comparison between Moses and Jesus is even hinted at in the words of the people who declare that "This is indeed the Prophet who is to come into the world!" (6:14b, itself alluding to Deut 18:15-19).

Where the comparison is broken, however, is in the attribution of testing to Jesus. After having displayed his power to save his people, his power over the natural forces of creation as well, God tells Moses that his intended purpose in sending them manna from heaven is to "...test them, whether they will walk in [his] law or not" (Exod 16:4). God is testing the people to see if they believe him and will, consequently, obey his law. John's record, however, identifies Jesus as the one who is present in leading his people, who are hungry for *bread*, in order to see what they will do. John demonstrates that Jesus, unlike Moses, is fully in control of the situation. Jesus, unlike Moses, is the one who is testing the professing believers. Jesus is testing Israel, just as Yahweh tested Israel in the wilderness. He will provide bread for Israel, just as Yahweh provided bread for Israel.

Implied by John is that Jesus is doing what only Yahweh does: He is testing the faithfulness of his people, of those who claim to love him and know him. Jesus' intention is to test his followers' faith and obedience to *himself,* just as Yahweh's intention was to test his followers' faith and obedience to himself.

It is a text which is often overlooked, with John 8:58 being given the more prominent role as a proof-text for the doctrines of Christ's deity and personal preexistence. The clarity of Christ' assertion - *viz.* "Before Abraham was, I Am" –renders the passage a very useful proof-text, as well as a favored target among anti-trinitarians. By ignoring John 8:58's biblical theological and systematic theological contexts, anti-trinitarians can muddy the interpretive waters enough to make their dismissal of truth at least *seem* plausibly justifiable. When understood in its canonical and immediate contexts, however, John 8:58 is an explicit declaration of what Jesus has already implied in John 8:40.

Hence, the importance of John 8:40's implied teaching. Jesus' short statement about what Abraham did not do *to him* implies what "I Am" in John 8:58 explicitly states—Jesus is Yahweh, the everlasting I Am. In what follows this will be demonstrated by an analysis of the text in in its canonical and immediate contexts.

John 8:30-47

John 8:40 is part of the second of Christ's three discourses with the Jews in John's Gospel. While these discourses vary with regard to their narrative content, they share a "loose structure" wherein the increasing blindness of the Jews is thrown into relief by increasing clarity of Christ's self-identification as Yahweh.[9] The equal and opposite increases in blindness and clarity occur in the individual pericopes, as well as in the three texts collectively (i.e. consecutively read).

More narrowly, our focus will be on John 8:30-47, which reads:

As he was saying these things, many believed in him.

---

[9] For a more in-depth treatment of these three passages, see Urban C. Von Wahlde, 1984. "Literary Structure and Theological Argument in Three Discourses With The Jews in The Fourth Gospel," *Journal of Biblical Literature*, 103/4, 575-584.

So Jesus said to the Jews who had believed him, "If you abide in my word, you are truly my disciples, and you will know the truth, and the truth will set you free." They answered him, "We are offspring of Abraham and have never been enslaved to anyone. How is it that you say, 'You will become free'?"

Jesus answered them, "Truly, truly, I say to you, everyone who practices sin is a slave to sin. The slave does not remain in the house forever; the son remains forever. So if the Son sets you free, you will be free indeed. I know that you are offspring of Abraham; yet you seek to kill me because my word finds no place in you. I speak of what I have seen with my Father, and you do what you have heard from your father."

They answered him, "Abraham is our father." Jesus said to them, "If you were Abraham's children, you would be doing the works Abraham did, but now you seek to kill me, a man who has told you the truth that I heard from God. This is not what Abraham did. You are doing the works your father did." They said to him, "We were not born of sexual immorality. We have one Father—even God." Jesus said to them, "If God were your Father, you would love me, for I came from God and I am here. I came not of my own accord, but he sent me. Why do you not understand what I say? It is because you cannot bear to hear my word. You are of your father the devil, and your will is to do your father's desires. He was a murderer from the beginning, and does not stand in the truth, because there is no truth in him. When he lies, he speaks out of his own character, for he is a liar and the father of lies. But because I tell the truth, you do not believe me. Which one of you convicts me of sin? If I tell the truth, why do you not believe me? Whoever is of God hears the words of God. The reason why you do not hear them is that you are not of God."

This discourse contains several antitheses which may be diagrammed as follows.

1. *Belief*	1. *Unbelief*
2. *Freedom*	2. *Slavery*
3. *Children of Abraham*	3. *Children of the Devil*
4. *Truth*	4. *Lies*
5. *Life*	5. *Murder*
6. *Hearing*	6. *Not-Hearing*

The overarching thematic antithesis is that of the children of Abraham (i.e. believers) and the children of the devil (i.e. unbelievers).

What one's genetic relationship to Abraham signifies is a salient theme of the entire New Testament[10] and the Gospel of John in particular. As early as John 1:11-13, John explicitly reveals that physical ancestry does not determine one's spiritual status. A child of God, i.e. a true Israelite/son of Abraham, is one who believes in Jesus Christ.[11] Nicodemus learns this when he is taught

---

[10] Cf. Matt 3:7-10, 8:5-13; Rom 1-3, 9 & 11; Gal 3-4.
[11] Like Zacchaeus in Luke 19:1-9 (spec. vv. 5-9), or Nathanael in John 1:45-51. Regarding Nathanael's status as a "true Israelite," see Trudinger, Paul L., 1982. "An Israelite In Whom There Is No Guile: An

by the Son of God that only those who are born *again* (i.e. spiritually reborn) will see and enter the kingdom of God.[12] The woman at the well in John 4, likewise, is taught that her Samaritan heritage does not exclude her from entering the kingdom of God by faith in Christ. For, Jesus says, "the hour is coming...when the true worshipers will worship the Father in spirit and truth, for the Father is seeking such people to worship him."[13]

Genetic ties to Abraham do nothing for one's spiritual condition. Christ's preaching undermined the Jewish tendency to locate spirituality in one's genetic ties to Abraham, a tendency so strong, in fact, that the Jews sought to discredit Christ by claiming that he was "a *Samaritan* and [had] a demon."[14] Conflict between Christ and the Jews in John's Gospel seems to be grounded in the two contrary doctrines of 1.) the spiritual impotency of being physically related to Abraham and 2.) one's spirituality being genetically inherited.

Genesis/John & Creation/Redemption

Scholars have long noted the relationship between John 1:1 and Genesis 1:1, both of which begin with the phrase "In the beginning." The relationship between these two texts is deeper, however, as the seven day schema of Gen 1-2 is paralleled by John's "deliberate, if somewhat artificial, [...] seven day schema in John 1:19-2:11,"[15] paralleling even some of the finer details of the creation narrative.[16] With this in mind, Jeannine K. Brown analyzes the *creation/re-creation* thematic paralleling of Genesis

---

Interpretive Note On John 1:45-51," *The Evangelical Quarterly* 54.2, 117-120.

[12] John 3:1-9.

[13] John 4:23.

[14] John 8:48. (emphasis added)

[15] Trudinger, Paul L., 1972. "The Seven Days of the New Creation in St. John's Gospel: Some Further Reflections," *The Evangelical Quarterly*, 44, 154.

[16] See Trudinger, "The Seven Days," 156-158.

and John in her essay "Creation's Renewal in the Gospel of John,"[17] deepening the roots of John's text in Genesis by drawing attention to Christ's role as the Last Adam,[18] as well as Creator of a new humanity made in his image.[19]

Most importantly, for our present purposes, we find that the first articulation of the seed of God and the seed of the devil is given in the *protoevangelium* of Genesis 3:15. This critical passage of Scripture succinctly describes the whole of human relationships throughout history in two ways. Firstly, humanity is ultimately divided into only two classes, *viz.* the seed of the woman and the seed of the serpent. As Thomas Davai notes, "the 'seed' [of the woman] refers to godly human descendants of Eve...[whereas the seed of the serpent are the] ungodly human descendants of Eve, who characterise the serpent."[20] Secondly, the seed of the woman are in perpetual conflict with the seed of the serpent. "The enmity is progressive...strife between the descendants of the woman and the serpent itself...The multitude of descendants on both sides will struggle [until the serpent's head is crushed]."[21]

The importance of the *toledot*[22] structure of Genesis, found in its emphasis on the promised seed of the woman, is a special point of emphasis in the New Testament. The primeval history of man unfolds, its genealogical focus gradually becoming narrower and narrower until Christ Jesus is born of a woman. Matthew and Luke

---

[17] 2010. *The Catholic Biblical Quarterly*, 72, 275-290.

[18] Ibid., 279-282.

[19] Ibid., 282-283. See also, Frayer-Griggs, Daniel, 2013. "Spittle, Clay, and Creation in John 9:6 and Some Dead Sea Scrolls," *Journal of Biblical Literature*, 132, No. 3, 659–670.

[20] 2012. "Analysis of 'Enmity' in Genesis 3:15," *Melanesian Journal of Theology*, 28-1, 85.

[21] Davai, "Enmity," 90.

[22] For more on this, see Derouchie, Jason S., 2013. "The Blessing-Commission, The Promised Offspring, and the *Toledot* Structure of Genesis," in *Journal of the Evangelical Theological Society* 56/2, 219–247.

explicitly connect Christ to the genealogies of Genesis as the Son of Abraham and Son of God[23] through whom God would bring salvation to the Gentiles, i.e. the entirety of the non-Jewish world, a theme which, as we have already noted, is given prominence in John's Gospel.

The Seed of Promise vs. The Seed of the Flesh

John's overall paralleling of many significant themes found in Genesis, we note, sets the broader immediate context in which we find John 8:40. The conflict between Jesus and the Jews is rooted in his denial of their self-ascribed titles of "sons of Abraham"[24] and "sons of God."[25] Christ states that they are indeed the physical offspring of Abraham,[26] but this physical relation does not make them free from slavery to sin (i.e. sons of God).[27] Those who are truly the children of Abraham, he reveals, are those who do the works that Abraham did, *viz.* believing the Gospel of the promised Seed and living in accordance with one's professed belief. The Jews were seeking to kill Jesus, a man who has told the truth, and this is *not* what Abraham did. Therefore, these Jews were not truly children of Abraham, but were children of the devil.

Here is where Christ implies his deity and personal preexistence. He asserts that the Jews are not children of Abraham because they are seeking to do what Abraham did not seek to do, *viz.* kill him. Exegetically, the word *this* (τοῦτο) can only be cogently interpreted as referring back to the actions of the Jews, *viz.* trying to kill Jesus.[28] Some commentators have unconvincingly

---

[23] Cf. Matt 1:1-17 & Luke 3:23-38.

[24] John 8:39-40.

[25] John 8:41-42.

[26] John 8:37.

[27] John 8:31-36.

[28] In email correspondence, Burgos explained:

νῦν δὲ ζητεῖτέ με ἀποκτεῖναι ἄνθρωπον ὃς τὴν ἀλήθειαν ὑμῖν λελάληκα ἣν ἤκουσα παρὰ τοῦ θεοῦ· τοῦτο Ἀβραὰμ οὐκ

argued that the assertion is either a Hebraism,[29] or an oddly phrased reference to Abraham's actions toward men who spoke the truth *in general*.[30] Others believe that Jesus is here alluding to Gen

---

ἐποίησε (John 8:40)

And now you are seeking to kill me, a man who spoke truth to y'all, which I heard from God. This Abraham did not do.
(Burgos' translation)

The continuative conjunction δὲ (and) is intended to mark the continuation of Jesus' argument against his interlocutors. These Jews are slaves to sin (v. 34), and despite being biological children of Abraham, they seek Jesus' death. In v. 38 Jesus announces that his words are what he has seen with his Father. The phrase παρὰ τῷ πατρὶ (with the Father) is one that demands from the reader recognition that Jesus is claiming to have been with (i.e., in the presence of) the Father presumably before his human birth. παρὰ with the dative noun is the same exact construction that is used twice in John 17:5 and many other places in Johannine literature to convey preexistence. In fact, virtually every single time παρὰ is with the dative appears in John it is indicative of someone being in the presence of someone else (e.g., John 1:39; 4:40; 14:17; 14:23, v. 25).

δὲ with the adverb νῦν signs that Jesus is dropping a bomb in this portion of his argument. You are a slave to sin (v. 35), and you are seeking to kill me because you don't like what I say (v. 37), and I have been with the Father and say what he tells me to say (v. 38), and now (νῦν δὲ) y'all are seeking to (ζητεῖτέ is a second person plural) kill (ἀποκτεῖναι – typically used for murder) me, a man who spoke the truth. Here, Jesus is alluding backward to those other men who spoke the truth and were likewise objects of murder by "Abraham's children" (cf. Matt 21:33-46; 23:34ff; Luke 11:47ff). Jesus reiterates his identity as a prophet—a man speaking words given to him from God precisely so that he can show that these Jews are in good company among the rest of the prophet murderers from times past. The last sentence is the bomb— this (τοῦτο—neuter demonstrative pronoun) Abraham did not do. The pronoun here is being used as a substantive, and when used this way it either points to an antecedent or a postcedent. In this context, it is clearly pointing backward, and the antecedent is Jesus' claim that the Jews wanted to murder him.

[29]J.C. Ryle does this in his *Expository Thoughts on the Gospel of John*.

[30] Including, but not limited to: *Ellicott's Commentary for English*

18, as well as 1st century traditions surrounding Abraham as the exemplar of Jewishness.[31]

Contextually, however, the word "this" points backward to a very specific action: Abraham did not seek to kill *Jesus*, the man who told him the truth. The grammatical structure of the text demands this interpretation, as do the central themes of this chapter. Specifically, Christ explains that he has been revealing his identity "from *the beginning*,"[32] a phrase which he uses again in reference to the devil's lying and murdering of Adam and Eve in the garden of Eden,[33] clearly placing himself in Genesis, as John himself does in his Gospel's prologue, and in conflict with the serpent.

Moses' use of the *toledot* structure brings the Seed/Serpent conflict into relief, as the broader "generations" narrow down to the generations of Abraham, Isaac, and Jacob. Specification of the lineage of the Seed of the Woman comes into view as Abraham is introduced to the reader and given the initial covenantal promises by Yahweh himself.[34] This is followed by the record of Abraham's attempt to fulfill God's promise to him in Genesis 16, an attempt which ends with "the son of the slave woman"[35] being cast out.

Jay Hess, along with Gunther Juncker, believes that Christ's response to the Jews alludes to Gen 18, convincingly arguing that the Jews assumed Abraham's seeing of Christ was a literal,

---

Readers, Matthew Poole's Commentary on the Holy Bible, John Gill's Exposition of the Entire Bible. More contemporary resources follow suit. See Carson, D.A., *The Gospel According to John,* (Grand Rapids: Eerdmans, 1991), 351-352; Ridderbos, Herman, *The Gospel of John: A Theological Commentary,* (Grand Rapids: Eerdmans, 1997), 312.

[31] See Kostenberger, Andreas J., *John,* (Grand Rapids: Baker Academic, 2004), 264-265.

[32] 8:25. (emphasis added)

[33] 8:44.

[34] See Gen 12:1-9; 15:1-6.

[35] Cf. Gal 4:22-31.

personal encounter.[36] These authors argue that Christ is one of the three men who meets Abraham and reveals his plans for Abraham, Sarah, and Sodom and Gomorrah, a traditional interpretation of the text that is historically rooted in the early post-apostolic era.[37]

Their identification of Gen 18 as the point of allusion, however, does not explain how Abraham did not seek to kill Christ. Thematically, the connection between Jesus' words and Gen 18 is lacking. While Yahweh tells Abraham "what he is about to do,"[38] and specifically mentions Abraham's moral character and its connection to his offspring,[39] what is lacking is what has been identified above as the seed conflict.

The only passage in which such a conflict comes into view, in fact, is found in Gen 17. There Yahweh "appeared to Abram" and revealed that he would establish his covenant between himself and

---

[36] See "What was Jesus' claim in John 8:56-58?," *Biblical Answers*. Accessed 09/08/2016. http://www.biblicalanswers.net/john8.html.

[37] In his article 1994. "Christ as Angel: The Reclamation of a Primitive Title" in *Trinity Journal* 15:2, 221–250, Gunther Juncker explains:

> Unknown to many, the early church fathers often referred to Jesus as an Angel. And they gave him this appellation long before the (alleged) distortions of Constantine, the Controversies, the Councils, and the Creeds. Due to its antiquity, its longevity, and the claim to being a primitive, if not an apostolic, Christological title… [222]

> …Hippolytus, Clement, Origen, Cyprian, Novatian, Victorinus, Eusebius, Athanasius, Hilary, Epiphanius, the Apostolic Constitutions: who through faith subdued kingdoms, wrote martyrdoms, obtained promises, stopped the mouths of heretics, quenched the violence of fire, turned to flight the armies of the demons. And these all referred to Christ by the title Angel (suggesting the paradoxical possibility that they still await the perfecting of our historical theology). [248]

[38] Cf. Gen 18:17.

[39] Cf. Gen 18:18.

Abraham and his offspring after him throughout their generations for an everlasting covenant, to be God to Abraham and to his offspring after him.[40] Having appeared to Abraham and made this promise, he then goes on to declare:

> "As for Sarai your wife, you shall not call her name Sarai, but Sarah shall be her name. I will bless her, and moreover, I will give you a son by her. I will bless her, and she shall become nations; kings of peoples shall come from her."[41]

Upon hearing these words,

> Abraham fell on his face and laughed and said to himself, "Shall a child be born to a man who is a hundred years old? Shall Sarah, who is ninety years old, bear a child?" And Abraham said to God, "Oh that Ishmael might live before you!"[42]

Abraham's desire to see his physical offspring receive the covenant blessings, however, is met with God's reply:

> "No, but Sarah your wife shall bear you a son, and you shall call his name Isaac. I will establish my covenant with him as an everlasting covenant for his offspring after him. As for Ishmael, I have heard you; behold, I have blessed him and will make him fruitful and multiply him greatly. He shall father twelve princes, and I will make him into a great nation. But I will establish my covenant with Isaac, whom Sarah shall bear to you at this time next year."[43]

---

[40] Gen 17:6-7.
[41] Gen 17:15-16.
[42] Gen 17:17-18.
[43] Gen 17:19-21.

God flatly denies Abraham's request to have the child born of the slave-woman, Hagar, receive the blessings of the covenant.

God's choice of Isaac, the child of promise, is not based on physical descent, for if that were the case then Ishmael would be the recipient of covenant blessings. Instead, God tells Abraham that those who are the recipients of the blessings of the covenant are the seed of promise, not the seed of the flesh. Ishmael, though the physical son of Abraham, is not the true son of Abraham, as God later implies.[44]

Despite having had his request regarding Ishmael's placement in the covenant denied, despite having been told that his own flesh and blood would not be a partaker of the covenant, "Abraham took Ishmael his son and all those born in his house or bought with his money, every male among the men of Abraham's house, and he circumcised the flesh of their foreskins that very day, as God had said to him."[45] His response to God's declaration that his own flesh and blood was rejected from the covenant was not anger, disbelief, or embitterment but faith and obedience to God's command. The dual lineage of Abraham, itself a narrowing of the dual lineage of believers/unbelievers mentioned in Gen 3:15, could have issued from Abraham a response of unbelief and antagonism toward Yahweh who *appeared to him*. However, Abraham, unlike his physical descendants millennia later, humbly accepted God's declaration that, in effect, not all who are Israel are Israel.[46] Unlike his descendants, according to the flesh, Abraham did not seek to kill Yahweh who revealed this hard truth to him.

Concluding Remarks

While John 8:40 is not the grand-finale of Christ's revelation of his deity, it is nevertheless an important stop along the way.

---

[44] See Gen 22:1-2.

[45] Gen 17:23.

[46] Cf. Rom 9:6.

Jesus has been revealing himself "from the beginning," i.e. since
the creation, from the beginning of the books of Moses[47] - from the
book of Genesis. This is not merely in prophetic revelation, but in
the very appearances of Yahweh recorded therein. Yahweh
appeared to Abraham and emphatically declared that the children
of the covenant were not those who were physical descendants of
Abraham but those who believed Yahweh's Word and lived in
light of that belief. This is the truth that Abraham was told: Not all
Israel is Israel. This is the same truth which the Jews would later
want to kill Yahweh for implying: "Neither circumcision counts
for anything, nor uncircumcision, but a new creation."[48] This is the
point of conflict between Jews and Gentiles that is addressed
throughout the New Testament subsequent to Jesus' ascension.

Understandably, Abraham desperately desired to see his son
Ishmael receive the promises of the covenant. Yet Abraham did
not do what his physical descendants sought to do millennia later.
Abraham, rather, submitted himself to Yahweh. He served
Yahweh, the man who told him the truth, in fact, providing him
with food, a foot-washing, and a place to replenish himself as he
continued on his journey to bring judgment to Sodom and
Gomorrah, as well as salvation to his elect.[49] Unlike their physical
progenitor, the unbelieving Jews fail to do these things for God the
Son as he passed through their land on his way to judge the world
and save his elect.[50]

John 8:40, in its canonical and immediate contexts implies that
what Abraham did not do is *seek to kill Christ*, Yahweh the Man
who told him the truth. The implicit nature of this revelation does
not diminish its importance, for this demonstrates that it is
foundational to the structure of the book of John, pointing forward
to Christ's explicitly stated grand finale in 8:58:

---

[47] Cf. John 5:39-47.
[48] Gal 6:15.
[49] Cf. Gen 18:1-8.
[50] Cf. Luke 7:44-50; Matt 25:31-46.

Before Abraham was, I AM.

FORMA DEI/FORMA SERVI: A NECESSARY CHRISTOLOGICAL DIALECTIC

Michael R. Burgos Jr.

Subordinationist Christology depends upon those passages within the New Testament that speak to the Son's inferiority to the Father. These texts are, from a subordinationist perspective, the most explicit statements which preclude orthodox Christology and the Trinity. For instance, Chang argued,

> "My Father is greater than all" (v.29). Do we imagine that "all" excludes Jesus himself? Is the meaning not plain enough: Absolutely no one is greater than my Father? Or in Paul's words, the Father is "God over all, blessed forever" (Rom.9.5). By saying that "the Father," not the Son, "is greater than all" Jesus had already precluded any claim to equality. He put this matter beyond dispute when he declared, "the Father is greater than I" (Jn.14.28).[1]

---

[1] Chang, *The Only True God*, 85. As an aside, Chang's interpretation of Rom 9:5 is incorrect. Paul's assertion that Christ belongs to the Israelites "according to the flesh" assumes that the derivation of Christ cannot be limited to flesh. Regarding the rendering,

Chang, like many subordinationists, understands Jesus to be speaking in definitive ontological categories. That is, on the unitarian view, when Jesus says the "Father is greater than all," he's saying that the Father is greater than himself in every sense.

The error involved in the subordinationist reading of these kinds of texts is that it does not take into account the Christological dialectic brought about by the incarnation. The claim of orthodoxy is that Jesus, who is eternally co-equal with God, took upon himself human existence, subordinating himself to the prescriptions of the law and conventional human existence. The incarnation created the occasion wherein the eternally glorious Son of God was made low and humiliated. Thus, the Son of God can be correctly assigned using both divine and creaturely descriptions.

In Philippians 2:5-11, the apostle uses the incarnation and humiliation of the Son of God to engender unity and humility in the Philippian church. Because this pericope demonstrates the aforementioned dialectic in vivid detail, an exegesis of the text is required. Thereafter, I will give several examples of how this Christological dialectic is appropriately applied.

An Exegesis of Philippians 2:5-11

> Have this mind among yourselves, which is yours in Christ Jesus, who, though he was in the form of God, did not count equality with God a thing to be grasped, but emptied himself, by taking the form of a servant, being born in the

---

the declaration that Christ belongs to the Israelites "according to the flesh" serves as the capstone of Paul's characterization of Israeli heritage—this is a classic Pauline *argumentum a fortiori*. Since a preexistent Christ is the antecedent, and since Paul puts Christ at the pinnacle of the blessings bestowed on Israel, the natural reading of the text refers to Christ as "God over all." See also Carraway, George W., *Christ is God Over All: Romans 9:5 in the Context of Romans 9-11*, (New York: Bloomsbury T & T Clark, 2013).

likeness of men. And being found in human form, he humbled himself by becoming obedient to the point of death, even death on a cross. Therefore God has highly exalted him and bestowed on him the name that is above every name, so that at the name of Jesus every knee should bow, in heaven and on earth and under the earth, and every tongue confess that Jesus Christ is Lord, to the glory of God the Father. (Philippians 2:5-11)

Τοῦτο φρονεῖτε ἐν ὑμῖν ὃ καὶ ἐν Χριστῷ Ἰησοῦ, ὃς ἐν μορφῇ θεοῦ ὑπάρχων οὐχ ἁρπαγμὸν ἡγήσατο τὸ εἶναι ἴσα θεῷ, ἀλλὰ ἑαυτὸν ἐκένωσεν μορφὴν δούλου λαβών, ἐν ὁμοιώματι ἀνθρώπων γενόμενος· καὶ σχήματι εὑρεθεὶς ὡς ἄνθρωπος ἐταπείνωσεν ἑαυτὸν γενόμενος ὑπήκοος μέχρι θανάτου, θανάτου δὲ σταυροῦ. διὸ καὶ ὁ θεὸς αὐτὸν ὑπερύψωσεν καὶ ἐχαρίσατο αὐτῷ τὸ ὄνομα τὸ ὑπὲρ πᾶν ὄνομα, ἵνα ἐν τῷ ὀνόματι Ἰησοῦ πᾶν γόνυ κάμψῃ ἐπουρανίων καὶ ἐπιγείων καὶ καταχθονίων καὶ πᾶσα γλῶσσα ἐξομολογήσηται ὅτι κύριος Ἰησοῦς Χριστὸς εἰς δόξαν θεοῦ πατρός. (Philippians 2:5-11, NA28)

In the beginning verses of chapter 2, Paul has sought unity and solidarity among the Philippian fellowship. He exhorts the congregation to have "the same mind, being in full accord and of one mind" (v. 2). In vv. 2-3 Paul provided practical instruction to accomplish unity, and in so doing he placed a prohibition on pride and a priority on the consideration of others. In v. 5, somewhat unexpectedly, Paul begins something of an object lesson, using Jesus as the exemplar for humility. He stated, "Have this mind among yourselves, which is yours in Christ Jesus." The first clause, "Have this mind among yourselves" points backward to v. 3 and 4, and thus indicates that the "mind" or attitude that is under consideration is the one that appropriates the aforementioned instruction (i.e., counting others more significant than oneself).

The second clause, "which is yours in Christ Jesus," indicates that the "mind" of humility was and is present in the person of Christ. This is a sentiment that finds continuity elsewhere within the Pauline corpus. Ephesians 5:1-2 states, "Therefore be imitators of God, as beloved children and walk in love, as Christ loved us and gave himself up for us..."

Paul's object lesson begins with the statement, "though he was in the form of God." Here, the ESV has sacrificed a literal reading. The Greek text reads ὃς ἐν μορφῇ θεοῦ ὑπάρχων. The best rendering is that of the *Christian Standard Bible*, which renders the clause, "Who existing in the form of God." What constitutes "the form of God"? In Greek texts, μορφῇ refers to the "external appearance," [2] and "something which may be perceived by the senses."[3] However, Hawthorne has well noted that "When this word is applied to God... such an understanding is quite inadequate. For God is the invisible God (Col 1:15; 1 Tim 1:17) and cannot be comprehended by the human senses."[4] So too, there is no external appearance that is particular to the "form of a slave." Warfield has well articulated the meaning of μορφῇ θεοῦ:

> Paul does not say simply, 'He was God.' He says, 'He was in the form of God,' employing a turn of speech which throws emphasis upon Our Lord's possession of the specific quality of God. 'Form' is a term which expresses the sum of those characterizing qualities which make a thing the precise thing that it is. Thus, the 'form' of a sword...is all that makes a given piece of metal specifically a sword, rather than, say, a spade. And 'the form of God' is the sum of the characteristics which make the being we call

---

[2] *TDNT*, Vol. 4, 742.

[3] Ibid., 745.

[4] Hawthorne, Gerald F., *Word Biblical Commentary: Philippians*, (Waco: Word Pub. 1983), 82.

'God,' specifically God, rather than some other being— an angel, say, or a man. When Our Lord is said to be in 'the form of God,' therefore, He is declared to be all that God is, to possess the whole fullness of attributes which make God God.[5]

The accompanying present active participle, ὑπάρχων, demands a certain temporal order to this pericope. Fee has noted, *"Prior* to his 'having taken the 'form' of a slave' he was in fact 'in the 'form' of God."[6] Thus, any interpretation of Philippians 2:6-9 that asserts that the "form of God" is something other than the Son's pre-incarnate state, must also assert that the Son existed on the earth sans the "form of a slave" (i.e., human existence). Hence, the Son's existence in the "form of God" occurred prior to and during his self-emptying (v. 7).

Although the Son was in the "form of God" and had equality with God, he "did not count equality with God a thing to be grasped" (v. 6). That is, being equal with God (τὸ εἶναι ἴσα θεῷ,), having all of the attributes commensurate with deity, the Son did not cleave to the full exercise of his position.[7] Such a construct itself refutes any unitarian theology. Instead (ἀλλὰ), "he made himself nothing" (ἑαυτὸν ἐκένωσεν, v. 7). The means by which

---

[5] Warfield, Benjamin B., *The Person and Work of Christ*, (Phillipsburg: Presbyterian & Reformed, 1950), 39. Similarly, with reference to the use of μορφῇ at Phil 2, *Louw-Nida* defines the term as "the nature or character of something." Louw, J. P., Nida, E., *Greek-English Lexicon of the New Testament Based on Semantic Domains*, 2nd ed., (New York: United Bible Societies, 1989), 2.58.

[6] Fee, *Pauline Christology: An Exegetical-Theological Study*, (Grand Rapids: Baker Academic, 2013), 377.

[7] On the meaning of the hapax ἁρπαγμὸν, see Wright's extensive study: Wright, N. T., *The Climax of the Covenant: Christ and the Law in Pauline Theology*, (New York: T & T Clark, 1991), 62-90. For a more concise study, see Fee, *Pauline Christology*, 381-383.

this self-emptying took place is supplied by the participial phrases that follow. He (i.e., the Son), emptied himself by means of "taking the form of a slave" (μορφὴν δούλου λαβών), "being made in the likeness of men" (ἐν ὁμοιώματι ἀνθρώπων γενόμενος). The timing of the text in conjunction with the reflexive pronoun demands the personal pre-incarnational existence of the Son.

After having taken upon himself the limitations of human existence, the Son humbled himself further, "by becoming obedient to the point of death, even death on a cross" (v. 8). Subsequently, God has highly exalted him (v. 9), and this exaltation resulted in the cessation of his humiliation, his reception of "authority over all flesh" and the receipt of the divine glory that he set aside for the purposes of accomplishing the work set before him.[8] Drawing from this same chronology, the apostle wrote in 2 Corinthians 8:9, "For you know the grace of our Lord Jesus Christ, that though he was rich, yet for your sake he became poor, so that you by his poverty might become rich."

Countering Dunn's Lame Interpretation

Dunn has argued that the hymn ought to be understood "as an allusion to Gen. 1-3."[9] On this view, the hymn becomes an implicit contrast between the disobedience of the first Adam and the obedience of the second Adam. According to this view, while the first Adam was given the "form of God" (i.e., the *imago Dei*), he attempted to become like God and ended up after the fall in the "form of a slave." Christ, the second Adam, did not seek to achieve equality with God, and thus achieved a status opposite of Adam. The difficulty with this interpretation, aside from the dubious assertion that the "form of God" is intended to invoke the image of

---

[8] John 17:2-5.

[9] Dunn, James D. G., *Christology in the Making: A New Testament Inquiry into the Origins of the Incarnation*, 2nd Ed., (Grand Rapids: Eerdmans, 1989), 115.

God, is that it is predicated upon the unfounded assumption that the comparison is between the human Christ and Adam. Wright has argued that the contrast between Adam and Christ "does not involve merely the substitution of one sort of humanity for another."[10] Rather, Wright has concisely articulated another form of comparison, one that is contextually and exegetically coherent: "Adam, in ignorance, thought to become like God: Christ, in humility, became man."[11] Moreover, Fee has pointed out that,

> Even if Paul might be contrasting Christ with Adam in this opening sentence, this phrase can scarcely be an allusion to Christ's *humanity* as being 'in God's image.' After all, it makes little sense to say that 'being already in God's likeness (as a human being), Christ emptied himself by coming to be (or 'being born') in human likeness.[12]

The overall intention of Paul's appeal to the example of Christ was to demonstrate humility to the Philippian church. Therefore, to suppose that it was humble for the human Christ not to cleave to equality with God employs a non-sequitur. Hawthorne has argued that to understand the "form of God" in terms of the second Adam motif "comes to grief fundamentally on the fact that it cannot be adopted for its second occurrence— μορφὴν δούλου."[13] That is, if one were to take Dunn's reading, there would necessarily be a time in the human life of Jesus wherein he did not subsist in the "form of a slave." When was that time?[14] So too, the explanatory participial phrase, "being born in the likeness of men," becomes a

---

[10] Wright, *The Climax of the Covenant*, 92.

[11] Ibid.

[12] Fee, *Pauline Christology*, 377.

[13] Hawthorne, *Philippians*, 82.

[14] Any soteriology that affirms the imputation of both the active and passive righteousness of Christ is at odds with Dunn's reading of Philippians 2:5-11.

redundant and clumsy appendage that has absolutely no relevance to a contrast between the obedient human Christ and the disobedient Adam.

Form of God & Form of a Slave

Because the incarnation of the Son of God resulted in his humiliation, texts which seem to subordinate the Son ought to be understood in terms of the functional subordination brought about by the incarnation.[15] Statements such as, "The Father is greater than I" (John 14:8), "But concerning that day and hour no one knows, not even the angels of heaven, nor the Son, but the Father only" (Matt 24:36), and "The Son can do nothing by himself" (John 5:19), are passages which need to be understood in terms of the Son's form of a slave.[16] These statements reflect Jesus' self-emptying—his state of incarnate humiliation. Statements which reflect his deity (e.g., John 1:1-3; 8:58; 20:28; 1 Cor 8:6; Gal 1:1, 12) must be understood in terms of his possession of the form of God.

When this incarnational dialectic is observed, the common unitarian objections to the deity of Christ become absurd. For

---

[15] There does exist an eternal functional subordination of the Son which was not caused by, nor does it depend upon, the incarnation. Rather, the incarnation is a product of the traits of leadership and humility that are displayed in the divine persons. Moreover, those passages which describe EFS (e.g., 1 Cor 11:3) are generally not the texts which subordinationists use against the deity of Christ. For more on how the 'Form of God/Form of a Slave' dialectic fits with ERAS, see Ware, Bruce A., Starke, John, *One God in Three Persons: Unity of Essence, Distinction of Persons, Implications for Life*, (Wheaton: Crossway, 2015), 82-87.

[16] For this chapter I am indebted to Augustine's *De Trinitate*, particularly 7.14.

instance, the claim that Christ cannot be God because God cannot die, when understood through the lens of Christ's possession of the form of a slave (i.e., genuine humanity), becomes senseless.[17] That is, God died because God the Son died a human death. The similar claim, Christ cannot be God because God cannot be tempted, when understood in light of the form of a slave, also becomes a non-sequitur. God can be tempted because Jesus Christ, the incarnate Son of God, was tempted. The common subordinationist quip, 'Jesus cannot be God because Jesus has a God,' also relies upon the same illogic. Jesus has a God because he entered into humanity and submitted himself wholly to God's law.[18]

The Exaltation of the Son & Unitarian Claims

> And now, Father, glorify me in your own presence with the glory that I had with you before the world existed. (John 17:5)

> καὶ νῦν δόξασόν με σύ, πάτερ, παρὰ σεαυτῷ τῇ δόξῃ ᾗ εἶχον πρὸ τοῦ τὸν κόσμον εἶναι παρὰ σοί. (John 17:5)

Whereas Philippians 2:6-8 depicts the Son's humiliation in

---

[17] This is an argument commonly articulated by subordinationists. E.g., Chang, *The Only True God*, 114, Chang, Eric H. H., *The Only Perfect Man: The Glory of God in the Face of Jesus Christ*, (Charleston: Createspace, 2016), 211, Graeser, Lynn,, Schoenheit, *One God & One Lord*, 14, Holmes-Sulton, Shirley, *Is Jesus God?*, 3rd Ed., (Bloomington: Trafford Pub., 2014), 4, Raddatz, Tom, *God is One and Christ is All: Biblical Truth Against the Trinity*, (1 Lord 1 Faith Publishing, 2012), 215ff.

[18] When it comes to the Jehovah's Witnesses version of this objection, the error is compounded by the mischaracterization of trinitarianism as modalism. See *Let God be True*, Rev. Ed. (Brooklyn: Watchtower Bible & Tract Society, 1952), 106. *Should You Believe the Trinity?*, (Brooklyn: Watchtower Bible & Tract Society, 1989), 27.

entering into human existence, Philippians 2:9-11 and John 17:5 depict his exaltation. John 17:5 consists of Jesus' petition for the glory previously possessed by the Son to be returned. This request occurs within the so-called 'High-Priestly Prayer,' which begins with Jesus' statement, "Father, the hour has come; glorify your Son that the Son may glorify you" (17:1). The verb δόξασόν (glorify) provides a contextual basis for understanding the nature of the Son's petition in 17:5. In the same way he had glorified his Father on the earth (17:2) by being completely obedient, Jesus petitions his Father to supply him with glory, so that he may again glorify his Father.

Throughout John 17 Jesus speaks proleptically, as if his sacrifice has already taken place. He stated, "you have given him authority over all flesh" (17:2), and "I glorified you on earth, having accomplished the work that you gave me to do" (17:4). These statements however, come just prior to the Son's arrest and subsequent crucifixion. The petition in 17:5, while predicated on an event yet to come (i.e., the passion), moves to the present. The phrase καὶ νῦν ("and now") is the marker of this transition. Hence, the restoration of glory "now" and the finished work both occur upon the cross. That is, the desolate humiliation and excruciating pain that Jesus endured was itself the restoration of his divine glory.

John 17:5 is composed of two general parts. The text begins with the imperative, "And now, Father, glorify me in your own presence," which is modified by "with the glory that I had with you before the world existed." The glory that was petitioned for is glory in the Father's presence. The utilization of the preposition παρὰ with the dative reflexive pronoun σεαυτῷ make this evident. παρὰ with the dative is defined as "a marker of nearness in space, at/by, beside, near, with."[19] So too, this glory that was to be had in the presence of the Father, was the same glory that was had in the

---

[19] *BDAG*, 757.

presence of the Father (παρὰ σοί) "before the world existed." Hence, John 17:5 indicates both the deity and personal preexistence of the Son of God.

Trinitarians have historically pointed to Jesus' authority as Lord of all (Matt 28:18) and his ability to give life to whomever he chooses (John 5:21) as evidence of his deity. On the trinitarian view, no one except God, not even an exalted agent, can possess the authority that Jesus has. Subordinationists reject such an interpretation, pointing to the accompanying statements wherein Jesus claims that such authority is given unto him by his Father so that he might act as the Father's agent. For example,

> There are many verses indicating that Jesus' power and authority was given to him by the Father. If he were the eternal God, then he would have always had those things that the Scripture says he was "given." Christ was given "all authority" (Matt. 28:18). He was given "a name above every name" (Phil. 2:9). He was given work to finish by the Father (John 5:36). He was given those who believed in him by the Father (John 6:39, 10:29). He was given glory (John 17:22 and 24). He was given his "cup" (his torture and death) by the Father (John 18:11). God "seated" Christ at His own right hand (Eph. 1:20). Christ was "appointed" over the Church (Eph. 1:22). These verses and others like them make no sense if Christ is "co-equal" with the Father, but make perfect sense if Christ was the Messiah, "a man accredited by God."[20]

The error in such an objection is the failure to recognize the existence of Jesus' humiliation and subsequent exaltation (i.e., the

---

[20] Graeser, Lynn,, Schoenheit, *One God & One Lord*, 588-589, cf. 244-245. See also Rees, Thomas, *Racovian Catechism*, (London: Longman, 1818), 57-58, 159-162.

form of God/form of a slave dialectic). Jesus was exalted upon the cross, receiving the glory that he veiled when he entered into the form of a slave. Thus, any argument that says Jesus' isn't God because his authority is derivative of the Father is circular reasoning. To assert Jesus' ontological inferiority to the Father upon the basis of his receipt of comprehensive dominion and Lordship is to miss the entire point of Paul's sermon illustration in Philippians 2:5-11. Such a position also precludes the gospel itself.

I AM: REDUCING UNITARIAN ARGUMENTATION TO ASHES

Michael R. Burgos Jr.

Unitarianism has attempted to repudiate the trinitarian contention that there is a meaning of the phrase 'I am' within Scripture that is outside of its normative function as a means of self-identification.

> So when he said to them, "I am *he*," they drew back and fell to the ground. (John 18:6)

The above text is one that trinitarians have understood to be evidence for the deity of Christ. Moreover, this text is one that trinitarians have understood to be the Son's identification of himself as Yahweh. The point of this study is to demonstrate the deity of Christ as made evident by a consideration of John 18:6 in light of an overview of the use of the phrase 'I am' in canonical and extra-canonical texts. Thereafter, several unitarian explanations for the text will be offered so as to magnify the harmony of trinitarian orthodoxy as it relates to the biblical identity of Christ.

The Old Testament background of "I Am"

The phrase 'I am' carries a special meaning outside of its common usage in Scripture. Within the Old Testament it is presented as a formula indicative of the God of Israel. In Exodus 3:13 Moses asks God, "if I come to the people of Israel and say to them, 'the God of your fathers has sent me to you,' and they ask me, 'what is his name?' what shall I say to them?" God answered Moses and said, "I Am Who I Am" (אֶהְיֶה אֲשֶׁר אֶהְיֶה). The Septuagint renders God's answer, ἐγώ εἰμι ὁ ὤν ("I am the being"). Since the Septuagint includes ὁ ὤν ("the being"), the participial form of ἐγώ εἰμι ("I am") in Exodus 3:14, a one to one parallel cannot be drawn to Jesus' usage of the phrase in John 18:6 upon that basis alone. However, within the Septuagint an atypical utilization of "I am" occurs repetitiously after Exodus 3:14 without the inclusion of ὁ ὤν.[1] The peculiarity of the usage stems from the fact that the phrase occurs without a predicate, being employed at the end of a clause or sentence in such a way that it tends to render the text awkward.

Deuteronomy 32:39 is a case in point. The text states, "See, see that I am, and there is no god except me."[2] Just as in Exodus, the phrase communicates exclusivity— a class of one. Yahweh is the living God because he is the "I am," the one existing.[3]

---

[1] While the phenomenon is certainly present within the Hebrew text via הוּא אֲנִי (*ani hu*), it is made even more explicit in the LXX. Also, it is inarguable that the translators of the Targums did not only observe, but also incorporated the formula so as to accentuate its effect. See Ronning, *The Jewish Targums and John's Logos Theology*, 194-223, Flesher, Chilton, *The Targums*, 490, and Boyarin, *Border Lines*, 126.

[2] Within this chapter, all OT citations marked NETS taken from Pietersma, Albert, Wright, Benjamin G., *A New English Translation of the Septuagint*, (New York: Oxford Univ. Press, 2007).

[3] Tantalizingly, Tg. PsJ. renders Deut 32:39, "When the Word of the Lord will be revealed to redeem his people he will say to all the nations: See now that I am he who is." The same sentiment is present in Rev 1:8:

Using the same style, Isaiah employs "I am" repetitiously and formulaically to indicate the exclusivity of Yahweh as the only living God.

Who has wrought and done these things? The one calling her from the beginning of generations has called her. I, God, am first, and for the things that are coming, I am. (Isaiah 41:4, NETS)

Be my witnesses; I too am a witness, says the Lord God, and the servant whom I have chosen so that you may know and believe and understand that I am. (Isaiah 43:10, NETS)

Hear me, O house of Iakob and everyone who is left of Israel, you who are being carried from the womb and trained from the time you were a child. Until your old age, I am. And until you grow old, I am. (Isaiah 46:3-4, NETS)

The Hebrew text of Isaiah 45:18 states, "I am the LORD, and there is no other." However, the Septuagint omits the tetragrammaton in favor of *egō eimi* alone. The Septuagint reads, "I am, and there is no other," thereby identifying that the ancient Jewish translators recognized the significance of "I am" as indicative and even synonymous with the name of the God of Israel. Moreover, in Isaiah 45:19 the Hebrew text states, "I the Lord speak the truth." The Septuagint renders this phrase as "I am, I am the Lord, speaking righteousness." In light of the rendering of verse 18, the insertion of "I am" a second time within the text is certainly an allusion to who was revealed to Moses at the bush, and this without the use of the participle.

In similar fashion, the Septuagint renders Isaiah 43:25 and

"I am the Alpha and the Omega," says the Lord God, "who is [ὁ ὢν] and who was [ὁ ἦν] and who is to come [ὁ ἐρχόμενος], the Almighty."

51:12 in such a way that the "I am" formula occurs in succession. These utilizations provide further evidence that *egō eimi* was a recognized title among the Jews, especially during the second temple period.

> I am, I am the one who blots out your acts of lawlessness. (Isaiah 43:25, NETS)

> I am, I am he who comforts you. (Isaiah 51:12, NETS)

Isaiah 47:8-10 states,

> But now hear these things, you delicate woman who sits securely, who says in her heart, 'I am, and there is no other; I shall not sit as a widow or know bereavement. But now both these things shall come upon you suddenly, in one day; widowhood and loss of children shall come upon you suddenly in your witchcraft, exceedingly in the strength of your enchantments. (NETS)

In this passage, we see that the "delicate woman" (i.e., Babylon) is characterized as making use of the phrase "I am" in the style and tenor that Yahweh uses it of himself.[4] The text is characterizing this people as being prideful to the extent that they believe that they possess sovereignty over their own circumstance like that of God. Therefore, their use of "I am" serves as a receptor of judgment; that the true Sovereign, the authentic "I am," will bring justice to this blaspheming people.[5]

---

[4] Cf. Isaiah 44:6; 44:8; 45:5-6; 45:21.

[5] There is also a very similar occurrence in Zeph 2:15 (3:1 LXX). Therein, Nineveh is characterized as arrogantly applying the "I am" formula to itself. This height of blasphemy is what precipitates the judgment of God much like that described in Isaiah 47:8-10.

Non-canonical Occurrences

Like the Old Testament, there exists a normative use of "I am" within the Jewish pseudepigrapha.[6] However, there is also present the formulaic use of the phrase that is an indicator of deity. Some of the most pronounced examples occur in the Apocalypse of Abraham:

...the voice of a Mighty One from heaven came down from the heavens in a stream of fire, saying and calling, 'Abraham, Abraham!' And I said: 'Here I am.' And He said, 'You art seeking in the understanding of your heart the God of gods and the Creator. I am He. (8:1-4)[7]

Fear not, for I am Before-the-World and Mighty, the God who created previously, before the light of the age. I am the protector for you and I am your helper. (9:1-4)[8]

Within the Apocalypse of Elijah there also exists the phrase "I am the Christ,"[9] which is in reference to an anti-Christ figure within an eschatological context. Wintermute suggests that the Coptic text, "probably translates an *ego eimi* statement." The statement is reminiscent of Mark 13:6 wherein Jesus warns of those falsely claiming to be Christ by saying "I am." Whether one accepts a second, third, or fourth century date for the text,[10] the

---

[6] E.g., Apocalypse of Moses 17:2-3.

[7] Charlesworth, James H., Ed., *The Old Testament Pseudepigrapha: Apocalyptic Literature and the Testaments,* Vol. I, (Peabody: Hendrickson, 1983), 693.

[8] Ibid.

[9] Ibid., 3:1, 744. Cf. Eth Enoch 108:12; Jub 24:22.

[10] The earliest witnesses for the text are of the fourth century. See VanDerKam, James C., Adler, William Eds., *The Jewish Apocalyptic Heritage in Early Christianity*, (Assen: Van Gorcum, 1996), 95.

presence of the formula by either a Christian or Jewish hand further demonstrates both the awareness and recognition of the phrase within antiquity.

The Synoptic Gospels and Acts

Unlike John, the synoptic writers were not nearly as concerned with portraying the Son as Yahweh by means of "I am" sayings.[11] However, being mindful of the precedent for the formula that is found within the Old Testament, there are a number of passages that bear consideration.

Upon terrifying his disciples by his early morning walk on water, Jesus stated in Mark 6:50, "Take heart: I am. Do not be afraid" (Θαρσεῖτε, ἐγώ εἰμι· μὴ φοβεῖσθε).[12] Catrin Williams has suggested that Jesus used ἐγώ εἰμι "in an ordinary sense..."[13] and "was probably understood...as an identification formula only."[14] Regarding the Johannine parallel, F. F. Bruce stated, "There are places within this gospel where the words *egō eimi* have the nature

---

[11] While the synoptic writers did not seek to emphasize Jesus' use of "I am," they did often indicate the deity of Christ by other means. For example, the application of Isaiah 40:3 to Jesus is found within all four gospels.

[12] Cf. Matthew 14:27; John 6:20. Anderson suggests that "In Mark the statement comes across as an identification...while in John it comes across as a theophany." Anderson does not substantiate this claim other than to say that "these represent two radically different perceptions and experiences." However, the two narratives are strikingly similar. The minuscule differences present can be accounted for by the differing perspectives of the respective author. See Anderson, Paul N., *The Riddles of the Fourth Gospel: An Introduction to John*, Minneapolis: Fortress Press, 2011), 176.

[13] Williams, Catrin H., *I am He: The Interpretation of 'Ani Hu' in Jewish and Early Christian Literature*, (Tubingen: Mohr Siebeck, 2000), 2.

[14] Fortna, Robert T., Thatcher, Tom Eds., *Jesus in Johannine Tradition*, (Louisville: Westminster John Knox Press, 2001), 346.

of divine designation…but here they simply mean 'It is I.'"[15] However, when one considers the background of the phrase and its place within the apex of the narrative, it becomes clear that while a self-identification is meant, it is that of the one who "trampled the waves of the sea."[16] Edwards rightly characterized Jesus as "treading only where God can walk."[17] The disciples reaction was one fitting for deity; "Those in the boat worshiped him, saying, "Truly you are the Son of God."[18]

Important to the narrative of Mark 6 and Jesus' use of *egō eimi* is the intention of Jesus to pass by the boat. The text states in Mark 6:48, "He meant to pass by them." This detail is one that is reminiscent of those times in which the God has passed by his people.[19] The characterization of one who passes by, having sovereign command of nature, making himself known by the phrase "I am," is one that purposefully invokes the revelations of God in the Old Testament. Edwards concluded,

> Jesus' walking on the water to his disciples is a revelation of the glory that he shares with the Father and the compassion that he extends to his followers. It is a divine epiphany in answer to their earlier bafflement when he calmed the storm, 'Who is this?'[20]

The most pronounced occurrence of *egō eimi* in Mark's gospel occurs during Jesus' trial. The High Priest asked, "Are you the

---

[15] Bruce, F. F., *The Gospel of John: Introduction, Exposition, and Notes*, (Grand Rapids: Eerdmans, 1983), 148.

[16] See Job 9:8. Cf. Job 38:16; Psalm 77:19.

[17] Edwards, James R., 1994. "The Authority of Jesus in the Gospel of Mark," *JETS*, Vol. 37, Num. 2, 223.

[18] Matthew 14:33. Cf. Luke 4:8.

[19] See Exodus 33:19, 22; 1 Kings 19:11.

[20] Edwards, James R., *The Pillar New Testament Commentary: The Gospel According to Mark*, (Grand Rapids: Eerdmans, 2002), 199.

Christ, the Son of the Blessed?" Jesus' response was a weighty combination of irony and eschatological punch. He stated in Mark 14:62, "I am, and you will see the Son of Man seated at the right hand of Power, and coming with the clouds of heaven."[21]

Jesus' response utilized the normative function of *ego eimi*, as the means of self-identification, and yet his response is reminiscent of Deuteronomy 32:39. Thus, Jesus' response held a rich double meaning; identifying himself as the divine Son by the very name of God.[22]

Hans Schwarz has noted,

> We may conclude that Jesus' use of *ego eimi* in Mark 14:62 is more than a simple affirmation. He uses a revelational phrase to disclose himself and identify himself with God. As the words following *ego eimi* show, the Messianic secret is lifted, and Jesus unashamedly admits his divine sonship.[23]

After Jesus' confession in Mark 14:62, "the high priest tore his garments and said, 'What further witnesses do we need? You have heard his blasphemy." Mark also documents that "they all condemned him as deserving death."[24] Jesus' "I am" statement was met with a reaction that gives the reader every reason to believe that there existed no ambiguity in the Jews understanding of the phrase as being particular to God.

---

[21] Ἐγώ εἰμι, καὶ ὄψεσθε τὸν υἱὸν τοῦ ἀνθρώπου ἐκ δεξιῶνκαθήμενον τῆς δυνάμεως καὶ ἐρχόμενον μετὰ τῶν νεφελῶν τοῦ οὐρανοῦ.

[22] Jesus' statement was an appeal to Daniel 7:11-14. Within that text the "Son of man" is depicted as receiving religious service from every human being, as He is the divine Judge with comprehensive eternal dominion (cf. Zec 14:5; Matt 16:27; Rev 1:7).

[23] Schwarz, Hans, *Christology*, (Grand Rapids: Eerdmans, 1998), 111.

[24] Mark 14:63.

The Johannine Background

Within the fourth gospel there are a number of occurrences wherein Jesus' use of "I am" is extraordinarily similar to those spoken by Yahweh within the Old Testament. It is not the point of this study to provide a detailed examination of those occurrences,[25] but rather it will suffice to consider these texts so that we might understand John 18:6 in light of them.

John 4:26 states, "Jesus said to her, 'I who speak to you am he.'"[26] In this particular instance, the *New International Version* actually provides a more literal translation, and in so doing the sense of the Greek text is rendered plainly. It states, "Jesus declared, 'I, the one speaking to you— I am *he*.'"[27] This is very similar to the Septuagint's rendering of Isaiah 52:6 which states, "I myself am the one who speaks: I am here."[28]

While I have labored above to communicate the importance of Jesus' *egō eimi* statement within Mark's depiction of the account of Jesus' walking on the water (Mark 6:45-52), there is sufficient reason to again appeal to this story as it appears within the John' Gospel. There are themes peculiar to John's account which nicely accent that which was recorded by Mark. While the two accounts are quite similar, John 6:16-21, particularly vs. 19-20, invokes certain themes that are entirely relevant to both the overall importance of the narrative and to those *egō eimi* occurrences which come later within John's Gospel. The text states,

When they had rowed about three or four miles, they saw Jesus walking on the sea and coming near the boat, and they were

---

[25] See bro. Dalcour in this volume, 232ff.

[26] ... λέγει αὐτῇ ὁ Ἰησοῦς· ἐγώ εἰμι, ὁ λαλῶν σοι.

[27] Italics have been added to note the lack of the pronoun within the Greek text.

[28] ... ὅτι ἐγώ εἰμι αὐτὸς ὁ λαλῶν.

frightened. But he said to them, "It is I; do not be afraid." (John 6:19-20)[29]

There is little doubt that Isaiah is on the mind of the apostle, as it appears throughout his gospel.[30] This is especially true of Isaiah 43 as it relates to Jesus' *ego eimi* statements.[31] However, as we have shown above, while the Septuagint played a significant role within John's gospel, the Targumic literature did as well. Regarding the John 6:16-21, Ronning has noted,

> In [Isaiah] 43:1, the LORD says to Israel, "Do not be afraid." In 43:2, he says he will be with them when they pass through the waters, which is what the disciples were doing at the time John 6:20 is spoken. In Isa 43:3, he says he is their savior. In 43:5, he says, "Do not fear, for I am with you." Finally, there is the "I am he" saying of 43:10, which is of great significance to other ἐγώ εἰμι sayings in John. *Targum Isaiah* 43:2 takes God's promise of being with his people when they cross through the waters to refer back to the crossing of the Red Sea. When Israel crossed the sea, it was dark, with a strong wind blowing as in John 6:16-21. Several *Pal. Tg.* Exod 14 passages point to the help of the divine Word in Israel's sea crossing. *Targum Isaiah* 43:2 says, "My Word was your help."[32]

---

[29] The last clause of John 6:20, "It is I, do not be afraid" (ἐγώ εἰμι· μὴ φοβεῖσθε), bears close resemblance in sentiment to the Septuagint's rendering of Isaiah 43:5 "Do not fear, for I am with you" (μὴ φοβοῦ, ὅτι μετὰ σοῦ εἰμι).

[30] See Carson, D. A., Williamson, Hugh G. M. Eds., *It is Written: Scripture Citing Scripture: Essays in Honour of Barnabas Lindars*, (New York: Cambridge Univ. Press, 1988), 254-264.

[31] See the discussion of John 8:24; 13:19 below.

[32] Ronning, *The Jewish Targums and John's Logos Theology*, 202-203.

John 8:24 states, "I told you that you would die in your sins, for unless you believe that I am you will die in your sins." This parallels Isaiah 43:10 which states, "Be my witnesses; I too am a witness, says the Lord God, and the servant whom I have chosen so that you may know and believe and understand that I am." John 13:19 provides a nearly identical parallel; "I am telling you this now, before it takes place, that when it does take place you may believe that I am."[33]

Because of the thematic union between Isaiah 43 and the above texts, it is not difficult to see John's intent in including an *egō eimi* statement at John 6:20, particularly in light of Ronning's comments.

When in John 8:58 Jesus states, "before Abraham was, I am" we ought not to be surprised at the response of the unbelieving Jews.[34]

---

[33] A comparison between the Septuagint's rendering of the relevant portion of Isaiah 43:10 (ἵνα γνῶτε καὶ πιστεύσητε καὶ συνῆτε ὅτι ἐγώ εἰμι) and of John 13:19 (ἵνα πιστεύσητε ὅταν γένηται ὅτι ἐγώ εἰμι) makes evident the intended parallel.

[34] The NWT's non-literal rendering, "Before Abraham came into existence, I have been," is highly problematic. The Watchtower Bible & Tract Society (WB&TS) has defended this reading by insisting that "Jesus' reply logically dealt with his age, the length of his existence." They further argued that A. T. Robertson supports such a reading from this quote: "The verb [*eimi*]...Sometimes it does express existence as a predicate like any other verb, as in [*ego eimi*] (Jo. 8:58)." *Reasoning from the Scriptures*, (Brooklyn: WB&TS, 1985), 418. First, the translation turns the present active verb in to a perfect active with no exegetical or contextual warrant. The WB&TS claim that *eimi* is a present of past action in progress (PPA, sometimes called the "durative present") is erroneous and is mitigated by the fact that the verb is an absolute. A PPA verb serves "to describe an action which, begun in the past, continues in the present." Wallace, *GGBB*, 519. However, PPA verbs are *always* accompanied with an adverb of time or duration in the New Testament. In John 8:58, *eimi* isn't accompanied by an adverbial

John 8:59 states, "therefore they picked up stones to throw at him." Not only does this usage of *egō eimi* demand the eternality of Jesus, but the response of the Jews was clearly an attempt at

---

phrase denoting time, but rather, the verb serves only as an absolute verb of being (hence, "I am"). The NWT *Study Edition* cites John 14:9 in support of their assertion regarding John 8:58: τοσοῦτον χρόνον μεθ᾽ ὑμῶν εἰμι ("So long a time I have been with you"). While this example follows the PPA construction perfectly, containing an adverbial phrase which indicates time, namely τοσοῦτον χρόνον, *eimi* at John 8:58 does not. Second, the correct translation (i.e., "Before Abraham was, I am") serves by implication to indicate "the length of his existence," or what Büchsel has called "supra-temporality." *TDNT*, Vol. II, 399. Thus, the argument made by the WB&TS doesn't follow. Third, Robertson's statement accords with the translation "I am," and it does not in any way give credence to the NWT's rendering. This is confirmed elsewhere by Robertson's actual exegesis of John 8:58:

> "Before Abraham came into existence or was born. I am" (*egō eimi*). Undoubtedly here Jesus claims eternal existence with the absolute phrase used of God.

Robertson, A. T., *Word Pictures in the New Testament*, Vol. V, (Nashville: Broadman Press, 1932), 158-159. It would seem therefore, that the WB&TS 'cherry picked' the quote from Robertson's grammar, making it seem as though he agrees with a theologically driven mistranslation. For a comprehensive evaluation and refutation of the WB&TS on John 8:58 incl. the PPA see Bowman, *Jehovah's Witnesses, Jesus Christ, and the Gospel of John*, 99-116. For more on the PPA see Dana, H. E., Mantey, J. R., *A Manual Grammar of the Greek New Testament*, (Toronto: Macmillan, 1957), 183, Robertson, A. T., *Grammar of the Greek New Testament in Light of Historical Research*, 3rd Ed., (Nashville: B & H, 1934), 879, and Köstenberger, Andreas J., Merkle, Benjamin L., Plummer, Robert L., *Going Deeper with New Testament Greek*, (Nashville: B & H Academic, 2016), 256-257.

execution, the punishment prescribed by God for blasphemy.[35]

The Armed Mob

The mob that sought Jesus on the night of his betrayal consisted of Judas Iscariot and, "a band of soldiers and some officers from the chief priests and the Pharisees (John 18:3). Carson has well elaborated that,

> ...in addition to bringing Jewish officials Judas Iscariot also guided a detachment of soldiers. The Greek (*ten speiran*) makes it clear that these were not Jews, but 'the cohort (of Roman auxiliaries)'... In practice a cohort normally numbered 600 men; but in any case the noun *speira* can refer to a 'maniple' of only 200 men, and it is not necessary to assume that an entire maniple was present. Roman auxiliary troops were garrisoned in the fortress of Antonia to the north-west of the temple complex. This move to Jerusalem not only ensured more efficient policing of the huge throngs that swelled the population of Jerusalem during the high feasts, but guaranteed that any mob violence or incipient rebellion, bred by the crowding and the religious fervour, would be crushed. That is probably the reason why they were called out to support the temple officials.[36]

The soldiers and officers are said to have been carrying "lanterns and torches and weapons" (John 18:3). In addition, it was a full moon.[37] Therefore, the amount of light available to the armed party was likely plentiful. Surely the Roman soldiers understood

---

[35] Whoever blasphemes the name of the LORD shall surely be put to death. All the congregation shall stone him. The sojourner as well as the native, when he blasphemes the Name, he shall be put to death. (Lev 24:16)

[36] Carson, *The Gospel According to John*, 577.

[37] It was Passover and thus the moon was full (cf. Numbers 26:18).

the importance of preparedness in a mission such as this. So too, the number of participants in the arresting mob, even if only a fraction of what Carson suggests, would serve to make the least courageous among the arresting party confident. Judas no doubt anticipated that Jesus would not be accompanied by a large crowd, but only a few disciples. He is characterized by John as "having taken the detachment of soldiers,"[38] thereby indicating that it was he who was their informant and guide.[39] Therefore, the mob likely expected a quick arrest with minimal resistance.

The Arrest

> Then Jesus, knowing all that would happen to him, came forward and said to them, 'Whom do you seek?' They answered him, 'Jesus of Nazareth.' Jesus said to them, 'I am he.' Judas, who betrayed him, was standing with them. When Jesus said to them, 'I am he,' they drew back and fell to the ground. So he asked them again, 'Whom do you seek?' And they said, 'Jesus of Nazareth.' Jesus answered, 'I told you that I am.' (John 18:4-8)

Within the above text we see a rather interesting response made by the mob at Jesus' utterance. John 18:6 begins with the adverbial conjunction ὡς ("when") thereby implying a causal nature to Jesus' utterance. That is, it was when Jesus said, "I am," that the arresting party drew back and fell to the ground. The plural verbs ἀπῆλθον ("they drew") and ἔπεσαν ("they fell") indicate that the entirety of the group not only "drew back" but also "fell to the ground." While the response of the well-equipped mob is

---

[38] … λαβὼν τὴν σπεῖραν.

[39] The apostle states in Acts 1:18, that Judas "became a guide (ὁδηγοῦ) to those who arrested Jesus." Hence, Judas served as an ideal informant for the arresting party thereby adding to their confidence.

admittedly fascinating, it is amplified by the fact that prior to the arrest Jesus knew "all that would happen to him." Jesus did not merely know of his pending arrest, but also the grim and fatal affliction he was to endure. It was on the basis of this knowledge that Jesus initiated contact with those that sought him, and it was on the basis of his knowledge that he asserted "I am." The divine power displayed through the utilization of the phrase demonstrated the authority Jesus had previously made known. In John 10:18 Jesus stated, "I lay down my life...no one takes it from me, but I lay it down of my own accord."

The Question

In acknowledgement of the background of *egō eimi*, the reaction of the mob is best explained as a display of the divine power of the Christ by way of his self-identification as Yahweh, the great 'I Am.' This understanding neither necessitates that the arresting crowd understood the implications of Jesus' statement, nor that the mob understood why they all fell at his word. This explanation is rejected by virtually all subordinationists, since they cannot allow for the deity of Christ. Subsequently, subordinationists have posed a number of explanations so as to refute the trinitarian understanding of the text. But do the explanations put forward satisfy the text?

Subordinationist Answers for the Collapse of the Mob

Greg Stafford has offered the following explanation:

...the reaction of the mob in 18:6 is no surprise given the confident, sudden self-identification Jesus makes. The soldiers present likely remembered hearing about how impressive Jesus was in his earlier encounter with the officers who were sent to 'get hold of him,' but failed to do so because of the way he spoke. Again, the context shows that Jesus' words caused the crowds to conclude, 'This is the Christ.' (John 7:41) The words 'they drew back and fell to the ground' need mean no more than that the men who came to make the arrest (some of whom at least did not previously know Jesus even by sight) were so overcome by his moral ascendancy that they recoiled in fear.

Most likely, then, when Jesus unhesitatingly revealed himself as the one who they sought, those coming to arrest him were taken aback by his fearless demeanor, particularly in light of their presuppositions about the man which were based upon what they heard or experienced.[40]

Stafford stated that "the men who came to make the arrest…were so overcome by his moral ascendency that they recoiled in fear." However, the text makes explicit that the mob did not simply recoil, but rather they "drew back and fell to the ground." Furthermore, the suggestion that Jesus' moral ascendancy was the means by which the mob fell to the ground is absurd. Surely Stafford would admit to Jesus' flawless moral behavior every moment of his existence. Why then is this the only time in which "his moral ascendancy" caused anyone, let alone an armed contingent of trained men to fall to the ground? Moreover, characterizing the drawing back and falling of the mob as merely being "taken aback" is at odds with the plain reading of the text.

Stafford has also raised the issue of an implied predicate regarding John 18:5. He argued that "a predicate is clearly implied by the context, for Jesus' response is to their request for 'Jesus the Nazarene.'"[41] Stafford is correct in pointing to the context so as to make sense of Jesus' response. However, the fact that Jesus' statement made grammatical sense does not constitute a refutation

---

[40] Stafford, Greg, *Jehovah's Witnesses Defended: An Answer to Scholars and Critics*, 3rd Ed., (Murrieta: Elihu Books, 2009), 311.

[41] Greg Stafford, *A Review of James White's "A Summary Critique: Jehovah's Witnesses Defended,"* http://jehovah.to/exe/general/cri_review.htm. Accessed 05/16/2018.

of the trinitarian contention regarding v. 6. Evidently, Stafford has failed to see the great irony present in not only the account of the arrest, but especially Jesus' response to those who sought him.

Stafford went further to point out that there exists a textual variant in John 18:5 wherein some important uncial manuscripts possess the reading, λέγει αὐτοῖς ὁ Ἰησοῦς ἐγώ εἰμι.[42] This can be legitimately rendered, "He said to them, I am Jesus," which in supplying the predicate, could have implications upon Jesus' *egō eimi* pronouncement in John 18:6. However, the more natural and hence more probable rendering puts ὁ Ἰησοῦς within the first clause (i.e., "Jesus said to them, I am.").[43] In addition, codex Vaticanus supplies Ἰησοῦς without the article after ἐγὼ εἰμι. While this reading would raise questions, it is dubious and otherwise unattested. Admittedly, the external support for the inclusion of (ὁ) Ἰησοῦς is strong, but its varied placement is indicative of a scribal addition.[44] On the other hand, because of the nature of the uncial text, written only with majuscule letters and without the benefit of spaces between words, it is possible that a scribe mistook AYTOICIC̄ for AYTOIC. But would a scribe be so careless so as to omit the *Nomen Sacrum*? It was not uncommon for a scribe to insert a name, particularly the name of Jesus, as an explanatory supplement to aid in clarifying the identity of the speaker.[45]

Ultimately, the fact that vv. 6 and 8 omit ὁ Ἰησοῦς while depicting Jesus repeating his response to the mob weighs heavily

---

[42] A, C, L, W, Δ, Θ, and Ψ have the articular reading, while ℵ has no article.

[43] Both the United Bible Societies 4th Ed. and the Nestle-Aland 28th Ed. place the variant within the first clause.

[44] Metzger, Bruce M., *A Textual Commentary on the Greek New Testament*, 2nd Ed., (New York: United Bible Societies, 1994), 251.

[45] See Aland, Kurt, Aland, Barbara, *The Text of the New Testament: An Introduction to the Critical Editions and to the Theory and Practice of Modern Textual Criticism*, 2nd Ed., (Grand Rapids: Eerdmans, 1989), 289-290.

against its inclusion.[46] Thus, unless Stafford wants to introduce evident discontinuity into the text, the reading present in the critical editions shall stand.

Patrick Navas, in his lengthy discussing of John 18:6, has offered the following explanation as found in the *Interpreter's Bible*:

> The moral majesty of Jesus astonished the captors, who recoiled in amazement, and some fell to the ground.[47]

Jesus was the perfect man. All of his speech and behavior were characterized by moral excellence all of the time. If the above statement is correct, why then is John 18:6 the only time in which such a reaction is given? Surely the arresting party was prepared for the unknown. Would not a trained soldier or officer, let alone an experienced soldier or officer, be ready not only for resistance but also surrender? In addition, the *Interpreter's Bible* errs in its characterization that "some fell to the ground," as the text gives no indication that anything less than the entirety of the arresting party fell to the ground.

Navas has also suggested,

> Some commentators, although not arguing that Jesus was uttering the name of God, believe that what occurred represented a characteristic manifestation of Jesus' supernatural power (the power of God working through him), the true cause of the soldiers falling-a powerful sign or miracle consistent with Jesus' walking on water, calming the sea during a storm, or opening the eyes of the blind, and

---

[46] Vv. 6 and 8 do not contain any relevant textual variation.

[47] Navas, Patrick, *Divine Truth or Human Tradition?: A Reconsideration of the Orthodox Doctrine of the Trinity in Light of the Hebrew and Christian Scriptures*, (Bloomington: AuthorHouse, 2011), 431.

raising people from the dead...Jesus may have wanted to demonstrate his power over the guards, showing that, in reality, they had no power to take him, and that he would only submit himself into their custody of his own accord, with view to the voluntary sacrifice he came into the world to give.[48]

While Navas ultimately concludes that the reason why the soldiers drew back and fell to the ground is difficult to ascertain,[49] this explanation at least finds evidence for the supernatural within the text. Essentially Navas' suggestion attributes the falling down of the soldiers at Jesus' utterance of *egō eimi* to coincidence.

Navas also denied the causal nature of Jesus' statement and the reaction of the arresting mob. He argued,

> John does not say 'because (Gk. *hoti*) Jesus said 'I am he' the soldiers fell,' as if the words in and of themselves were the direct cause of their reaction.[50]

The above claim is precluded by the text itself. As previously mentioned, the text states, ὡς οὖν εἶπεν αὐτοῖς, Ἐγώ εἰμι, ἀπῆλθον εἰς τὰ ὀπίσω καὶ ἔπεσαν χαμαί ("*When* Jesus said to them, 'I am he,' they drew back and fell to the ground"). ὡς is defined as "a temporal conjunction"[51] and "a point of time which is prior to another point of time, with the possible implication in some contexts of reason or cause—'when.'"[52] By means of time, the conjunction indicates a causal connection between the act of Jesus' declaration and the reaction of the mob. Hence, ὡς is normatively translated "when" at John 18:6. While John did not use the

---

[48] Ibid.

[49] Ibid., 435.

[50] Ibid.

[51] *BDAG*, 1105.

[52] *Louw-Nida*, 634.

conjunction ὅτι, he did indicate the causal nature of Jesus'
statement by other means. Williams has noted that John 18:6 "is
phrased in such a manner as to give the impression that the
captors' reaction is inextricably linked to Jesus' *egō eimi*
response."[53]

In addition to denying the causal nature of Jesus' words, Navas
sees *egō eimi* not as a name indicative of the living God, but rather
merely a means of self-identification. However, there is a second
temple account which, in light of the data examined thus far, is
relevant. The writings of the second temple Jewish historian
Artapanus have survived in fragmentary form within the works of
Eusebius and Clement of Alexandria.[54] Artapanus recorded an
account of Moses, who in declaring his intention to deliver the
Israelites from Egypt, was promptly imprisoned by Pharaoh. The
text then states,

> But when it was night, all of the doors of the prison-house
> opened of their own accord, and of the guards some died,
> and some were sunk in sleep, and their weapons broken in
> pieces. So Moses passed out and came into the palace; and
> finding the doors open he went in, and the guards here also
> being sunk in sleep he woke up the king. And he being
> dismayed at what happened bade Moses tell him the name
> of the God who sent him: but Moses bent down and
> whispered in his ear, and when the king heard it he fell
> speechless, but was held fast by Moses and came to life
> again.[55]

---

[53] Williams, *I am He*, 292.

[54] See Eusebius of Caesarea, *Praeparatio Evangelica*, 9.18.1;
9.23.1-4; 9.27.1-37. See also Clement of Alexandria,
Stromata 1.23.154.2-3.

[55] Gifford, E. H., *English Translation of Eusebius of Caesarea's
Praeparatio Evangelica*, (Typographeo Academico, 1903), 218.

Artapanus' account consists of an early Jewish depiction wherein Pharaoh fell down at the hearing of the divine name. Given the background of *egō eimi* within the Septuagint, and its utilization within the New Testament, there is an interesting similarity in the account of Pharaoh's collapse and the collapse of the arresting party.

David Kroll has suggested that the soldiers "probably drew back and fell to the ground simply in response to Jesus offering himself to them without resistance, something they probably weren't used to."[56] However, given the background of *egō eimi* within Scripture, can the response of the soldiers really be attributed to a bit of surprise by Jesus' surrender? Kroll's explanation implies that these soldiers were derelict half-wits, who being so amazed by Jesus' surrender, drew back and fell to the ground. Like those explanations offered previously, Kroll's theory is far-fetched at best.

Jason BeDuhn has argued that,

> In John 18, Jesus asks the soldiers whom they have come for. When Jesus answers they say they are looking for Jesus of Nazareth, Jesus answers 'I am (he)' (*ego eimi*). In other words, 'I am Jesus, the one you are looking for.' Now when he says this the first time, the soldiers fall back in shock. But there is no reason to think that Jesus has used some sort of verbal spell on them. There is nothing in the words of *ego eimi* themselves that have power; it is Jesus who has the power.[57]

---

[56] Kroll, David, *The God of Jesus: A Comprehensive Examination of the Nature of the Father, Son, and Spirit*, (Bloomington: Westbow Press, 2012), 173.

[57] BeDuhn, Jason, *Truth in Translation: Accuracy and Bias in English Translations of the New Testament*, (Lanham: Univ. Press, 2003), 109.

BeDuhn has assumed that the trinitarian contention is that the actual phrase of *egō eimi* contains some kind of divine power akin to a "verbal spell." In so doing, BeDuhn has presented a straw-man as virtually all orthodox trinitarians recognize that the words are powerless. However, it was those very words that were uttered by the Author of life.[58] The text says nothing about the soldiers falling "back in shock." Rather John indicates that the well-prepared mob drew back and fell to the ground at Jesus' utterance. Far from a "verbal spell," John 18:6 was a display of the sovereign authority of the incarnate Son by means of his name.

Buzzard and Hunting have provided the following explanation of John 18:6:

> There is good evidence that John incorporates into his portrait of Jesus as Messiah, ideas drawn from the Messianic Psalm 45. In answer to Pilate, Jesus declared that he was a king whose task was to bear witness to the truth (John 18:37). There is an Old Testament background to this theme. Psalm 45 is written in praise of the Messiah (Heb. 1:8), who is addressed as 'most mighty,' and urged to 'ride prosperously in the cause of Truth' (vv. 3, 4). The psalmist foresees that the king's enemies 'will fall under you' (v. 5). The royal status of this leader is emphasized when the writer addresses him with the words 'O God' (Ps 45:6). The career of the Messiah outlined in Psalm 45 is reflected in John's observation that Jesus' enemies recoiled at his claim to be the Messiah and 'fell to the ground' (John 18:6).[59]

Buzzard and Hunting have assumed that Jesus' "I am" statement consisted merely of a claim to be an exclusively human Messiah.

---

[58] See Acts 3:15.

[59] Buzzard, Hunting, *The Doctrine of the Trinity*, 291-292.

This conclusion is unfounded even if one rejects the entirety of the biblical data concerning *egō eimi* since the soldiers sought "Jesus of Nazareth." Within the relevant pericope Jesus makes no explicit claim to be the Messiah, and therefore Buzzard and Hunting's contention amounts to an unfounded assumption. The text of John 18 does not indicate that the reason the soldiers fell to the ground was due to a Messianic claim. So too, this explanation ignores both the Old and New Testament background of *egō eimi*. Even if one were to grant that John has incorporated Psalm 45 so as to communicate the events within his gospel, it would not logically follow that a Messianic claim was responsible for the soldiers falling to the ground. The text of Psalm 45:5 states, "Your arrows are sharp in the heart of the king's enemies the peoples fall under you." Would not the literal fulfillment of "the peoples fall under you" require the literal fulfillment of "your arrows are sharp in the heart of the king's enemies"?

From the perspective of this writer, the above correlation with Psalm 45:5 is strained and would seem to require an atypical hermeneutic.[60] If one were to look to the Psalms, Psalm 9 would seem like a far more logical choice due to the apparent similarities between Psalm 9:4 and John 18:6. Ronning has noted,

"The sequence, "they drew back and fell to the ground" agrees with something David wrote about the fate of his enemies as a consequence of the presence of God: "When my enemies turn back, they will stumble and perish at your presence" (Ps 9:3). In the upper room, Jesus described his friends as those who keep his commandments, who love one another, and who remain in him. Jesus described Judas as one who has perished (John

---

[60] Buzzard and Hunting's work contains a seven page discussion (218-224) of Jesus' "I am" statements within John. Disappointingly, John 18:6 is never discussed in that section. John 18:6 is briefly mentioned in the provided quotation within a discussion of John 20:28.

17:12), and John reminds us of this in 18:9. The fact that the arresting officials draw back and fall to the ground at the "I am he" thus indicates, when read against the backdrop of Ps 9:3, the presence of the LORD. In David's experience, the presence of the LORD refers to the LORD's personal intervention on his behalf. *Targum Psalms* 9:7 has David say, "As for the Word of the LORD, his seat is in the highest heavens forever; he has established his throne for judgement."[61]

Conclusion

There is a theme that runs throughout John's gospel which utilizes the currency of the language of the Old Testament. This theme is a means unto communicating just what is meant by the phrase, "Son of God," as it relates to Jesus. For John, Jesus is the living God, the I Am.

---

[61] Ronning, *The Jewish Targums and John's Logos Theology*, 221-222.

NOT FROM MEN, NOR THROUGH MEN

Hiram R. Diaz III

Paul's Defense of His Apostleship: The Deity of Christ

In his epistle to the Galatians, Paul sets out to defend the gospel of Jesus Christ. Before doing this, however, he establishes his credentials as a real apostle. Thus, he begins the letter as follows:

> Paul, an apostle—not from men nor through man, but through Jesus Christ and God the Father, who raised him from the dead[1]

Paul's authority comes neither *from men* nor *through man*, but is given by God the Father and Jesus Christ his Son. His primary focus here is on the authenticity of his apostleship, using the universal ἄνθρωπος (*anthropos*, man) to exclude himself and all other men as the source of his authority. He has not appointed himself to be an apostle, nor has any other man appointed him to this role.

The careful reader should at this point be aware of the logical implication of Paul's assertion. If the universal ἄνθρωπος denies

---

[1] Gal 1:1.

that Paul's apostleship is derived from and through *any* man, then this implies that Jesus Christ, though truly man, is more than a mere man. For if Paul does not imply that Christ is more than a mere human being, then he is contradicting himself by saying:

A. His apostleship came neither from men nor through man.

~A. His apostleship came from and through a particular man, viz. Christ.

These two assertions cannot simultaneously be true. Therefore, Christ is not merely human. The Son of God is *more than* human. Christ's authority and the authority of the Father, moreover, as classed together by Paul, further implying the co-equality of Son of God and God the Father. Thus, Christ is not a mere human being but man who is more than merely human, who shares in the same authority with God the Father to appoint apostles and empower them to authoritatively teach and preach the authentic gospel.

At this point, Paul's words do not clearly identify Christ as God, perhaps leading some to believe that Paul's implied meaning is that Christ is something more than a mere human but less than God, e.g. an angel. Yet Paul goes on to state the following:

I am astonished that you are so quickly deserting him who called you in the grace of Christ and are turning to a different gospel—not that there is another one, but there are some who trouble you and want to distort the gospel of Christ. But even if we or an angel from heaven should preach to you a gospel contrary to the one we preached to you, let him be accursed.[2]

---

[2] Gal 1:6-8.

Paul here states that neither men nor angels have the authority, he right, to preach a gospel contrary to the one Paul received from Christ and the Father. Christ's authority, once again, is clearly equal to that of the Father, seeing as even the good angels can only speak in accordance with his and the Father's gospel message, and any demons who preach another gospel are, as Paul says, *accursed*. Jesus Christ, therefore, is excluded from the category of mere humans, and he is excluded from the category of angels - but he is not excluded from the category of divinity. Paul has identified Jesus Christ as God.

This becomes even more clear in Paul's following verse:

> For am I now seeking the approval of man, or of God? Or am I trying to please man? If I were still trying to please man, I would not be a servant of Christ.[3]

Paul declares that he is not seeking the approval of *man* but of *God*. He is not trying to *please men* but is being *a servant of Christ*. Again, the contrast between mere men and God places Christ alongside of the Father, identifying him as the non-angelic, more-than-human object of service and faithfulness, to the exclusion of men. Christ and the Father receive the exclusive devotion and service of the apostle Paul, placing them in the same divine category. Jesus Christ is God.

The apostle confirms this identification of Christ as the God-Man once again in vv.11-12, declaring:

> ...I would have you know, brothers, that the gospel that was preached by me is not man's gospel. For I did not receive it from any man, nor was I taught it, but I received it through a revelation of Jesus Christ.

---

[3] Gal 1:10.

Once again, Christ is excluded from the category of mere humans with the universal ἄνθρωπος (anthropos, man). The Son of God is neither a mere human, nor an angel, but one in power and authority with God the Father - Christ is God the Son.

Concluding Remarks

The apostle Paul's defense of his apostleship to the Galatians consists in identifying the source of his authority in God the Father and his Son. Jesus Christ and God the Father occupy the same unique category, sharing equal authority over men and angels. Either this is the case, or Paul is contradicting himself when he states that he received his apostleship neither from men nor through man (ἄνθρωπος). Yet the Scriptures are never self-contradictory. Therefore, Paul identifies Jesus Christ as the God-Man, equal in authority over men and angels with God the Father, yet personally and economically (i.e. functionally) distinct from the Father.

DON'T CALL IT A COMEBACK: UNITARIANISM REFUTED BY DIVINE FATHERHOOD

Michael R. Burgos Jr.

It was his final appeal. Just as the Israelite High Priest bore the people of God upon his heart on the Day of Atonement,[1] the Son of God went before his Father in prayer for his people. It was then that he divulged the identity of "the only true God" as Father.[2] Ironically, it is this declaration that the subordinationist apologetic has implemented to defy the teaching of orthodoxy.[3] Like the dogmatic postmodernist, unitarianism has engaged in self-refutation by not recognizing the obvious implication of pinning the title "only true God" upon the one who is unrelentingly Father.

When we consider the nature of God we are rightly compelled to look to the person and teaching of the Son of God who is the only one, who is himself God, who makes the Father known.[4] John

---

[1] Exodus 28:15-29.

[2] John 17:1-3.

[3] E.g., Stafford, *Jehovah's Witnesses Defended*, 129. Also see Buzzard, *Jesus Was Not a Trinitarian*, 20.

[4] John 1:18. There is substantial reason to affirm the reading μονογενὴς θεός. The reading is found in two 2nd century papyri, P[66] and P[75], as well as several important uncials (e.g., ℵ, B, C, & L). Given the

characterizes the Son of God as the divine Word, for it is he who has explained the Father. Whoever has seen the Son has seen the Father,[5] as it is the Son who is the exact representation of the Father.[6] Therefore, to settle the question of the nature of God we look to the Son.

The teaching of Christ was marked by the characterization of God as Father. Jesus taught that prayer is to be offered not merely to God, but to "our Father."[7] Jesus made known his own identity by revealing the unique relationship he has to God the Father. He claimed to be the one who was sent from the Father,[8] on whom "God the Father has set his seal,"[9] and the one who is glorified by the Father.[10] The level of dependence and the specificity of this relational aspect of God employed by Jesus is a departure from the generalized characterization of God as Father in the Old Testament. Jesus' teaching superseded the Old Testament's conception of God as Father by means of his depiction of his unique relationship—a relationship that was understood by the theological establishment as a claim of equality with God.[11] Jesus came to make God known to man, and he revealed God as Father.

Poythress has noted that, "There is an analogy between God the Father and human fathers."[12] This analogy stands in one

---

difficulty of μονογενὴς θεὸς and the harmonizing tendency of the Byzantine tradition, especially in the gospels, and given that John already applied θεὸς to the same subject in the prologue (v. 1), there remains no substantive textual critical reason to object to the earliest attested reading.

[5] John 14:9.

[6] Heb 1:3.

[7] Matt 6:9.

[8] John 10:36.

[9] John 6:27.

[10] John 8:54.

[11] John 5:18.

[12] Poythress, Vern S., *Logic: A God Centered Approach to the*

direction as God the Father is the one "from whom every fatherhood in heaven and on earth is named."[13] Earthly fathers derive their office from one Exemplar, and therefore the Father's identity precedes that of all earthly fathers. The only true God is Father, and that identity is absolutely essential to human existence. Men receive the title because they have engaged in procreation. That is, they have entered into a particular relationship with someone that is unique to those who bear the name. The title father therefore, is one that is necessarily relational. Men are fathers because they uniquely relate to their offspring. It is this office that men derive from God.

Fatherhood assumes the existence of a relationship that is unique to those that bear the name. To be consistent, unitarianism must contend that the concept of God as Father is one that is deployed within the confines of the economy of creation and redemption. This is due to that fact that the natural estate of the unitarian God is an entirely solitary enterprise wherein the concepts of relationship and love are completely unrealized. Relationality is foreign to the unitarian God as any subject-object existence can only be a convention of creation. Unitarianism therefore subjects the primary revelation of God by Christ to the confines of creation. Yet, unitarians insist that, "The overwhelming testimony of Scripture leads one to conclude that none other than

---

Foundation of Western Thought, (Wheaton: Crossway, 2013), 53.

[13] Ephesians 3:14-15. While the Greek text states, "πατέρα, ἐξ οὗ πᾶσα πατριὰ ἐν οὐρανοῖς καὶ ἐπὶ γῆς ὀνομάζεται," the ESV has translated πατριὰ as "family." However, it includes a footnote stating, "Or *from whom all fatherhood.*" I have chosen to follow Wycliffe and render πατριὰ "fatherhood" because of its close association with πατέρ, and because within the patriarchal context of the apostle, the father was the representative for the entirety of a family. The term is defined as "people linked over a relatively long period of time by line of descent to a common progenitor." *BDAG*, 788.

the Father is the one true God."[14] To this assertion, trinitarian orthodoxy hardly agrees. The Nicene Creed stands as one of the historic statements of trinitarian orthodoxy, and it begins by confessing, "We believe in one God, the Father Almighty, Maker of all things visible and invisible."[15] Thus, the unitarian affirmation of the one true God as Father is in fact, an affirmation of trinitarian orthodoxy.

The incompatibility of unitarianism with Christ's revelation of God as Father is evident. Jesus taught that he personally pre-existed with his Father, having been with his Father prior to the existence of the world.[16] Jesus revealed that the natural estate of God is not the unbridled solitude of unitarianism, but rather a state wherein the Father was in loving relationship with his Son.[17] Michael Reeves has remarked,

> Ask what God was doing before creation. Now to the followers of the goat-path that is an absurd, impossible question to answer; their wittiest theologians reply with the put down: 'What was God doing before creation? Making hell for those cheeky enough to ask such questions!' But on the lane it is an easy question to answer. Jesus tells us explicitly in John 17:24. 'Father,' he says, 'you loved me before the creation of the world.' And that is the God revealed by Jesus Christ. Before he ever created, before he ever ruled the world,

---

[14] Barron, *God and Christ*, 25.

[15] See Burgos Jr., Michael R., *Credo*, (Winchester: Church Militant, 2017), 104-107.

[16] Cf. John 8:38; 17:5. It must be emphasized that the Trinitarian contention is not merely the existence of two divine persons who are temporally titled "Father" and "Son," but rather that the relationship depicted by the appellations are essential to the nature of God.

[17] John 17:24.

before anything else, this God was a Father loving his Son.[18]

God did not need to depend upon creatures to experience relationship. Rather, God is Father and therefore God is eternally relational. Thus, God the Father's eternity presupposes the Son's eternity. However, suppose unitarianism affirmed the eternality of the Father while denying the eternality of the Son.[19] Such a position would require the redefinition of the term "father." Instead of being characterized by the giving of life and love, the term "father" would have to be recast so as to denote a natural state of utter isolation. Alternatively, some unitarians have rooted the eternality of God as Father in his identity as the origin of creation.[20] This position renders the Father dependent upon his own creation for his identity.

Theological Repercussions of Unitarianism

When the biblical revelation of God as Father is rejected, far reaching repercussions result. Unitarianism results in a God who

---

[18] Reeves, Michael, *Delighting in the Trinity: An Introduction to the Christian Faith*, (Downers Grove: InterVarsity Press, 2012), 21.

[19] In a dialogue with Dr. Robert Bowman Jr., Greg Stafford took this position. He stated, "The fact that the Father is eternal has nothing to do with whether or not the Son is eternal." Thus, Stafford has affirmed either the theological equivalent of a married-bachelor (i.e., a Father is not a progenitor), or a God who is dependent upon his creation for his very identity. See
http://www.jehovah.to/exe/discussion/stafford_bowman_2.htm.

[20] This was the view of the ancient Arians. According to Athanasius, the Arians understood the name Father primarily in terms of his role as the unoriginate Creator. However, as Athanasius argued, "[the Son] says not, 'When you pray, say, O God Unoriginate, 'but rather, 'When ye pray, say, our Father...'" Philip Schaff and Henry Wallace Eds., *Nicene and Post Nicene Fathers: Second Series*, Vol. IV- Athanasius: Selected Works and Letters, (New York: Cosimo, 2007), 326.

said of his image bearer, "It is not good that the man should be alone," and yet the one to whom the image belongs has known nothing but eternal loneliness. Moreover, if the relationship between the unitarian God and his Messiah is one that is predicated upon the difference between Creator and creation, then the relational dynamic is rooted in the ontological superiority of God and the inferiority of Jesus Christ.[21] However, because we are told, "the head of every man is Christ, the head of a wife is her husband, and the head of Christ is God,"[22] unitarianism therefore, demands the ontological superiority of husbands and the inferiority of wives.[23]

To the people of Israel, God most often mediated his revelation through his creatures (i.e., the prophets). At times he would appear himself and provide direct revelation. For example,

---

[21] See for example the "Biblical Unitarian" article "Who is Jesus Christ?," wherein the primary relationship between the Father and Son is portrayed by means of an ontological division (i.e., the exclusively human Jesus as he relates to God). http://www.biblicalunitarian.com/articles/jesus-christ/who-is-jesus-christ. Accessed 06/05/2018.

[22] 1 Cor 11:3.

[23] In an effort to mitigate the argument, one could appeal to the egalitarian contention that "head" (Gk. κεφαλή) communicates "source" and not "authority over" as in Mickelson, Alvera Ed., *Women, Authority, & the Bible*, (Downers Grove: Intervarsity Press, 1986), 97-110. However, there exists no biblical lexical source that supports such a definition. For example, see the exhaustive *BDAG*, 541-542. Mickelson, and many who follow her, engage in special pleading in order to usurp the semantic range recognized in lexicons of biblical literature for those that support their needed definition. For a further discussion of the term see Wayne Grudem, 1985. "Does ("Head") κεφαλή Mean 'Source' Or 'Authority Over' in Greek Literature? A Survey of 2,336 Examples," *Trinity Journal*, 6.1, 38-59. See also D. A. Carson, *Exegetical Fallacies*, 2nd Ed., (Grand Rapids: Baker Academic, 1996), 36-37.

Exodus 24:9-11 states,

> Then Moses and Aaron, Nadab, and Abihu, and seventy of the
> elders of Israel went up, and they saw the God of Israel. There
> was under his feet as it were a pavement of sapphire stone,
> like the very heaven for clearness. And he did not lay his hand
> on the chief men of the people of Israel; they beheld God, and
> ate and drank.

While this kind of occurrence was the exception and not the rule in
the Old Testament, a direct revelation of God to man was not
unprecedented.[24] In light of this, suppose one were to accept the
theology of unitarianism. The New Testament would then depict a
new paradigm wherein the Father is exclusively mediated through
his created Son. In these last days the Father has spoken by his
Son,[25] and therefore a relationship with the Father is restricted to
that which is mediated through creation. Not only does this present
a reversal of progressive revelation, the unitarian contention also
places the burden of revealing the nature of God upon a creature-
thereby rendering God truly unknowable to mankind.[26] If the
revelation of the nature and character of God is filtered through the

---

[24] It is beyond disputation to suggest anyone other than YHWH
himself appeared in the relevant text. The text itself, Exodus 33:11 and
Numbers 12:6-8 preclude the possibility of a created agent acting in
place of Yahweh.

[25] See Heb 1:1-2.

[26] Unsurprisingly, this was the view of Arius. Stephen Holmes has
noted that, "There is no question Arius' theology was profoundly
apophatic. God is unknowable, spiritual, simple, and eternal, and in the
beginning exists alone." Holmes, Stephen R., *The Quest for the Trinity:
The Doctrine of God in Scripture, History and Modernity*, (Downers
Grove, IL: InterVarsity Press, 2012), 86. For a further discussion of
Arius' apophaticism see Williams, Rowan, *Arius: Heresy and Tradition*,
(Grand Rapids: Eerdmans, 2001), 156; 207ff.

dim lens of creaturely finitude; Immanuel has failed to live up to his name and role as the one who makes God known.[27]

The Son of Scripture is altogether different than that of unitarianism. He has perfectly revealed the Father as it is he is who is "the radiance of the glory of God and the exact imprint of his nature." In the same way in which God has always had his glory, the Father has always been in relationship with his Son.[28] The Son is so very much like his Father that it is foolish to ask of him, "Lord, show us the Father."[29] To see the Son is to see the Father as the Father is in the Son and the Son is in the Father.[30] When we look to the Son of Scripture, we see in him the authentic revelation of God to man because to the same degree the Father knows his Son, the Son knows his Father and has made his Father known to those whom he has willed.[31]

The Misguided Use of a Proof-Text

> And this is eternal life, that they know you the only true God, and Jesus Christ whom you have sent. (John 17:3)

Non-trinitarians of all stripes tend to make John 17:3 the centerpiece of their polemic.[32] However, given the above, the use

---

[27] Cf. John 1:18; Matthew 11:27.

[28] John 14:8.

[29] See John 14:9-11. Cf. John 12:45; John 15:24.

[30] Matthew 11:27

[31] Matt 11:27.

[32] Navas, *Divine Truth or Human Tradition?*, 73-74, 163-166. Gill, *The One*, 206. Graeser, Lynn,, Schoenheit, *One God & One Lord*, 67. Buzzard, *Jesus Was Not a Trinitarian*, 28. Kerrigan, Jason, *Restoring the Biblical Christ: Is Jesus God?*, (Charleston: CreateSpace, 2016), 36ff. George, Robert, *The Trinity's Weak Link*, (New York: iUniverse, 2007), 112. Chang, *The Only True God*, 26. Bernard, David K., *The Oneness View of Jesus Christ*, (Hazelwood: Word Aflame, 1994), Kindle, loc.

of John 17:3 to prove unitarianism is misguided and self-refuting. One cannot pin the title "Father" upon the one true God without entering into the aforementioned dilemma. In a unitarian system, either God is Father because of creation, thereby nullifying the cornerstone of Jesus' teaching, or God is Father eternally, and is subsequently the equivalent of a married-bachelor in eternity past.

One of the points of common ground between trinitarians and most subordinationists is an affirmation of monotheism. That is, both trinitarians and unitarians (e.g., Muslims, Christadelphians, Oneness Pentecostals, Socinians) agree that there is only one God at all times and in all places. Therefore, it is not monotheism that is under dispute, but the nature of God. Although, there are a significant number of unitarians who, by ignorance or by malice, claim, despite the teaching of Christians for 2000 years, that trinitarianism is polytheism. However, trinitarianism denies such a claim. Aside from the human nature of Christ, the Father and Son are only differentiated relationally. That is, "The only distinctions between the members of the Trinity are in the ways they relate to each other and to the creation."[33] Thus, the unitarian argument that John 17:3 teaches that the Father is God to the exclusion of the Son depends upon a mischaracterization of trinitarianism. Since the Father, Son, and Holy Spirit are one and the same God, to affirm the exclusive deity of the *Father* is to simultaneously affirm the deity of the Son and Holy Spirit.

A logical problem emerges by insisting that John 17:3 asserts the deity of the Father to the exclusion of the Son. Such a construal engages in the fallacy of denying the antecedent (i.e., the fallacy of inverse error).[34] The fallacy takes the following form:

---

867. Norris, David, *I Am*, loc. 1782.

[33] Grudem, *Systematic Theology*, 250. See also Frame, John M., *A Theology of Lordship: The Doctrine of God*, Vol. 2, (Philipsburg: Presbyterian & Reformed, 2002), 622-625

[34] For further description of the fallacy of denying the antecedent

Premise: If A, then B.
Premise: Not A.
Conclusion: Not B.

An example of this fallacy is as follows:

Premise: If one is human, one is mortal.
Premise: Duke is not human.
Conclusion: Duke is not mortal.

Premise: If one is Father, then one is the only true God.
Premise: Jesus is not the Father.
Conclusion: Jesus is not the only true God.

Both of these arguments are fallacious since the conclusions wrongly assume the inverse of Premise 1 to be true (i.e., the exclusivity of Premise 1 beyond its stated parameters). Subsequently, the unitarian claims from John 17:3 do not follow and do not prove either that the Father is God to the exclusion of the Son, or that God is unitarian.

The above conclusion may be shown by the inconsistency of subordinationist hermeneutics regarding Jude 1:4:

> For certain people have crept in unnoticed who long ago were designated for this condemnation, ungodly people, who pervert the grace of our God into sensuality and deny our only Master and Lord, Jesus Christ.

Jude identifies Jesus as τὸν μόνον δεσπότην καὶ κύριον ἡμῶν ("The only Master and Lord of us"). The same attributive adjective

---

see Damer, T. Edward, *Attacking Faulty Reasoning*, 7th Ed., (Boston: Wadsworth, 2013), 82-83.

is used by John in John 17:3 when he writes of the Father, σὲ τὸν μόνον ἀληθινὸν θεὸν ("You, the only true God"). If subordinationists held a consistent hermeneutic, they would be required to affirm the Lordship and Mastery of Jesus Christ to the exclusion of the Father. Clearly, such a wooden reading is not intended in either Jude 1:4 or John 17:3.

Jesus is True God

> And we know that the Son of God has come and has given us understanding, so that we may know him who is true; and we are in him who is true, in his Son Jesus Christ. He is the true God and eternal life. (1 John 5:20)

> οἴδαμεν δὲ ὅτι ὁ υἱὸς τοῦ θεοῦ ἥκει, καὶ δέδωκεν ἡμῖν διάνοιαν ἵνα γινώσκωμεν τὸν ἀληθινόν: καὶ ἐσμὲν ἐν τῷ ἀληθινῷ, ἐν τῷ υἱῷ αὐτοῦ Ἰησοῦ Χριστῷ. οὗτός ἐστιν ὁ ἀληθινὸς θεὸς καὶ ζωὴ αἰώνιος. (1 John 5:20, NA28)

The above passage also serves to further mitigate the subordinationist contention regarding John 17:3. While some interpreters understand the appellation "true God" to refer to the Father, the demonstrative pronoun points back to the antecedent, namely Jesus Christ. Wallace has noted that,

> The demonstrative pronoun, οὗτός, in the gospel and the Epistles of John seems to be used in a theologically rich manner. Specifically, of the approximately seventy instances in which οὗτός has a personal referent, as many as forty-four of them (almost two-thirds of the instances) refer to the Son. Of the remainder, most imply some sort of positive connection with the Son. For what its worth, this datum increases the probability that Ἰησοῦ Χριστῷ is the antecedent in 1 John

5:20.[35]

In addition to the above observation, there are four reasons why it is apparent that John is referring to Jesus as "true God:"

1. The most natural reading suggests that the pronoun refer to its immediate antecedent, namely Jesus Christ.[36]

2. John identifies Jesus as "true,"[37] "truth,"[38] "God,"[39] as well as "full of truth."[40] Whereas Christ is repeatedly identified as "life" and "eternal life"[41] that title is *never* used of the Father.

3. The same construction occurs earlier in the chapter (i.e., οὗτός ἐστιν in 1 John 5:6) and refers to Jesus.

4. The Father is identified as "true" twice already in the verse. The addition of "true God" would be redundant and superfluous.[42] That is, calling God "true" as in 5:20 c-d, and

---

[35] Wallace, *GGBB,* 327.

[36] Lindars, Barnabus, Edwards, Ruth B., Court, John M., *Johannine Literature*, (Sheffield: Sheffield Academic Press, 2000), 160. Yarbrough, Robert. W., *Baker Exegetical Commentary on the New Testament: 1-3 John*, (Grand Rapids: Baker Academic, 2008), 320.
Bultmann, Rudolph K., *The Johannine Epistles*, (Philadelphia: Fortress Press, 1973), 90.

[37] John 1:9; 6:32; 15:1; 1 John 2:8; Rev 3:7; 19:11.

[38] John 14:6.

[39] John 1:1; 1:18; 20:28.

[40] John 1:14.

[41] John 6:48; 14:6; 1 John 1:1-2;

[42] Akin, Daniel L., *The New American Commentary: 1, 2, 3 John*, (Nashville: Broadman & Holman Pub., 2001), 214. Jobes, Karen H., *Exegetical Commentary on the New Testament: 1, 2, & 3 John*, (Grand Rapids: Zondervan, 2014), 241.

then "true God" is tautological.

5. The titles "true God and eternal life" bookend the Epistle since Jesus is identified as "eternal life" early in 1:2. John has coupled that title with the identification of Jesus' absolute deity in a manner that invokes the climax of his gospel (i.e., John 20:28).

A thorough recognition of the Fatherhood of God in conjunction with the exegetical witness to the divine nature of the Son preclude subordinationist theology. That Jesus is not only "true God," but also the "only Master and Lord," require a stable hermeneutic that isn't dependent upon isolated proof texts. Rather, orthodox theology, especially trinitarian Christology, is a product of an evenhanded pan-canonical approach to hermeneutics.

THE PREEXISTENCE OF THE PERSON OF THE SON

Edward L. Dalcour[1]

But of the Son he says..."You, Lord, in the beginning laid the foundation of the earth, and the heavens are the works of your hands. . . ." (Heb. 1:8, 10) [2]

The preexistence and deity of the distinct person of the Son, Jesus Christ, has been a main theme in Christian education as well as the basis of many hymns of the Christian faith. The preexistence of the Son has been a laser light in early Christian councils and resulting creedal documents. That Christ preexisted with the Father and the Holy Spirit is the very foundation of historic biblical

---

[1] Dr. Edward Dalcour holds a Master in Apologetics at (Columbia Evangelical Seminary) and a Doctorate of Philosophy in Dogmatic Theology at (North-West University). He is the president and founder Department of Christian Defense (a counter-cult apologetic ministry). He is the lead administrator and faculty member at Grace Bible University and serves as Mentor of Theology and Senior lecturer at Greenwich School of Theology (London, Eng.).

[2] Unless otherwise indicated, I have utilized the *New American Standard Bible* (1996).

Christianity. Christ Jesus clearly affirmed the magnificent truth of both his deity and preexistence many times in his earthly life.[3] In addition, according to various passages in the NT, the preincarnate Christ is identified as the YHWH of the OT in many places.[4]

In point of verifiable fact, the NT evidence of the preexistence of the Son is massive and unambiguous. We will examine some of the more significant passages that clearly and exegetically affirm this:

- John 1:1
- John 1:18 and the significance of the articular participle ὁ ὤν.
- The "sent from heaven" passages
- The eternal ἐγώ εἰμι ("I am") claims of the Son
- John 17:5
- The *Carmen Christi* (Phil 2:6-11)
- The Son as the agent of creation, the Creator himself (esp. John 1:3; Col 1:16-17; and Heb 1:10-12)

Unitarian Assumption: Being vs. Person

When discussing the Trinity and/or the deity of the Son with unitarian[5] groups, we must be aware of their starting theological

---

[3] E.g., Matt. 8:26; 12:6, 18; Mark 14:61-62; John 2:19; 3:13; 5:17-18; 6:35-40 [esp. v. 38]; 8:24, 58 *et al.*; 10:28-30; 16:28; Rev. 1:8, 17; 22:13.

[4] For example, compare Psalm 102:25-27 with Hebrews 1:10-12; Isaiah 6:1, 3, 10 with John 12:39-41 (thus, Isa 6:8); Isaiah 8:12-13 with 1 Peter 3:14-15; Isaiah 45:23 with Philippians 2:10-11; Joel 2:32 with Romans 10:13 and many more (cf. also Dan 7:9-14; Isa 9:6; Mic 5:2). Aside from the NT affirmation, which identifies Christ as the YHWH of many OT passages, the OT identifies the Angel of the Lord as YHWH (e.g., Gen 16:10-11; 19:24; Exod 3:6, 14; Judg 6:11-24; 13:16, 21 *et al.*).

[5] A unitarian or unipersonal belief of God is a radical view of

commitment—namely, God is one person. In other words, every time "one" is applied to God, the unitarians read into the term "one" as person (e.g., Deut 6:4; Mark 12:29; 1 Tim 2:5; etc.). Hence, by default, the unitarian reinterprets *monotheism* to mean *unipersonalism,* although, there is no passage in the OT or NT, which clearly identifies God as "one person."[6] It is on that fundamental premise which unitarian groups such as Muslims,

---

monotheism (μόνος, "one," and θεός, "God"), which sees God as "one person." Thus, a distinction needs to be made between religious groups that are unitarian in their doctrine of God and the official Unitarian religion itself. The former would include such religious systems as Judaism, Islam, the Watchtower Bible and Tract Society (i.e., Jehovah's Witnesses), Oneness Pentecostals, etc., while the latter is applied exclusively to the Unitarian Church as a religious denomination. Thus, unitarian (in lower case) will be used throughout this work to refer to the unipersonal theology, but not necessarily the Unitarian Church.

[6] The OT uses many plural nouns, verbs, adjectives, and plural prepositions to describe the one true God emphasizing His multi-personal nature. Note these examples: plural nouns—Gen 1:26 ("Our image, likeness"); plural verbs—Gen 1:26; 2:18 (LXX); 11:7; Isa 6:8; 54:5 (Heb., "Makers," "Husbands"); Psalm 149:2 and Job 35:10 (Heb., "Makers"); Ecc 12:1 (Heb., "Creators"); plural prepositions—Gen 3:22 ("one of Us"); and plural adjectives—Prov 30:3 (Heb. and LXX, "holy Ones"). Also, there are many places in the OT where YHWH interacts with or does something on behalf of "another" (distinct) YHWH as in Gen 19:24 (cf. Hosea 1:7-8); the Angel of the Lord references who was identified as YHWH (e.g., Gen chaps. 18-19; 22:9-14; Exod 3:6-14; 23:20-21; Num 22:21-35; Judg 2:1-5; 6:11-22; 13:9-25; Zech 1:12; etc.). Further, places such Heb 1:10-12, we read of YHWH (the Father) interacting with, that is, directly addressing, the Son as the YHWH of Psalm 102:25-27, the unchangeable Creator of all things. Many other examples can be cited clearly showing that the true God of biblical revelation is multi-personal. In point of fact, these plural references of God and YHWH to YHWH correspondences can only be consistent with biblical monotheism in the of context trinitarianism.

Jehovah's Witnesses, and Oneness Pentecostals launch their attacks on the doctrine of the Trinity and the deity of Christ, thus, rejecting any notion that "another" person (Jesus) is God.

This misunderstanding of biblical monotheism also confuses "being" with "person." Simply stated, "being" (an ontological reference) is *what* something is, while "person" is *who* someone is. Scripture presents one eternal God, that is, one being, revealed in three distinct persons, the Father and the Son, and the Holy Spirit. Hence, because the Scripture presents a Triune God, the Christian church has consistently and tenaciously held to and affirmed the Trinity and preexistence of the person of God the Son.

Biblical Data of the Preexistence of the Person of the Divine Son

John 1:1

In the beginning was the Word, and the Word was with God, and the Word was God.[7]

From a theological and grammatical standpoint, the three clauses of John 1:1 powerfully and effectively refute the theology of every non-Christian group that denies the full deity of Jesus Christ and his distinction from God the Father. Consider the three clauses of John 1:1:

A. Ἐν ἀρχῇ ἦν ὁ λόγος (lit., "In [the] beginning was the Word").

---

[7] Ἐν ἀρχῇ ἦν ὁ λόγος, καὶ ὁ λόγος ἦν πρὸς τὸν θεόν, καὶ θεὸς ἦν ὁ λόγος, *En archē ēn ho logos, kai ho logos pros ton theon, kai theos ēn ho logos.* Unless indicated, my citations from the Greek NT are from the *Novum Testamentum Graece: Nestle-Aland,* 28th Rev. Ed., (Stuttgart: Deutsche Bibelgesellschaft, 2012).

In the first clause, we find the affirmation of eternality of the person of the Word (Christ). First, unlike the Stoic view that the impersonal *Logos*/Word was merely the rational principle of the universe, in the prologue (vv. 1-18), John presents the preexistent Word as possessing personal attributes. Thus, the content of the prologue radically and clearly militates also against the Oneness Pentecostal impersonal abstract thought or concept view of the Word. Thayer says of the *Logos* of 1:1, "ὁ λόγος denotes the essential Word of God, i.e., the personal (hypostatic) wisdom and power in union with God."[8] "The *Logos* is not," says Lenski, "an attribute inhering in God...but a person in the presence of God..."[9] Simply, the first verb ἦν ("was") here is the imperfect indicative of εἰμι ("I am, exist"). The force of the imperfect tense indicates a *continuous action* (or repeated action) normally occurring *in the past.* Hence, the Word did not *originate* at a point in time, but rather in the beginning of time, the Word ἦν already existed. Thus, linguistically, the Word was existing ("ἦν the Word") prior to the time of the ἀρχῇ—before "the beginning." Also, note the verbal contrast between ἦν and the aorist ἐγένετο[10] ("came into being," cf. v. 3). The aorist indicative normally indicates a punctiliar action normally occurring in the past.[11] In the prologue of John, ἦν is exclusively applied to the eternal Word in vv. 1, 2, 4, 9, and 10, while in vv. 3, 6, and 10, the aorist ἐγένετο is applied to everything created. Not until verse 14 does ἐγένετο refer to the Son denoting

---

[8] Thayer, Joseph H., *Thayer's Greek-English Lexicon of the New Testament*, (Peabody: Hendrickson, 1996), 381-2.

[9] Lenski, Richard C. H., *The Interpretation of John's Gospel*, (Minneapolis: Augsburg Fortress Press, 1943), 32

[10] From γίνομαι ("to become").

[11] Cf. Greenlee, Herold J., *A Concise Exegetical Grammar of New Testament Greek,* 5th Ed., (Grand Rapids: Eerdmans, 1986), 49.

his new added nature—"the Word *became* flesh."[12]

B. καὶ ὁ λόγος ἦν πρὸς τὸν θεόν (lit., "and the Word was with the God").

The second clause of John 1:1 teaches the absolute personal distinction between the eternal Word and τὸν θεόν (i.e., the Father).[13] John envisages a marked distinction between two persons.[14] Of all the prepositions that John could have utilized, which can mean "with" (e.g., ἐν, μετά, παρά, σύν), he chose πρὸς (lit., "facing"/"toward," with the accusative, θεόν as the object of the preposition). Hence, πρὸς with the accusative clearly indicates that the Word was "at, with, in the presence of . . . God."[15] Robertson explains the significance of the preposition in John 1:1b:

With God (πρὸς τὸν θεόν). Though existing eternally with God, the *Logos* was in perfect fellowship with God. Πρὸς with

---

[12] The same verbal contrast (εἰμι vs. γίνομαι) is seen in John 8:58.

[13] Generally, articular (with the article) nouns point to identification, while anarthrous nouns point to essence, nature, quality.

[14] The preposition πρὸς ("toward") generally denotes intimate fellowship between person(s). In relationship to John 1:1b, the specific phrase πρὸς τὸν θεόν occurs twenty times in the Greek NT. In each occurrence, πρὸς differentiates between a person or persons and God. The only exception is the three times where the neuter plural article precedes the phrase (viz. Rom. 15:17; Heb. 2:17 and 5:1). Thus, they are not syntactically the same as John 1:1b. In John 1:1b, εἰμί (in the imperfect form, ἦν) precedes the phrase, whereas in Romans 15:17; Hebrews 2:17 and 5:1, the neuter plural article τὰ ("the things") precedes the phrase. Πρὸς τὸν θεόν expresses the distinct personality of the Logos, which other prepositions (such as, ἐν, μετὰ, παρά, or σύν) would have obscured.

[15] Greenlee, *Exegetical Grammar,* 39.

the accusative presents a plane of equality and intimacy, face to face with each other. In 1 John 2:1 we have a like use of πρὸς. . . .[16]

Though existing eternally with God the *Logos* was in perfect fellowship with God. *BDAG* specifically points out that πρὸς at John 1:1b indicates the meaning of "by, at, near; πρὸς τίνα εἶναι: be (in company) with someone."[17] Thus, the distinct person of the Word was always in intimate loving fellowship with the Father, before time.

C. καὶ θεὸς ἦν ὁ λόγος (lit., "and God was the Word").

The third clause of John 1:1 teaches the deity of Jesus Christ. Here we read one of the clearest and unequivocal affirmations of the deity of the person of the Word in the NT. John accentuates his high Christology by first showing that the person of the Word (the Son) was eternal, that is, preexisting (1:1a) and that the eternal Word was distinct from Father (1:1b). Then, John presents the very marrow of the gospel: "The Word was God" and "the Word became flesh (v. 14).

That the Word was fully God and distinct from the Father (τὸν θεόν) is clearly accentuated by the context and grammar. In the inspired syntax of the clause John uses the "emphatic" conjunction (i.e., "especially, in fact") followed by the anarthrous [18] θεὸς (καὶ θεὸς ἦν ὁ λόγος). Grammatically, the anarthrous θεὸς is a preverbal predicate nominative. The PN describes the class or category to which the subject (λόγος) belongs.[19] Hence, the anarthrous preverbal PN θεὸς points to the "quality" (essence) of the Word,

---

[16] Robertson, *Word Pictures in the New Testament,* Vol. 5, 4.

[17] *BDAG*, 875.

[18] A noun that lacks the article is anarthrous.

[19] Cf. *GGBB*, 262, 265.

not the identity (person). In view of John's theology, along with the grammar and context, the highest semantical possibility for θεὸς in 1:1c is qualitative.[20]

If John would have written θεὸς as articular in 1:1c (ὁ θεὸς), then, John would have been saying that the λόγος is the same person as in 1:1b, τὸν θεόν (viz. God the Father)—but he did not. Even more mismatched is an indefinite rendering of θεὸς ("a god") in 1:1c, as we find in the Jehovah's Witnesses' NWT ("and the Word was a god"). Of course, this idea of the Word being a created indefinite god ("a god") clearly clashes with John's own view of the Word within the content of his literature. In the prologue, the Word is presented as eternal (1:1a), the Creator of all things (v. 3), Life (v. 4), the "one and only/unique God" who is always [ὁ ὢν][21] at the Father's bosom (v. 18). Hence, an indefinite rendering ("a god") although grammatically possible, would be theologically impossible in light of John's own monotheistic theology. John 1:1 expresses the marvelous truth of the preexistent person of the Word—who was God and existing with God. He is "the true God and eternal life" (1 John 5:20), the Creator of all things who became flesh in order "to give his life a ransom for many" (Mark 10:45). "In three crisp sentences," says Warfield,

He declares at the outset his eternal subsistence, his eternal intercommunion with God, his eternal identity with God...In some sense distinguishable from God, he was in an equally true sense identical with God. There is but one eternal God; this eternal God, the Word is; in whatever sense we may distinguish him from the God whom he is "with," he is yet not another than this God, but himself is this God...John would have us realize that what the Word was in eternity was not

[20] Ibid., 196, 269.

[21] See discussion below pertaining to the linguistic import of the articular participle ὁ ὢν in both John 1:18 and Romans 9:5.

merely God's coeternal fellow, but the eternal God's self.[22]

John's own commentary of John 1:1 in 1 John 1:1-2:

What was from the beginning, what we have heard, what we have seen with our eyes, what we have looked at and touched with our hands, concerning the Word of Life—and the life was manifested, and we have seen and testify and proclaim to you the eternal life, which was with the Father and was manifested to us. (1 John 1:1-2)

Note the remarkable similarities with John 1:1, both attesting to the deity, preexistence, and unipersonality (a distinct person) of the Word:

In the beginning [ἀρχῇ] was the Word [ἦν ὁ λόγος], and the Word was with God [ἦν πρὸς τὸν θεόν]. (John 1:1)

What was [ἦν] from the beginning [ἀρχῆς] . . . concerning the Word [περὶ τοῦ λόγου] of Life. . . . which was with the Father [ἦν πρὸς τὸν πατέρα]." (1 John 1:1-2)

Both John's gospel and epistle use the same and highly significant Greek nouns, prepositions, and verbs to denote "the Word" and his relationship *with* the Father. Both use ἀρχῇ and the imperfect verb ἦν indicating the preexistence of the person of the Word. And both use πρὸς indicating the eternal Word's intimate relationship with (distinct from) God the Father. Further, the prepositional phrase in 1 John 1:2 (the Word was πρὸς τὸν πατέρα) identifies "God" in John 1:1b as the Father, who was *with* the Word: "and the Word was with God"—that is, the Word was *with*

---

[22] Warfield, Benjamin B., *Biblical Doctrines*, (Carlisle: Banner of Truth, 1988), 190-92.

the Father, not *was* the Father.[23] Also note that in both John's gospel and epistle, the Word is referred to as "Life," which is a distinguishing epithet used of the Son throughout John's literature (cf. John 11:25; 14:6; 1 John 5:12) and "nowhere else used of the Father."[24]

John 1:18

No one has seen God at any time; the only begotten God who is in the bosom of the Father, he has explained him.[25]

This passage is the bookend of John's prologue: "The Word was God"—the "one and only God who is [always] in the bosom of the Father, he has explained him." John makes the assertion that God the Father is invisible and the "the only God"[26] has revealed him. John presents the Son as distinct from the Father in intimate fellowship being continuously at the Father's bosom. John also points out that it is the "unique"[27] God the Son, the eternal Word

---

[23] Both nouns, "God" in John 1:1b and "Father" in 1 John 1:2 are articular, thus, both signifying identification—viz. the person of the Father, with whom the Son preexisted, ἦν πρὸς τὸν θεόν/πατέρα.

[24] Wallace, *GGBB*, 327.

[25] θεὸν οὐδεὶς ἑώρακεν πώποτε· μονογενὴς θεὸς ὁ ὢν εἰς τὸν κόλπον τοῦ πατρὸς ἐκεῖνος ἐξηγήσατο.

[26] This is the ESV rendering. While the updated NIV incorporates both variants (μονογενὴς θεὸς and ὁ μονογενὴς υἱός): "the one and only Son, who is himself God."

[27] The adjective μονογενὴς points to the uniqueness of the Son (from μονος and γένος). He is the "one and only" or "one of a kind" God the Son, that is, "The unique God who was near the heart of the Father" (Wallace). The Lexical evidence of the compound Greek adjective is quite weighty. For example, *BDAG*:

Pertaining to being the only one of its kind or class, unique (in kind)

of something...μονογενὴς υἱὸς is used only of Jesus. The renderings only, unique may be quite adequate for all its occurrences...See also...vs. 18 where, beside the reading μονογενὴς θεὸς (considered by many the orig.) an only-begotten one, God (acc. to his real being; i.e. uniquely divine as God's son...or a uniquely begotten deity.

Louw and Nida:

μονογενὴς, pertaining to what is unique in the sense of being the only one of the same kind or class —'unique, only."
Liddle and Scott: "μονο.γενὴς, μουνο- (γένος) the only member of a kin or kind: hence, generally, only, single.

Newman: "Unique, only."

Lightfoot (Epistles):

μονογενὴς, unicus, alone of His kind and therefore distinct from created things. The two words express [πρωτότοκος and μονογενὴς] the same eternal fact; but while μονογενὴς states it in itself, πρωτότοκος places it in relation to the Universe...The history of the patristic exegesis of this expression is not without a painful interest. All the fathers of the second and third centuries without exception, so far as I have noticed, correctly refer it to the Eternal Word.

International Standard Bible Encyclopedia (ISBE):

In these passages, too, it might be translated as "the only son of God;" for the emphasis seems to be on His uniqueness, rather than on His Sonship. . . He is the son of God in a sense in which no others are. "μονογενὴς describes the absolutely unique relation of the Son to the Father in His divine nature; πρωτότοκος describes the relation of the Risen Christ in His glorified humanity to man.

TDNT:

made flesh who "explains"[28] the Father.

ὁ ὢν

As it relates to John's recurring presentation of the preexistence (and deity) of the person of the Son (cf. 1:1a, 3, 10), the apostle now affirms the Son's timeless existence in the bosom of the Father. In the phrase μονογενὴς θεὸς ὁ ὢν εἰς τὸν κόλπον τοῦ πατρὸς ("only begotten God who is in the bosom of the Father"), the articular participle, ὁ ὢν ("who is") is used to affirm the very same thing as in John 1:1b—namely, the person of the Son preexisted *with* the Father. Just as the present active participle ὑπάρχων in Philippians 2:6 communicates the perpetual existence of the divine Son (as discussed below), more than a few passages, where the context is warranted, contain the present active participle ὢν (from εἰμί), which also linguistically denotes the Son's eternal

---

What Jn. means by ὁ μονογενὴς υἱός...When Jn. speaks of the Son of God, he has primarily in view the man Jesus Christ, though not exclusively the man, but also the risen and pre-existent Lord. The relation of the pre-existent Lord to God is that of Son to Father. This comes out indisputably in 17:5...Jesus is aware that He was with God, and was loved by Him, and endued with glory, before the foundation of the world. This is personal fellowship with God, divine Sonship...in Jn. the Lord is always the Son. Because He alone was God's Son before the foundation of the world, because the whole love of the Father is for Him alone, because He alone is one with God, because the title God may be ascribed to Him alone, He is the only-begotten Son of God." To maintain that in Jn. the pre-existent Lord is only the Word, and that the Son is only the historical and risen Lord, is to draw too sharp a line between the preexistence on the one side and the historical and post-historical life on the other.

[28] The verb ἐξηγήσατο (from ἐξηγέομαι) is from which we get the English term, "exegete." Thus, God the Son is the one who exegetes the Father perfectly and continuously (cf. John 14:6; Heb 1:3).

existence.[29] In explicit reference to the Son's eternality, the present active participle is used both articularly (ὁ ὤν) and anarthrously (ὤν). Two such examples of the articular form of the participle are in John 1:18 and Romans 9:5 both pointing to the Son's eternality.

No one has seen God at any time; the only begotten God **who is** [ὁ ὤν, i.e., "the One who is/being always"] in the bosom of the Father, He has explained Him." (John 1:18)

Whose are the fathers, and from whom is the Christ according to the flesh, **who is** [ὁ ὤν, i.e., "the One who is/being always"] over all, God blessed forever. Amen. (Rom 9:5)

Note that within the defining context of both passages, both authors refer to the Son as θεὸς, which further supports the affirmation of the Son's deity and his preexistence. Systematic theologian, Robert Reymond remarks on the significance of the articular participle in John 1:18: "The present participle ὁ ὤν . . . indicates a continuing state of being: 'who is continually in the bosom of the Father.'"[30] In the LXX of Exodus 3:14, we find the articular present participle ὁ ὤν to denote YHWH's eternal existence: ἐγώ εἰμι ὁ ὤν, literally, "I am the eternal/always existing One." Also note, the ἐγώ εἰμι phrase precedes the participial phrase here (cf. also John 8:58 *et al.*).

We moreover find the use of the anarthrous present active participle ὤν, in contexts where the deity of the Son is clearly in view. In Hebrews 1:3,[31] the present active participle (i.e., ὅς ὤν)

---

[29] Cf. Harris, Murray, *Jesus as God: The New Testament Use of Theos in Reference to Jesus* (Grand Rapids: Baker Book House, 1992), 157-158.

[30] Reymond, Robert L., *A New Systematic Theology of the Christian Faith* (Nashville: Thomas Nelson, 1998), 303.

[31] As noted below, the prologue of Hebrews provides a marked

"marks the Son's continuous action of being, which denotes total and full deity."[32]

It "refers to the absolute and timeless existence."[33] Furthermore, the present participle ὤν (εἰμί) in Hebrews 1:3 is set in contrast with the aorist participle γενόμενος ("having become" from γίνομαι) in verse 4.

This same verbal contrast (present/continuous past vs. a punctiliar action) is also seen, as mentioned above, in the prologue of John where the imperfect indicative ἦν (εἰμί) is set in contrast with aorist indicative ἐγένετο; as in John 8:58, where the present indicative εἰμί is set in contrast with the aorist infinitive γενέσθαι; and, as in Philippians 2:6-8, where the present participle ὑπάρχων in verse 6 is set in contrast with the following aorist verbs in verses 7 and 8—ἐκένωσεν, λαβών, γενόμενος, and εὑρεθείς. In each case, we find a vivid linguistic contrast between the preexistent Son and *all things that came to be.* Lastly, in Revelation 1:4, 8; 11:17; 16:5, the articular participle ὁ ὤν is used to denote the "timeless existence" of God. In 1:8, articular participle applied to the "Lord God" is especially amplified by the title, "Alpha and Omega": "'I am the Alpha and the Omega,' says the Lord God, 'who is [ὁ ὤν] and who was and who is to come, the Almighty.'" As to the speaker in verse 8, some have pointed to the Father (cf. v. 4). However, identifying the Son as the speaker is more compelling and more contextually apparent (esp. in light of vv. 7 and 22:13). Adding to that is the fact that the articular participle ὁ ὤν is applied

---

contrast between things created (viz., angels, the heavens, and the earth) and the eternal divine Son (cf. vv. 3, 8) whom the author presents as the unchangeable Creator of all things (cf. vv. 2, 10-12).

[32] Robertson, *Word Pictures*, 5:17-18.

[33] Rogers Jr.. Cleon, Rogers III, Cleon L., *New Linguistic and Exegetical Key to the Greek New Testament* (Grand Rapids: Zondervan 1998), 516.

specifically to the Son at John 1:18 and Romans 9:5 (and the anarthrous participle at Heb. 1:3).

Therefore, John 1:18 is an excellent example of the preexistence of the person of Christ. As the theological bookend of the prologue, John ends as he began—with the affirmation of the Son's deity. Both passages present the person of the Word, the Son of God, as θεὸς; a distinct person from the Father (πρὸς τὸν θεόν - ὁ ὢν εἰς τὸν κόλπον τοῦ πατρὸς); and his preexistence. The articular participle ὁ ὢν in John 1:18 (as well ὑπάρχων in Phil. 2:6) carries the same linguistic idea as that of the imperfect ἦν in John 1:1a—namely, the Son's preexistence.

The Divine Son "Sent From Heaven"

> I came forth from the Father and have come into the world; I am leaving the world again and going to the Father. (John 16:28).

In the NT, there are countless examples of the person of the Son as being "sent" from heaven. In fact, at least forty times in the gospel of John we find references of the Son who was sent by the Father (cf. John 3:13, vv. 16-17; 6:33, vv. 38, 44, 46, 50-51, 62; 8:23, vv. 38, 42, 57-58; 16:28). The many passages that present the sending of the preincarnate person of the Son are written plainly and in normal language. Further, in John chapter 6 alone, nine times Jesus specifically refers to himself as coming down "out/from the heaven": ἐκ τοῦ οὐρανοῦ ("out of, from the heaven"; vv. 32 [twice], 33, 41, 42, 50, 51); ἀπὸ τοῦ οὐρανοῦ ("from, out of the heaven," v. 38); and ἐξ οὐρανοῦ ("from heaven," v. 58). These passages naturally affirm that the preincarnate Son came out from heaven down to earth.

John 6:38 is most remarkable in its claim. Jesus said that that he came down out of heaven not to do his own will, but the will of the one having sent him. The text reads: ὅτι καταβέβηκα ἀπὸ τοῦ οὐρανοῦ οὐχ ἵνα ποιῶ τὸ θέλημα τὸ ἐμὸν ἀλλὰ τὸ θέλημα τοῦ πέμψαντός με· (lit., "For I have come down from out of the heaven not in order that I should do the will of me, but the will of the one having sent me." Note that grammatically an aorist participle is usually antecedent to the main verb.[34] Here the main verb is the perfect indicative καταβέβηκα ("I have come down") and πέμψαντός ("having sent") is an aorist participle. Consequently, the Father's action of *sending* his Son, signified by the aorist participle, occurred *before* the Son's incarnation—thus, before the action of *coming down* from heaven to earth.[35]

Even more, this shows clearly that even before the incarnation, the person of Christ, God the Son, possessed his own will distinct from the Father's will, yet in perfect harmony—destroying the Oneness Pentecostal position of a unipersonal God.[36] In other

---

[34] See DeWitt Burton, Ernest, *Syntax of the moods and tenses in New Testament Greek* (Univ. of Chicago Press, 1892), sec. 134. Mounce: "The aorist participle indicates an action occurring prior to the time of the main verb" (Mounce, William D., *Basics of Biblical Greek Grammar* [Grand Rapids: Zondervan 2003], 237). Wallace: "The aorist participle, for example, usually denotes antecedent time to that of the controlling verb" (Wallace, *GGBB*, 614; cf. also 555). See also Robertson, A. T., *A Grammar of the Greek New Testament in the Light of Historical Research*, (Nashville: Broadman Press, 1934), 860.

[35] A similar construction to John 6:38 is found in the last clause of John 8:42: ἐγὼ γὰρ ἐκ τοῦ θεοῦ ἐξῆλθον καὶ ἥκω· οὐδὲ γὰρ ἀπ' ἐμαυτοῦ ἐλήλυθα, ἀλλ' ἐκεῖνός με ἀπέστειλεν (lit., "I indeed from the God came forth and am here, not even indeed of myself have I come, but he, me sent." The aorist indicative ἀπέστειλεν ("sent") is antecedent to the perfect indicative ἐλήλυθα ("I have come"). As in 6:38, the sending of the Son was before the coming to earth.

[36] For an exegetical refutation to Oneness unitarian theology see Dalcour, Edward L., *A Definitive Look at Oneness Theology: In the Light of Biblical Trinitarianism,* 4th ed., available at www.christiandefense.org.

words, before coming down from heaven and becoming flesh, this text reveals that the person of the Father and the person of the Son each possessed his "own" will: ποιῶ τὸ θέλημα τὸ ἐμὸν ("to do the will of me") - τὸ θέλημα τοῦ πέμψαντός με ("the will of the one having sent me"). We see the same in Philippians 2:6 where the preexistent Son performed the action of the verb ἡγήσατο ("consider, suppose") before the action of his self-emptying (ἑαυτὸν ἐκένωσεν), that is, his incarnation. Hence, in John 6:38 (and Phil. 2:6-8), the preexistence of the Son and Triune nature of God is clearly being expressed.

The Son's claim to be the Eternal ἐγώ εἰμι

> Therefore I said to you that you will die in your sins; for unless you believe that I am He, you will die in your sins. (John 8:24)

There are several places in the OT where the LXX records YHWH as referring to himself as ἐγώ εἰμι (cf. Deut 32:39; Isa 41:4; 43:10; 46:4; 48:12, etc.).[37] At these places, the LXX translates the Hebrew phrase, *ani hu* ("I am he"), as the unpredicated ἐγώ εἰμι, "I am." This was an exclusive and recurring title for YHWH, which the Jews clearly understood. Plainly, the

---

[37] Although the LXX of Exodus 3:14 is not an exact equivalent to 8:58, it does provide a stark presentation of eternality that is tantamount in meaning to Jesus' ἐγώ εἰμι statements. In the LXX, YHWH responds to Moses' question, not as ἐγώ εἰμι, as in John 8:58, rather, as ἐγώ εἰμι ὁ ὤν. Both ἐγώ εἰμι and ὁ ὤν are incorporated. As we saw in John 1:18 and Romans 9:5, the articular participle, ὁ ὤν, in these contexts, denotes timeless existence—"the One eternally existing." While Exodus 3:14 and John 8:58 are not strictly equivalent in wording, they are indeed equivalent in meaning. And to say again, in such places as Deuteronomy 32:39; Isaiah 41:4; 43:10; and 48:12 (LXX) we do see the precise equivalent of the unpredicated phrase ἐγώ εἰμι as in John 8:58 *et al.*

phrase ἐγώ εἰμι was a recurring linguistic epithet of YHWH denoting his eternal existence. So, when Christ makes this unmistakable claim of himself, we find the response of the Jews was most appropriate according to their theological understanding of the title and their denial of Christ as God.

The ἐγώ εἰμι ("I am") declarations of Jesus mainly appear in the gospel of John (viz. John 8:24, vv. 28, 58; 13:19; 18:5, vv. 6, 8). However, other gospels recorded them (e.g., Mark 6:50). It should also be considered that Jesus' claims to be the ἐγώ εἰμι was not only seen in John 8:58 (as many assume), but there is marked progression starting in 8:24 and climaxing in 18:8. Keep in mind, the full deity (and full humanity) of Jesus Christ, Son of God, was a main theme in John's literature (cf. John 1:1, v. 18; 5:17-18; the "I am" clauses; 10:30; 20:28; 1 John 5:20; Rev. 1:8, v. 17; 22:13; etc.). However, I will say at the outset that the deity and preexistence of the person of the Son does not rest merely on Jesus' ἐγώ εἰμι affirmations nor on any other single passage. Rather, the entire content of biblical revelation in both the OT and NT unambiguously presents Christ as Lord and eternal God.

Regarding the several occurrences of Jesus' ἐγώ εἰμι claims, most translations see John 8:58 as an absolute unpredicated claim.[38] However, most add the pronoun "He/he" (e.g., NKJV, NASB, NIV et al.) after the "I am" clause at John 8:24, v. 28; 13:19; 18:5, vv. 6, 8 (and Mark 6:50) in spite of the fact that the pronoun is not contained after ἐγώ εἰμι in any Greek manuscript. These instances of ἐγώ εἰμι lack a clear supplied predicate. Hence, the ἐγώ εἰμι phrases such as, for instance, "I am the door," "I am the shepherd," "I am the gate," etc. all have clear predicates following ἐγώ εἰμι. Whereas, as exampled above, the specific ἐγώ εἰμι claims of the Son (and of YHWH in the LXX) have a

---

[38] As previously shown, Jesus contrasts Abraham's origin: πρὶν Ἀβραὰμ γενέσθαι ("before Abraham was born") with his eternal existence: ἐγὼ εἰμί ("I am").

definitive context[39] justifying an unpredicated ἐγώ εἰμι—namely, an unmistakable claim of deity (again, as the Jews clearly perceived, cf. John 8:59).

As acknowledged by the mass of scholarship, the particular ἐγώ εἰμι statements of YHWH in the LXX[40] and Jesus in the NT are crystal clear affirmations of deity and thus, eternality. For example, along with John 8:58, R. E. Brown sees 8:24 and verse 28 as non-predicated, that is, absolute.[41] Anderson observes that John 8:24, vv. 28, 58; 13:19 and 18:5, vv. 6, 8 occur "in the absolute having no predicate."[42] See also Robertson[43]; Jamieson-Fausset-Brown[44] Daniel Wallace[45]; Philip Harner[46] et al. all who attest to the unpredicated absolute ἐγώ εἰμι claim of Christ.[47]

---

[39] The recorded ἐγώ εἰμι claims by the Christ in John 8 begin in v. 24.

[40] As seen (e.g., Deut 32:39; Isa 41:4; 43:10; and 48:12). Note that in Isaiah 41:4 and 48:12, YHWH claim to by the ἐγώ εἰμι are in apposition with the title "First and the Last," which are only applied to Christ in Revelation. See Burgos in this volume, "I Am: Reducing Unitarian Argumentation to Ashes," 175.

[41] Brown, R. E., *The Gospel According to John* I-XII (Anchor Bible Series, vol. 29; Garden City: Doubleday, 1966), 1:533-38.

[42] Anderson, Paul N., *The Christology of the Fourth Gospel* (Eugene: Wipf & Stock Publishers, 2010), 21.

[43] Cf. Robertson, *Grammar*, 879-880.

[44] In their *Commentary Critical and Explanatory on the Whole Bible,* it pointed out that the language of John 8:24 as "so far transcending what is becoming in men, of those ancient declarations of the God of Israel, 'I AM HE' (Deut 32:39, Isa 43:10, v.13, 46:4; 48:12)" (Volume 3: Matthew to Ephesians).

[45] Cf. Wallace, *GGBB*.

[46] Cf. Harner, Philip B., *The 'I Am' of the Fourth Gospel: A Study in Johannine Usage and Thought* (Minneapolis: Fortress Press, 1970), 4.

[47] Even more, the early church saw Jesus' "I am" claims as an absolute claim to deity (e.g., Irenaeus, *Against Heresies*, in Schaff, Philip, *Ante-Nicene Fathers: The Writings of the Fathers down to A.D.*

John 17:5

> Now, Father, glorify Me *together with Yourself,* with the glory which *I had with You* before the world was.[48]

In Jesus' High Priestly prayer to the Father, he *commands*[49] or requests the Father to glorify himself together with the Father with the glory that he *had* or *shared* (ἣ εἶχον) *with* (παρὰ) the Father *before the world was* (πρὸ τοῦ τὸν κόσμον εἶναι). According to the Son's own words, he preexisted *with* the Father *before time.* The exegetical significance is undeniable:

The glory was shared, between the Father and the person

325, 1:478; Origen [ibid., 4:463]; Novatian [ibid., 5:624-625]; Chrysostom [ibid., 14:199]).

[48] Καὶ νῦν δόξασόν με σύ, πάτερ, παρὰ σεαυτῷ τῇ δόξῃ ᾗ εἶχον πρὸ τοῦ τὸν κόσμον εἶναι παρὰ σοί.

[49] The first part of the text reads, Καὶ νῦν δόξασόν με σύ, πάτερ (lit., "And now glorify Me You, Father"). Note the aorist imperative verb, δόξασόν. The most common usage of the imperative mood is for commands. However, the imperative can also denote a request. On occasion, "the request imperative will be used by a superior when addressing an inferior" (Wallace, *GGBB,* 485). Here in this text, the imperative is in the aorist (δόξασόν) stressing the urgency of the command or request. Since the Son is biblically presented as ontologically coequal with the Father (cf. John 1:1c; Phil 2:6-11; Heb 1:3), his "commanding" the Father to glorify him would not infringe on the doctrine of the Trinity—one divine person commanding another divine person of the same ontological class or category. Although it is possible that the imperative here can be one of request, it is the assumption of unipersonalism, denying that the Son is a divine person coequal with Father, that we find a natural and automatic rejection of the imperative of command. Even though the plainness of the passage cannot be denied (the Father and the Son sharing glory before time).

of the Son: It is the divine glory that YHWH does "not share" with anyone else (cf. Isa 42:8). Notice that the glorification applies to both the Father and the Son here, which they shared before the creation. It is not glory *apart* from the Father; rather the Son possesses glory *alongside* the Father. The glory of which Jesus speaks is a "me *with* you" glory. No creature can make this claim. This unique glory here is a defined glory exclusive to YHWH alone (as in Isa. 42:8). The Apostle John applies the "glory" that Isaiah saw (cf. Isa 6:1-3, LXX) to the Son in John 12:41. John even uses the same terms as the LXX of Isaiah.[50]

The Son is presented as a distinct person from the Father— παρὰ with the dative: The glory that the Son had was "with" the Father. Grammatically, when the preposition παρὰ ("with") is followed by the dative case, which occurs twice in this passage (παρὰ σεαυτῷ, "together with yourself," παρὰ σοί, "together/with You"), especially in reference to persons, it indicates "near," "beside," or "in the presence of."[51] In fact, in John's literature, παρὰ with the dative is used ten times (John 1:39; 4:40; 8:38; 14:17, 23, 25, 17:5 [twice]; 19:25; and Rev 2:13).

In every place, παρὰ with the dative carries a meaning of a literal "alongside of" or "in the presence of," that is, "with" in a most literal sense —thus, nowhere in John's literature does para with the dative denote "in one's mind—unless one sees John 17:5 as some kind of exception. In point of fact, all *standard* lexicons (regarding παρὰ + dat.),[52] recognized Greek grammars,[53] as well as

---

[50] John 12:41, εἶδεν τὴν δόξαν αὐτοῦ ("he [Isaiah] saw the glory of Him [Jesus]") - Isaiah 6:1, 3: εἶδον. . . . τῆς δόξης αὐτοῦ ("I saw. . . . the glory of Him [YHWH]").

[51] Cf. Wallace, *GGBB,* 378; *BDAG,* 757.

[52] Cf. Thayer, *Lexicon,* "II. [παρὰ] with the dative," as applied to John 17:5.

[53] Cf. Wallace, *GGBB.*

and the mass of biblical scholarship[54] firmly attest to the fact that John 17:5 exegetically presents an actual preexistence of the divine Son who shared glory *together with* (in the presence of) the Father, before time.

Regarding the particular grammar of John 17:5, Ignatius in his letter to the Magnesians (*c.* A.D. 107) uses the same prepositional phrase, as in John in 17:5 to affirm the preexistence of the divine Son: "Jesus Christ, who *before the ages* [πρὸ αἰώνων] was *with the Father* [παρὰ πατρὶ] and appeared at the end of time" (6). Specifically, Ignatius uses παρὰ with the dative, as in John 17:5, denoting a marked distinction between Jesus and the Father. And he employs the preposition πρὸ to indicate that their distinction existed from eternity—"before time." Thus, Ignatius, following the apostolic tradition, envisages the Son as preexisting παρὰ ("with/in the presence of") the Father, πρὸ αἰώνων—"before time."

The glory that the Son had/possessed (ῇ εἶχον)[55] was in his preexistence: We read that the glory that the Son possessed and shared *together with* (παρὰ) the Father was πρὸ τοῦ τὸν κόσμον εἶναι ("before the world was"). The preexistence (and deity) of the Son is a running theme in John's literature: The person of the Son was sent from heaven (cf. John 6:38; 3:13; *et al.*); existing before the beginning (ἀρχῇ, John 1:1a); was the Creator of all things (cf. John 1:3, as discussed below); the μονογενὴς θεὸς ὁ ὢν, that is, the unique God, the one who is/being always in the bosom of the Father (cf. John 1:18); the "Alpha and the Omega, the first and the last, the beginning and the end" (Rev 22:13). So that the Son possessed glory with the Father before the world was is consistent with John's theology. It was "not just ideal preexistence," says

---

[54] Cf. Reymond, *Systematic Theology,* 230.

[55] The imperfect εἶχον denotes that the Son possessed this glory; the glory that the preincarnate Son "Actually possessed" (Vincent, Marvin R., "Commentary on John 17:5" in *Word studies in the New Testament,* 6 vols. [Nabu Press, Charleston: 2010]).

Robertson, "but actual and conscious existence at the Father's side …'before the being as to the world.'"[56] Likewise, Reymond further comments on the Son's eternal preexistence as taught in John 17:5:

> The gospel of John witnesses that Jesus claimed eternal preexistence: "Glorify me, Father," Jesus prayed, "with yourself, with the glory which I had with you before the world was" (John 17:1, 5), indeed, with "my glory which you have given me because you loved me before the foundation of the world" (John 17:24). This claim in Jesus' part to an eternal preexistence with the Father is not an aberration, for he speaks elsewhere, though in somewhat different terms, of that same preexistence.[57]

The exegesis of John 17:5 reveals that the person of the Son shared glory with the Father, corresponding with 1:1b: πρὸς τὸν θεόν. This divine glory, says Christ, ᾗ εἶχον ("I had"), that is, always possessed it πρὸ τοῦ τὸν κόσμον εἶναι ("before the world was"), corresponding with Hebrews 1:3: ὃς ὢν ἀπαύγασμα τῆς δόξης καὶ χαρακτὴρ τῆς ὑποστάσεως αὐτοῦ. Hence, the Son *is* (ὢν –always, timelessly) the radiance or effulgence of the Father's *glory* and the "exact representation of the nature of him." Hence, vividly consistent with the Christology of the NT, John 17:5 underlines the Son's preexistence, deity, and distinction from the person of the Father.

Philippians 2:6-11—Carmen Christi

> Who [Christ], although He existed in the form of God, did not regard equality with God a thing to be grasped, but [He] emptied Himself, taking the form of a bond-servant, and being

---

[56] Robertson, *Word Pictures*, 5:275-76.

[57] Reymond, *Systematic Theology*, 230.

made in the likeness of men. Being found in appearance as a man, He humbled Himself by becoming obedient to the point of death, even death on a cross. For this reason also, God highly exalted Him, and bestowed on Him the name which is above every name, so that at the name of Jesus EVERY KNEE WILL BOW, of those who are in heaven and on earth and under the earth, and that every tongue will confess that Jesus Christ is Lord, to the glory of God the Father.

Philippians 2:6-11, known as the *Carmen Christi* ("Hymn to Christ") and also as the Kenosis Hymn (from κενόω, "to make empty") was utilized by the early Christian church to teach and magnify the preexistence, incarnation, and the full deity of the Son of God, Jesus Christ. The context of Philippians 2 is clear: Paul stresses to the Philippians that they ought to act in a harmonious and humble way. Paul then instructs them to have an attitude in themselves "which was also in Christ Jesus"—humility (v. 5). Which then leads Paul in verse 6 to present the ultimate act of humility: Christ, who was always subsisting as God, emptied himself taking the form/nature of a bond-servant and becoming obedient to the point of death.

In these seven short verses, Paul provides a beautiful delineation of the gospel of Jesus Christ. This Hymn to Christ *as God* systematically encapsulates Jesus' nature as subsisting as God (preexisting), his incarnation, his cross-work, his exaltation, and his distinction from God the Father whom he glorifies. Unquestionably, Paul positively affirmed the two natured person of the Son implicitly and explicitly in virtually every one of his epistles (e.g., Rom 1:3-4; 9:5; 1 Cor 2:8; 2 Cor 8:9; Gal 4:4; Eph 2:18ff; Phil 2:6-11; Col 2:9; 1 Tim 3:16; Titus 2:13).

ὃς ἐν μορφῇ θεοῦ ὑπάρχων. In verse 6, Paul utilizes very specific terms to bolster his case in which he plainly asserts that Jesus was *always subsisting* as God: "Who although he *existed* in the *form of God*." The active participle, ὑπάρχων denotes a *continuous existence* or state of continually subsisting.[58] Hence, Jesus, the Son of God (cf. 1:2; 2:9, v. 11), did not *become* the very form or nature of God at a certain point in time, rather he always existed as God, just as Paul definitely expressed. While μορφῇ ("form," NASB, "nature," NIV) denotes the specific qualities or essential attributes of something. Here, it denotes "the expression of divinity in the preexistent Christ."[59] It expresses that which is intrinsic and essential to the thing. Thus, here it means "that our Lord in his preincarnate state possessed essential deity."[60] "The noun μορφῇ implies not the external accidents, but the essential attributes."[61] Warfield clearly expresses its semantic force:

"Form" is a term, which expresses the sum of those characterizing qualities which make a thing the precise thing that it is... When Our Lord is said to be in "the form of God," therefore, He is declared, in the most expressed manner possible, to be all that God is, to possess the whole fullness of attributes which make God God.[62]

To deny that the Son was truly the μορφῇ of God is to deny that the Son was truly the μορφῇ of man "taking the form of a bond-servant."

οὐχ ἁρπαγμὸν ἡγήσατο τὸ εἶναι ἴσα θεῷ. We then read that the person of the Son did not ἡγήσατο ("consider, regard") "equality with God a thing to be grasped." Although the noun

---

[58] Cf. Thayer, 638; *BDAG*, 1029.

[59] *BDAG*, 659.

[60] Ryrie, Charles C., *Basic Theology: A Popular Systematic Guide to Understanding Biblical Truth*, (Wheaton: Victor Books 1986), 261.

[61] Lightfoot, J. B., *St. Paul's Epistle to the Philippians* (London: Macmillan, 1894), 108.

[62] Warfield, *Biblical Doctrine,* 177.

ἁρπαγμὸν ("a thing to be grasped") has been a point of continuous discussion among biblical scholarship, the term must be interpreted in light of the participial phrase μορφῇ θεοῦ ὑπάρχων, which safeguards against any denial of the Son's personhood and deity.

ἀλλ᾽ ἑαυτὸν ἐκένωσεν μορφὴν δούλου λαβών. In v. 7, we read that the person of the Son, who was always subsisting in the nature of God, voluntarily ἑαυτὸν ἐκένωσεν ("made himself nothing") μορφὴν δούλου λαβών (lit., form/nature of a slave having taken").

Note the reflexive pronoun ἑαυτὸν ("himself"). The force of the reflexive pronoun here indicates that the subject (the Son) is also the object (i.e., the one receiving the action of the verb— "emptied"). Hence, it was the Son who emptied himself. We see the reflexive pronoun in verse 8, ἐταπείνωσεν ἑαυτὸν (lit., "He humbled himself") denoting the Son's self-humiliation in his glorious self-emptying incarnational work and obedience to death on the cross. The aorist active participle λαβών (semantically, a *participle of means*)[63] describes the means or manner of the Son's emptying. Thus, the Son emptied himself *by means of* "taking the form of a bond-servant, and being made in the likeness of men." The Son's incarnational work was not an emptying or subtraction of deity, again, verse 6 shields against such a notion. Rather, it involved an addition to his divine nature—God the Word became flesh.

The divine Son preexisted before performing the action of the participles describing his incarnation. In verse 6, the Son, in his prior existence as God, performed the action of ἡγήσατο *before* performing the actions of the three following aorist participles in verses 7 and 8 (λαβών, γενόμενος, εὑρεθείς) describing his self-emptying. In other words, syntactically, the participial phrase, μορφῇ θεοῦ ὑπάρχων and the verb ἡγήσατο are antecedent to the participles in vv. 7 and 8 denoting his self-emptying incarnational

---

[63] Cf. Wallace, *GGBB,* 630.

work: "having taken," "having been made," having been found"—namely, verse 6 indicates his preexistence as the person of God the Son in his preincarnate state (see notes on John 6:38 above). Verse 6, points to the preexistent Son as *asarkos*, in μορφῇ θεοῦ, and in contrast, verses 7-8 points to the Son as *ensarkos*, μορφὴν δούλου.[64]

In verses 10-11, Paul concludes his high Christological Hymn with the affirmation that Christ the Son was the fulfillment of the "future" prophecy in Isaiah 45:23. Starting in verse 9, Paul states the *purpose* of God highly exalting the Son and bestowing on him "the name which is above every name," which was for the *result* that (note the ἵνα clause in v. 10) "at the name of Jesus every knee will bow . . . and that every tongue will confess that Jesus Christ is Lord to the glory of God the Father" (vv. 10-11). In Greek, κύριος in the *emphatic position* (κύριος Ἰησοῦς χριστός), intensifying his argument that Jesus is the κύριος, that is, the YHWH and fulfillment of the future prophecy of Isaiah 45:23.[65]

---

[64] 2 Corinthians 8:9 contains the same contextual-linguistic regarding the Son's incarnational work. Note that both passages contain present tense participles denoting the Son's prior existence as God: πλούσιος ὤν ("rich being") - μορφῇ θεοῦ ὑπάρχων ("in the nature of God being") and both contain aorist indicatives denoting the Son's self-emptying: ἐπτώχευσεν ("became poor") - ἑαυτὸν ἐκένωσεν ("He emptied himself").

[65] Paul cites Isaiah 45:23 in both Romans 14:11 and loosely here in Philippians 2:10-11. both Isaiah 45:23 (LXX) and Romans 14:11 contain future indicatives: "every knee *will bow* [κάμψει] . . . every tongue *will confess* [ἐξομολογήσεται]" indicating the future certainty of the event. However, Paul modifies the original tenses and moods of the verbs in Isaiah and Romans (to aorist subjunctives) to make Philippians 2:10-11 a *purpose and result* clause (cf. Wallace, *BBGG,* 474). The *purpose* of God the Father exalting the Son and bestowing on Him "the name which is above every name" was for the *result* of every knee bowing and every tongue confessing that "Jesus Christ is Lord," thus, the YHWH of Isaiah

Jesus Christ the Son, the Unchangeable Creator of all Things

The Scriptural evidence for the full deity and humanity of Jesus Christ, the Son of God, is overwhelming. Both the OT and NT present the Son as the very object of divine worship (cf. Dan 7:14; Matt 14:33; John 9:38; Heb 1:6; Rev 5:13-14). In addition, the NT presents that the Son was the agent[66] of creation, thus, the unchangeable Creator of all things. That Jesus was the Creator of all things is additional and irrefutable proof that he preexisted as God. For if the Son were the actual Creator, that would mean that he 1) existed before time, thus, was not a part of creation, 2) coexisted *with* the Father, and hence, 3) is a distinct person *alongside* the Father, as co-Creator.

We will examine John 1:3; Colossians 1:16-17; and Hebrews 1:2, 10, which contain a weighty amount of exegetical substance affirming the Son as the actual Creator.

45:23—*hence the fulfillment of Isaiah's (future) prophecy.*

[66] In the NT, *agency* is commonly expressed in three ways: *ultimate* agency (the ultimate source of the action; the one directly responsible for the action— ἀπὸ παρά, ὑπὸ + the genitive); *intermediate* agency (that which the ultimate agent uses to *carry out* the action— διά + the genitive); and *impersonal* agency (that which the *ultimate* agent uses *to perform* the action— ἐκ, ἐν + the dative; cf. Wallace, *GGBB*, 431-32). Biblically, then, the Father was the *source* (*ultimate* agent) of creation, the Son being the *intermediate* agent in that he *carried out* the act for the ultimate agent (cf. ibid., 431). That the Son is the *intermediate* agent of creation does not mean that he was a mere "helper" of sorts, or a secondary agent of God, but rather, he was the actual agent of creation— namely, that which the *ultimate* agent (the Father) used to *carry out* the action—namely, the Creator of all things. This grammatically point is specifically revealed in several NT passages (viz. John 1:3, δι' αὐτοῦ; 1 Cor 8:6 [δι' οὗ]; Col 1:16 [δι' αὐτοῦ]; Heb 1:2 [δι' οὗ]; 2:10 [δι' οὗ]).

John 1:3

All things came into being through him, and apart from him nothing came into being that has come into being.

That the Son was the actual Creator is entirely consistent with the Christ that John preached. As shown, in 1:1, John presents the Word as the eternal God distinct from the Father. In verse 18, the apostle refers to the Son as the μονογενὴς θεὸς ("unique God") who *is always existing* (ὁ ὢν) in the bosom of the Father. As previously discussed, in the prologue, the apostle presents a well-defined contrast between *all things created or that had origin* (signified by the aorist ἐγένετο; cf. vv. 3, 6, 10, 14) and the *eternal* divine Word (signified by the imperfect ἦν; vv. 1, 2, 4, 9).

In verse 3, the apostle further declares of the divine Word that πάντα δι᾽ αὐτοῦ ἐγένετο (lit., "All things through Him came to be"). We see the creative activity viewed as "one event in contrast to the continuous existence of ἦν in verses Jo [hn] 1, 2. . . . Creation is thus presented as becoming (γίνομαι) in contrast with being (εἰμι)."[67] What fortifies the argument even more is John's usage of the preposition διά followed by the genitive αὐτοῦ. This is a very significant aspect as it relates to the exegesis of the passage. In Greek, διά followed by the genitive indicates *agency* (or *means*).[68] The preexistent Son was not a mere helper of sorts, or mighty helper, rather he was God the Creator of all things as the apostle so clearly states. In such a comprehensible and undeniable way, the Apostle John presents the Son, the eternal Word, as the Creator of all things.[69]

---

[67] Cf. Robertson, *Word Pictures*, 1932: 5:5).

[68] Cf. Greenlee, *Exegetical Grammar*, 31; Wallace, *GGBB*, 368; *BDAG*, 225)

[69] Another interesting note pertaining to our contention that the Targum may have been the source of John's Logos theology. Both the

Colossians 1:16-17

> For by Him all things were created, both in the heavens and on earth, visible and invisible, whether thrones or dominions or rulers or authorities—all things have been created through Him and for Him. He is before all things and in Him all things hold together.

To interpret properly these (and any) passages in Colossians, a coherent understanding of Paul's main purpose for writing the book must be first apprehended. Mainly, this letter was written to serve as meaningful refutation to the proto-Gnostic spirit *versus* matter ideology. The Gnostic system did not allow Jesus to be the Creator of something as inherently evil as "matter." In light of this, Paul provides a clear anti-Gnostic polemic by firmly demonstrating that Jesus the Son of God did *in fact* create all things.

Note the clear and forceful (and even redundant) way he literally presents this:

> That *in/by him* [ἐν αὐτῷ] *the all things* [τὰ πάντα] were create...*the all things* [τὰ πάντα] have been created *through him* [δι᾽ αὐτοῦ] and *for Him* [εἰς αὐτὸν].[17] *He is before all things* [αὐτός ἐστιν πρὸ πάντων], and *the all things in him* [τὰ

Targum and John present the "Word" as the Creator of all things. For example, note the Targumic rendering of Isaiah 44:24: "I am the LORD, who made all things; I stretched out the heavens by My Memra." And Isaiah 45:12: "I by My Memra made the earth, and created man upon it; I by My might stretched out the heavens." In fact, there are many other places where the Targum identifies the "Word" (Memra) as the Creator of all things, as John explicates in 1:3 (cf. also Gen 14:19 [*Neofiti*]; Ps. 33:6; Isa 48:13; Jer 27:5; etc.).

πάντα ἐν αὐτῷ] hold together.[70]

Along with John 1:3, Paul employs the *neuter* adjective πάντα, which indicate that the Son was the actual Creator of all-encompassing things (cf. Eph. 1:11). To reinforce his refutation, Paul definitizes the adjective, τὰ πάντα—Jesus is the Creator of "the all things." Paul utilizes four different prepositions to magnify his affirmation that the Son was the Agent of creation: All things were created "by/in him" (ἐν + dative; vv. 16, 17); "through him" (διά + genitive; v. 16); "for him" (εἰς + accusative; v. 16); and, he is "before all things" (πρὸ + genitive; v. 17). Cleary, Paul is speaking here of the Son, not the Father (cf. v. 14).

As a final point, as with John 1:3, Paul specifically states that "the all things" were created δι' αὐτοῦ ("through him"). As observed above, we find the preposition διά followed by the genitive grammatically revealing that the Son was the actual Creator himself. There is no stronger way in which Paul could have articulated that the Son was the real and actual agent of creation.[71] If Paul wanted to convey the idea that the Son was

---

[70] It is worth mentioning how Oneness Pentecostals erroneously treat these and other passages that speak of the Son as the Creator. They argue that it was unitarian God, the Father alone (Jesus' divine mode), who created all things. However, it was the mere "plan" of the future "Son" (i.e., Jesus' human mode) that the Father had in mind. UPCI authority and Oneness author David Bernard explains: "Although the Son did not exist at the time of creation except as the word in the mind of God, God used his foreknowledge of the Son when he created the world." Bernard, David K., Series in *Pentecostal Theology Vol. 1: The Oneness of God,* (Hazelwood: Pentecostal Pub. House, 1986), 116, cf. 117. Thus, their exegesis of the Scripture always starts with their assumption of unitarianism.

[71] In 1 Corinthians 8:6 and, as discussed below, in Hebrews 1:2, διά is followed by the genitive signifying the Son as the agent of creation (cf. Heb 2:10).

merely "in view" of the Father or an absent mere conceptual *instrument* of creation (as Oneness advocates assert[72]), he would not have used διά with genitive.[73]

Hebrews 1:2, 10

In these last days [God the Father] has spoken to us in His Son, whom He appointed heir of all things, through whom also He made the world...And, "You Lord, in the beginning laid the foundation of the earth, and the heavens are the works of Your hands..."

---

[72] Oneness teachers along with other unitarian groups (esp. Jehovah's Witnesses and Muslims) argue that the Son could not have been the Creator because passages such as Isaiah 44:24 and 1 Corinthians 8:6 teach that God (viz. the Father) *alone* created all things. But as consistently pointed out, Oneness teachers assume unitarianism/unipersonalism in that they envisage God as one person— the Father. The doctrine of the Trinity, in contrast to a unitarian assumption, teaches that God is one undivided and unquantifiable being who has revealed himself as three distinct coequal, coeternal, and coexistent persons. The three persons *share* the *nature* of the one being. As fully God it can be said that the Father is the Creator (cf. Acts 17:24), the Son was the Creator (cf. John 1:3; Col 16-17; Heb 1:2, 10), and the Holy Spirit is the Creator (cf. Job 33:4). For the one God is indivisible and inseparable (cf. Deut 6:4; Isa 45:5). Therefore, passages like Isaiah 44:24, which speak of God creating *by himself* and alone are perfectly consistent with Trinitarian theology. Again, the three persons are not three *separate* beings; they are distinct self-conscious persons or selves sharing the nature of the one being. Unless one clearly realizes what the biblical doctrine of the Trinity actually teaches, the doctrine will be confounded and misrepresented ether as tritheism or Modalism.

[73] Although Paul does use the accusative case in verse 16 (αὐτὸν), but he uses it after the preposition εἰς meaning "for" or "because of" and not after διά.

The prologue of Hebrews systematically affirms the preexistence and deity of the person of the Son, Jesus Christ whom the Father commands "all the angels" to worship (v. 6). Relative to the preexistence and creatorship of the Son, verses 2 and 10 communicate both truths in an exceptional way. As with John 1:3 and Colossians 1:16-17, the prepositional phrase, δι᾽ οὗ ("through whom") affirms the apostolic teaching that the Son was the agent of creation. Here we have again, the preposition διά followed by the genitive case: "In these last days has spoken to us in his Son, whom he appointed heir of all things, *through whom* [δι᾽ οὗ] also he made the world" (emphasis added).[74]

Contextually, as we saw in the prologue of John (ἐγένετο vs. ἦν), the core line of evidence that the author presents of the eternality of the Son is a precisely crafted and defined contrast between creation (viz., angels and the heavens and the earth) and the eternal divine Son (cf. vv. 2-3, 8-10).

Since verse 5, the author has been exclusively quoting the Father. In verses 10-12, in reference to the divine Son (πρὸς δὲ τὸν υἱόν, ὁ θρόνος σου ὁ θεός, v. 8), God the Father applies Psalm 102:25-27[75] to the Son. Notice first, the Psalm is a reference to YHWH as the unchangeable Creator of all things. Second, the Father is speaking *to the Son* and not merely *about* the Son.[76] Specifically, the referential identity of the pronoun σὺ at the beginning of verse 10 ("And, You") we find back in verse 8, πρὸς δὲ τὸν υἱόν–"But of the Son he [the Father] says." Irrefutably, *it is God the Father directly addressing the Son*. In verse 8, θεὸς appears in the *nominative* for the *vocative of address* (ὁ θρόνος

---

[74] As seen above (esp. n. 65), διά with the genitive denoting the Son as the agent of creation appears in John 1:3; 1 Corinthians 8:6; Colossians 1:16; Hebrews 1:2; and 2:10.

[75] From the LXX of Psalm 101:25-27.

[76] Here the Father clearly differentiates Himself from the Son (esp. in light of vv. 8-9).

σου ὁ θεός).[77]

However, in verse 10, the actual vocative of κύριος (κύριε) is used, which bolsters the author's argument even more: "You, Lord [κύριε], in the beginning laid the foundation of the earth, and the heavens are the works of Your hands." This so unequivocally and irrefutably verifies that the person of the Son preexisted as "the God" and as the YHWH of Psalm 102, the unchangeable Creator of all things.

Conclusively, the prologue of Hebrews is one of the most theologically devastating prologues in all of the NT for Oneness defenders. Not only does the prologue affirm the deity and eternality of the Son as well as the distinction between the Father and the Son, but also it clearly presents the Son as the actual agent of creation, the Creator himself.

Conclusion

To deny the deity and preexistence of the person of the Son is to deny the Son of God of biblical revelation. "Whoever denies the Son," says the apostle, "does not have the Father; the one who confesses the Son has the Father also" (1 John 2:23; cf. John 5:23; 8:24; 1 John 5:20). Scripture is crystal clear:

1. The OT presents the preincarnate person of the Son who is identified as YHWH and the Angel of the Lord (cf. Gen 16:10-11; 19:24; Exod 3:6, v. 14; Judg 6:11-24; 13:16, 21;

---

[77] The fact that the nominative θεὸς with the vocative force is used does not remove in any way the meaning of *direct address*. The usual way of addressing God in both the LXX and the NT was the nominative for the vocative (cf. Reymond, *Systematic Theology*, 272; Wallace, *GGBB,* 1996: 56-57; also cf. John 20:28; Rev 4:11). So common was the nominative for the vocative that every time θεὸς was directly addressed in the NT, only in one verse (Matt 27:46) does θεὸς actually appear in the vocative case: θεέ μου θεέ μου— "My God, My God."

Isa 6:3, vv. 8, 10 [cf. John 12:39-41]; Dan 7:9-14 *et al.*).

2. John 1:1 (and 1 John 1:1-2): The Logos was existing *prior to the beginning*. He was a distinct person, who was πρὸς τὸν θεόν, and he was θεὸς as to his nature who became flesh.

3. John 1:18: The Son is the μονογενὴς θεὸς and ὁ ὢν (always existing) in the bosom of the Father.

4. John 6:38: The person of Christ exercised his own will distinct from the Father's will, in his preincarnate existence, that is, before coming to earth.

5. John 8:24 *et al*: Christ the Son claimed he preexisted as the eternal God— ἐγώ εἰμι.

6. John 17:5: The person of the Son shared/possessed divine glory παρὰ (together with) the Father, πρὸ τοῦ τὸν κόσμον εἶναι—*before the world came to be.*

7. Philippians 2:6-11, the ultimate act of humility: Jesus Christ, the Son of God, who was always being in the nature of God, emptied himself *by* having taken the very nature of man and became obedient to death on a cross; he was the fulfillment of the Isaiah 45:23 prophecy, the YHWH before whom every knee shall bow and every tongue shall confess—"to the glory of God the Father."

8. John 1:3; Colossians 1:16-17; and Hebrews 1:2: God the Son was the agent of creation—the Creator of all things.

9. Hebrews 1:10-12: God the Father directly addressed the Son as the YHWH of Psalm 102:25-27, the unchangeable

Creator of all things.

THE UNITY OF GOD IN CHRISTIANITY & ISLAM

Rudolph P. Boshoff[1]

Introduction

It was theologian A.W. Tozer, who, in his book *The Knowledge of the Holy*, stated,

> What comes into our minds when we think about God is the most important thing about us. The history of mankind will probably show that no people has ever risen above its

---

[1] Rudolph is also currently the director of Ad Lucem Ministries (Towards the light), a ministry that investigates theological trends and apologetic questions in an African and global context. Rudolph has completed his Bachelor's degree in Theology at the South African Theological Seminary as well as his Bachelor's degree in Theology Honors at the same institution. Rudolph is also actively pursuing his Masters in Theology with a specific emphasis on Islam under the supervision of Dr. Richard Schumack (Melbourne School of Theology) and Dr. Kevin Smith (South African Theological Seminary). Rudolph is also happily married to Candice, who is actively involved behind the scenes of this ministry and have been married for 10 years. They are currently parents to two Rottweiler's, Cody & Dub.

religion, a man's spiritual history will positively demonstrate that no religion has ever been greater than its idea of God. Worship is pure or base as the worshiper entertains high or low thoughts of God. For this reason, the gravest question before the Church is always God Himself, and the most portentous fact about any man is not what he at a given time may say or do, but what he in his deep heart conceives God to be like.[2]

The Scope of this chapter is not to define the broad contours of some pseudo-intellectual perspectives of the Christian understanding of God, but rather to account for a common understanding between the Christian trinitarian and Islamic monotheistic worldviews. I have used the terms Allah [Arabic – *'Allāh'*] to describe and highlight the Muslim conception of God as described in the Qur'an, and YHWH/God [*Yahweh* or יהוה] to point to the understanding of the Judeo-Christian tradition.

A Christian understanding of God:

Biblically we would define the Christian understanding of God as both three (*tri*) and one (*une*). The three biblical doctrines that flow directly into the river that is the Trinity are as follows:

1) There is one and only one God, eternal, and immutable (Deut 4:32-35; cf. v. 39, 6:4-5, 32:39; Isa 44:6-8, cf. 45:21).

2) There are three eternal persons described in Scripture; the Father, the Son, and the Spirit. These persons are never identified with one another; that is, they are carefully differentiated as 'persons' (Isa 48:16; 63:9-10, John 14:16-18, 26; Acts 10:38).

---

[2] Tozer, A. W., *The Knowledge of the Holy*, (New York: HarperOne, 2009), 1.

3) The Father, the Son, and the Spirit, are identified as being fully deity—that is, the Bible teaches the deity of Christ (John 1:1, 18; 20:28, Rom 9:5, Titus 2:13, Heb 1:8) and the deity of the Holy Spirit (Acts 5:3-4, 2 Cor 3:17-18) as well as the deity of the Father (John 17:3, 1 Cor 8:6). White mentions that it is important to emphasize the fact that, "We are not saying that the Father is the Son, or the Son the Spirit, or the Spirit the Father."[3]

It is very common for people to misunderstand the doctrine to mean that we are saying Jesus is the Father or the Father is in fact the Spirit. The doctrine of the Trinity does not in any way say this! When we recognize the reality of their distinct roles in Scripture we realize that there is an order and economy between the persons of the Trinity (Matt 28:19; John 15:26; Eph 1:3-14) and a functional subordination between them. Bosserman writes:

First, in addition to creating the universe (Mark 13:19), and predestining believers unto salvation (1 Pet 1:2), the Father is responsible for directing the Son and the Spirit in their creative and redemptive work (Luke 11:13; John 3:16). Second, the Son is the mediator between God and creation (John 17:23; 1 Tim 2:5) and especially between the Father and believers, as the vessel through whom the Holy Spirit is poured out (John 15:26; Luke 3:16). Third, the Spirit glorifies and completes the work of the Father and the Son by directing the creation back unto God in praise and worship (John 14:26; Gal 4:6). In fact, the Spirit is the archetypal glory of God (1 Pet 4:14; Gen 1:2 with Exod 24:16-17) and the chief object of the Father and the Son's

---

[3] White, James R., *The Forgotten Trinity: Recovering the Heart of Christian Belief*, (Grand Rapids: Bethany House, 1998), 30.

affection (Isa 43:7, Matt 12:31-32).[4]

Biblically we can identify that each member of the Triune God has distinct roles but also different functions. It is also important to note that a difference in function or economy between the three persons does not denote inferiority in essential nature. We see that each person of the Triune God equally exhausts the one divine nature but assigns to themselves definite tasks. For example, the Father is the ultimate source or cause of the universe (1 Cor 8:6; Rev 4:11), of divine revelation (Rev 1:1), of salvation (John 3:16-17), and of Jesus' human works (John 5:17; 14:10). The Son is the agent through whom the Father does the following works: The creation and maintenance of the universe (1 Cor 8:6; Joh 1:3; Col 1:16-17); divine revelation (John 1:1, 16:12-15; Matt 11:27; Rev 1:1); and salvation (2 Cor 5:19; Matt 1:21; John 4:42). The Holy Spirit is the means by whom the Father does the following works: creation and maintenance of the universe (Gen 1:2; Job 26:13; Ps 104:30); divine revelation (John 16:12-15; Eph 3:5; 2 Pet 1:21); salvation (John 3:6; Tit 3:5; 1 Pet 1:2); and Jesus' works (Isa 61:1; Acts10:38). Thus, the Father does all these. The Christian finds his very core self in a trinitarian atmosphere. Tim Chester writes;

> Everywhere we look, we find this trinitarian structure to Christian truth and Christian living... Trinity is the Christian name of God...To fully understand [Christianity] you must learn its language, and its language is the Trinity. The Trinity is the language in which Christian truth is spoken. It gives shape to truth. The Trinity is not peripheral, let alone optional. It is the marvelous,

---

[4] Bosserman, Brant A., *The Trinity and the Vindication of Christian Paradox: An Interpretation and Refinement of the Theological Apologetic of Cornelius Van Til*, (Eugene: Pickwick Pub., 2014), 182-183.

wonderful heart of our faith.[5]

The biblical Christian is a Triune Christian because the work, person, and sufficiency of God find its fullest expression in the revelation of this central Christian truth. The most common objection biblical trinitarians have to contend with is that the very idea of God being three-in-one violates the sole assumptions of absolute monotheism. Biblical trinitarians should follow with the following resolve:

If we say:

A) God is one and

B) God is not one;

It would clearly be a logical contradiction.

Also; if we said:

1). God is three persons but also say

2). God is not three persons that would also be a contradiction.

However, biblical trinitarians do not affirm 'A' and 'B' nor 1 and 2. We affirm both 'A' and 1 and therefore, there is no logical contradiction. A logical contradiction is to affirm both 1 and 2 or 'A' and 'B' but not 1 and 'A'. It should also be noted that biblical trinitarians shouldn't overemphasize the "threeness" within the Trinity because it will seemingly become "Tritheistic" and neither ought we overemphasize the oneness of God it tends to become "Modalistic". It is important to understand that historically biblical

---

[5] Chester, Tim, *Delighting in the Trinity: Just Why are Father, Son, and Spirit Such Good News?*, (Epsom: Good Book Company, 2005), 14-15.

trinitarians affirm the Athanasian Creed that stipulates in line 4, "That we worship one God in Trinity, and the Trinity in unity. Neither confounding the Persons, nor dividing the Substance."[6]

As the fourth century Archbishop of Constantinople Gregory of Nazianzus (329-390 A.D) noted,

> No sooner do I conceive of the One than I am illumined by the Splendor of the Three; no sooner do I distinguish Them than I am carried back to the One. When I think of any One of the Three, I think of Him as the Whole, and my eyes are filled, and the greater part of what I am thinking of escapes me. I cannot grasp the greatness of That One so as to attribute a greater greatness to the Rest. When I contemplate the Three together, I see but one torch, and cannot divide or measure out the Undivided Light.[7]

For biblical trinitarians, the economies of the three persons in the one being of God clearly denotes a God sufficient in himself,

---

[6] Kelly, J. N. D., *The Athanasian Creed: Quicunque Vult*, (London: Adam & Charles Black, 1964), 17.

[7] Orations 40.41 in Schaff, Philipp, Wace, Henry Eds., *Nicene & Post-Nicene Fathers*, 2nd Series, Vol. 7, (Peabody: Hendrickson, 1994), 375. Nazianzus continued:

> This I give you to share, and to defend all your life, the One Godhead and Power, found in the Three in Unity, and comprising the Three separately, not unequal, in substances or natures, neither increased nor diminished by superiorities or inferiorities; in every respect equal, in every respect the same; just as the beauty and the greatness of the heavens is one; the infinite conjunction of Three Infinite Ones, Each God when considered in Himself; as the Father so the Son, as the Son so the Holy Ghost; the Three One God when contemplated together; Each God because Consubstantial; One God because of the Monarchia.

being ultimately free to express his likeness and relations through the sovereignty of his own self-revelation. Bosserman writes,

> The Triune God is a harmony between unity and diversity, but unlike the ideal absolute, he is (a) strictly eternal, and (b) exhaustively personal. The first point indicates that the Trinity is not in any measure dependent on an opposing, ever incomplete temporal sphere that would compromise the finality of his knowledge and being. The second point indicates that the Triune God is not married to any sort of unconscious being that would resist, and fail to fully express his own eternal self-awareness and self-direction. With these observations in mind, God is justly regarded as at once uni-personal (Exod 20:3; Isa 35:10, 44:24), and tri-personal (Matt 28:19; 2 Cor 13:14).[8]

The Christian conception of the biblical revelation of God is that he is essentially a Triune community of love, and because he is essentially love, we are assured of the consistency of his actions towards us and therefore we can know God through the self-revelation of his Son Jesus Christ by the revelation of the Holy Spirit.[9]

---

[8] Bosserman, *The Trinity and the Vindication of Divine Paradox*, 87.

[9] Bosserman writes,

> Ontologically, the "one" God cannot recede into oblivion as an abstract and indistinct universal, for he is concretely and infinitely defined in relationship to the "three" persons. Nor can the "three" degrade into irrational "particulars" that evade definition at some point, for they are exhaustively defined by the one Trinitarian dynamic. Nothing, then, would fall outside of God's personal comprehension, including the relationship between His trifold being and his comprehensive self-

The Muslim understanding of Allah

Islamic scholar Abdul Saleeb mentions that the whole system of Muslim theology, philosophy, and religious life is summed up in these seven words:

La ilaha illa Allah, Muhammad rasul Allah.

In English it reads:

There is no god but Allah, and Muhammad is Allah's prophet (apostle / messenger).[10]

This is the *Shahada,* and to recite it with sincerity of belief is all that one must do to become a Muslim. Belief in Allah as the one true God is the first of the five *imam* or articles of faith for a Muslim.

Surah Al-Ikhlas (112.1) describes the very heart of Islam when it says,

"*Qul huwa Allahu ahad 'Allahu assamad Lam yalid walam yoolad Walam yakun lahu kufuwan ahad.'*"

"Say, 'He is God, the One. God, the Absolute. He begets not, nor was he begotten. And there is nothing comparable to him.'"

Ayatullah Murtaza Mutahhari states, The Islamic world view is the

---

knowledge. God would be a self-contained, self-defined, and self-sufficient person.

Ibid., 87.

[10] Geisler, Norman, Saleeb, Abdul, *Answering Islam: The Crescent in Light of the Cross,* Updated & Rev. Ed., (Grand Rapids: Baker, 2002), 13.

world view of *tawhid*.[11] There are three categories of *Tawheed*:

1. *Tawheed ar-Ruboobeeyah* (Maintaining the Unity of Lordship).
2. *Tawheed al-Asmaa was Sifaat* (Maintaining the Unity of Allah's names and attributes).
3. *Tawheed al-'Ebaadah* (Maintaining the Unity of Allah's Worship).[12]

Dr. Abu Ameenah Bilal Philips mentions the importance of *Tawhid* when he explains that:

> Literally *Tawheed* means "unification" (making something one) or "asserting oneness," and it comes from the Arabic verb (*wahhada*) which itself means to unite, unify or consolidate. However, when the term *Tawheed* is used in reference to Allaah (i.e. *Tawheedullaah*), it means the realizing and maintaining of Allaah's unity in all of man's actions which directly or indirectly relate to Him. It is the belief that Allaah is One, without partner in His dominion and His actions (*Ruboobeeyah*), One without similitude in His essence and attributes (*Asmaa wa Sifaat*), and One without rival in His divinity and in worship (*Ulooheeyah/'Ebaadah*). These three aspects form the basis for the categories into which the science of *Tawheed* has been traditionally divided. The three overlap and are inseparable to such a degree that whoever omits any one aspect has failed to complete the requirements of *Tawheed*. The omission of any of the above-mentioned aspects of Tawheed is referred to as "*Shirk*" (lit. sharing); the

---

[11] Mutahhari, Ayatyllah Murtaza, Trans. by Campbell, R., *Fundamentals of Islamic Thought*, (Berkley: Mizan Press, 1985), 75.

[12] Philips, Bilall, *The Fundamentals of Tawheed*, (Riyadh: International Islamic Publications House, 2005), 18.

association of partners with Allaah, which, in Islamic terms, is in fact idolatry.

It is important to note that in the Islamic conception of Allah, he is absolutely one and unequivocally unique. On the Islamic view, Allah's uniqueness makes him the only one worthy of Worship with which nothing should be associated. The absolute unity and oneness of Allah is so critical to Muslim belief that the only unpardonable sin, called *Shirk*, is to associate any other god or partners with Allah. This message is summarized in the word *tawhid*. *Tawhid* is essential when espousing Muslim theology (*kalam*) which always concerns itself with maintaining the oneness of Allah especially relating to his attributes. Historically there are two perspectives prevalent when looking at the Islamic understanding of *Tawhid*. The first adherent vastly influenced by Greek rationalism was the *Mu'tazilites* or the people of justice (*adl*) and divine unity (*tawhid*) who championed the primacy of reason as well as the necessity of man's free will.[13]

> They argued on behalf of God's absolute unity and transcendence, and they denied the reality of any human attributes ascribed to him by the Quran (such as his hearing, seeing, knowing, etc.). To recognize these attributes as anything other than metaphors, they thought, would compromise God's essential unity.[14]

The second perspective that is now the dominant position in Sunni theology since the 12th century is the *Ash'arite* position. This school, known as the scriptural literalists, argued that Allah's

---

[13] O'Reilly, Robert, *The Closing of the Muslim Mind: How Intellectual Suicide Created the Modern Islamist Crisis*, (Wilmington: Intercollegiate Studies Institute, 2010), 21.

[14] Campo, Juan E., *Encyclopaedia of Islam*, (New York: Facts on File Pub., 2009), 664-665.

attributes are essential, even if we cannot explain how these attributes can be apparent to elucidate the 'personality' of Allah. This is expressed through the *Hanbalite-Ash'arite* formula, *'bila kayfa wala tashbih'* (without inquiring how without making comparison) and mentions that the Quran was Allah's speech 'eternally and uncreated like he, yet, not essentially he'.[15] Here, we will contend with this dominant Muslim perspective on the attributes of Allah. In my evaluation of both the Christian and Muslim understanding of Allah, I will show that our ideas about God bring a clear distinction between how both communities function in their devotion towards their God and what difference these doctrines make.

I will consider three points in this outline:

1. God as an absolute Unity and Compound Unity.
2. Love of Yahweh and the love of Allah.
3. The knowability of Yahweh and the knowability of Allah.

1. Absolute Unity and Compound Unity?

Christian conception of God's Unity:

As we have seen in the earlier introduction, the Bible clearly speaks of the unity of God. Moses wrote "Hear, O Israel! The Lord is our God, the Lord is one!" *Sh'ma Yisra'eil Adonai Eloheinu Adonai echad*, Deut 6:4). DeHaan mentions that this declaration was a clear affirmation of the One God of Israel and their distinctiveness as God's holy people that would be free from any polytheistic errors.[16] In this confession, the indivisibility of God is not compromised, as the *Shema* is an affirmation of sole allegiance to the one existing God. There has been a great emphasis on this

---

[15] O'Reilly, *The Closing of the Muslim Mind*, 54.

[16] DeHaan, Richard W., *The Living God*, (Grand Rapids: Zondervan, 1967), 80-82.

confession to identify the numeric value of Israel's one god but I will show that the intention of this declaration was not to account for the absolute numerical value of YHWH. Wright mentions that;

> From the Maccabean revolt to Bar-Kochba – there is no suggestion that 'monotheism', or praying the *Shema*, had anything to do with numerical analysis of the inner being of Israel's god himself. It had everything to do with the two-pronged fight against paganism and dualism. Indeed, we find strong evidence during this period of Jewish groups and individuals who, speculating on the meaning of some difficult passages in scripture (Daniel 7, for example, or Genesis 1), suggests that the divine being might encompass a plurality.[17]

Orthodox Christians maintain that God is a composite being made up of three distinct persons. As a unity, this God should not be divided because He is indivisible and one in number. The Christian God is not made up of multiple substances and is not conceived to be separate beings within one divine essence. When we approach Muslims in our witness to them we need to show that the God of the Old Testament is a compound unity, and not an absolute unity as demanded in the Quran. In earlier Judaism the understanding of the word '*echad*' (one) does not note or explain an absolute unity or even a 'monadic' one as some would have us believe. Brown mentions,

> Actually, *'echad* simply means 'one,' exactly like our English word 'one.' While it can refer to compound unity (just as our English word can, as in one team, one couple, etc.), it does not specifically refer to compound unity. On the other hand, *'echad* certainly does not refer to the

---

[17] Wright, N. T., *The New Testament and the People of God*, (Minneapolis: Fortress Press, 1992), 259.

concept of absolute unity, an idea expressed most clearly in the twelfth century by Moses Maimonides, who asserted that the Jewish people must believe that God is *yachid*, an 'only' one. There is no doubt that this reaction was due to exaggerated, unbiblical, 'Christian' beliefs that gave Jews the impression Christians worshiped three gods. Unfortunately, the view of Maimonides is reactionary and also goes beyond what is stated in the Scriptures. In fact, there is not a single verse anywhere in the Bible that clearly or directly states that God is an absolute unity.[18]

Spangler & Tverberg noted that the priority emphasized in the Old Testament Scriptures has always been to "obey" the Lord our God. The *Shema* was prayed every day to declare the individual obedience of the adherent to the One God of Israel.

> In the Bible, the Word *Shema* is widely used to describe hearing and also its outcomes: understanding, taking heed, being obedient, doing what is asked... Every place we see the word "obey" in English in the Bible, it has been translated from the word Shema. To "hear" or "listen" is to "obey."[19]

What is described in the *Shema* is what is called a "monolatrous" confession. Again, this highlights God's uniqueness amongst other superficial 'gods.' Bird writes,

> Monotheism entails monolatry, the Worship of the one true God to the exclusion of others...make[ing] up the

---

[18] Brown, Michael L., *Answering Jewish Objections to Jesus: Theological Objections*, Vol. II, (Grand Rapids: Baker, 2000), 4.

[19] Spangler, Ann, Tverberg, Lois, *Sitting at the Feet of Rabbi Jesus: How the Jewishness of Jesus Can Transform Your Faith*, (Grand Rapids: Zondervan, 2009), 177.

substance of Jewish Monotheism.[20]

Another interesting point is how the *Shema* reads in the Hebrew. Dunn and Rogerson note,

> [The *Shema*] most likely refers to Yahweh's uniqueness. He alone is God, and he needs no other gods to assist him. However, this unique and incomparable God is also, for Israel, our God, not because of what Israel deserves or merits but because of God's graciousness (cf. 7:7).[21]

The ultimate myopic means in which scholars narrowly interpret the *Shema* is seemingly void of any meaningful substance once it is deduced as a mere confession of Yahweh's sole unity. When we look at the historical intention of the *Shema*, biblical trinitarians can wholeheartedly confirm God is one and personally one as a self-sufficient complex unity being the sole recipient of our obedience. Let us now turn to the Islamic understanding of Allah's unity.

Islamic conception of Allah's Unity:

As noted earlier, the Islamic conception of Allah is that he is the ultimate sole undivided creator who is absolute one. The problem arises when we see clear inconsistencies with this idea. Muslims that hold to the absolute eternality of Allah find it hard to recognize the Quran itself have negated distinctions within God's absolute Unity, which implies a direct violation of his essential unity. Jan Peters introduces this central perceived dilemma.

> The Quran is God's [Allah] speech. About this point of

---

[20] Bird, Michael F. et. al., *How God Became Jesus: The Real Origins of Belief in Jesus' Divine Nature—A Response to Bart D. Ehrman*, (Grand Rapids: Zondervan, 2014), 29.

[21] Dunn, James D. G., Rogerson, John W., *Eerdmans Commentary on the Bible*, (Grand Rapids: Eerdmans, 2003), 157.

view there is no disagreement amongst Muslims throughout the centuries. The discussion, however, centered upon the question whether the Quran is eternal or temporal and created, have led to fierce disputes and even to the persecution of the adherents of one or the other of the two positions. The question at stake was: did the Quran coexist with God, uncreated, in all eternity, so that God could send it down to his prophet and reveal it to mankind, or did God create it in time and it have a beginning, "it was not, afterwards it was", (*lam yakun, tumm kân*) as the traditional formula says.[22]

The Quran clearly depicts the eternal Quran preserved on a tablet with Allah. Sura al- Burūj (85) 21-22 states:

> No indeed, (but) it is an Ever-Glorious Qur'an, in a preserved Tablet (Ghali).

Sura al-Zukhruf (43) 3-4 reads:

> We have made it a Qur'an in Arabic, that ye may be able to understand (and learn wisdom). And verily, it is in the Mother of the Book, in Our Presence, high (in dignity), full of wisdom (Ali). (cf. Sura 13:39).

Muslims agree that the Quran in heaven is uncreated perfectly expressing the mind of Allah yet, not in essence Allah. In other words, Allah is deemed as the only volitional "eternal" but the Quran is quintessentially also deemed as being "eternal" without violating the idea of the One God. Dr G. F. Haddad writes in *The Uncreatedness of the Divine Speech: The Glorious Qur'an* that;

---

[22] Peters, J. R. T. M., *God's Created Speech; a Study in the Speculative Theology of the Mu'tzili Qadi l-Quadat Abu l-Hasan Abd al-Jabbar Bn Ahmad al-Hamadani*, (Leiden: Brill, 1976), 1.

Ahl al-Sunna agrees one and all that the Qur'an is the pre-existent, pre-eternal, uncreated Speech of Allah Most High on the evidence of the Qur'an, the Sunna, and faith-guided reason.[23]

Another interesting fact affirmed in the Hadith is that the Quran expresses the personal attribute of intercession on the day of judgement.

Abu Umamah said that he heard Allah's Messenger (saws) say: Recite the Qur'an, for on the Day of Resurrection it will come as an intercessor for those who recite it.[24]

Allah's Messenger (saws) said, "Fasting and the Qur'an will intercede for man (on the Day of Judgment). Fasting says, 'O my Lord, I have kept him away from his food and his passions by day, so accept my intercession for him.' The Qur'an says, 'I have kept him away from sleep by night, so accept my intercession for him.' Then their intercession is accepted.[25]

Muslims seem to be very charitable towards themselves in spite of this immense difficulty, in that another eternal entity is seemingly more than just a notional idea with Allah; yet, it is not identified as Allah. Is this mere personification to make a theological point or an actual indication of the nature of Allah's word? Trying to account for this obvious difficulty the early Mu'tazilites argued that the Quran was not eternal because it is not an attribute of Allah but an act of him. They leaned on various

---

[23] Haddad, G. F., "The Uncreatedness of the Divine Speech: The Glorious Qur'an," *As-Sunnah Foundation of America*, http://www.sunnah.org/aqida/uncreatedness_quran.htm. Accessed 02/21/2018.

[24] *Sahih Muslim* Hadith, 1757, Narrated by Abu Umamah.

[25] *Al-Tirmidhi* Hadith, 1963, Narrated by Abdullah ibn Amr.

passages within the Quran that described it as created and not eternal.[26] Opposing any such notion Jon Hoover describes the Asharite position as follow:

> The Ash'ari tradition affirms that God's essential attributes such as knowledge, speech, and power are real and eternal. However, this introduces a certain ontological multiplicity into the being of God. How do God's real, eternal attributes fit with the simplicity of God's essence? The traditional Ash'ari response is that God's attributes are not identical with God and yet not other than God. So, for example, God's attribute of power is not identical to God himself; yet, God's power is not other than God. This does not provide a rational solution to the problem. Rather, it simply sets linguistic boundaries for what may be said of God, and it leaves unanswered the question of how God's many attributes subsist in God's single essence.[27]

Orthodox Muslims maintains that the speech of Allah is an eternal attribute like his knowledge that is infinitely preserved with him but not identified with him. The Christian cannot but notice the lack of charity given by the Muslim then when we explain Christ as the *logos* with the *theos* without being the same personal person with the *theos*. John describes this reality beautifully in his gospel account when he writes:

> In the beginning was the Word, and the Word was with God, and the Word was God. He was in the beginning with God. All things were made through him, and without him was not anything made that was made. (John 1:1-3)

---

[26] Shahrastani, Al, *Al-Milal wa al-Nihal* (Leipzig: Otto Harrassowitz,1923), 38, 46, 68.

[27] Hoover, Jon, 2009. "Islamic Monotheism and the Trinity," *The Conrad Grebel Review*, 57-82.

Ἐν ἀρχῇ ἦν ὁ λόγος, καὶ ὁ λόγος ἦν πρὸς τὸν θεόν, καὶ θεὸς ἦν ὁ λόγος. οὗτος ἦν ἐν ἀρχῇ πρὸς τὸν θεόν. πάντα δι' αὐτοῦ ἐγένετο, καὶ χωρὶς αὐτοῦ ἐγένετο οὐδὲ ἕν. ὃ γέγονεν. (John 1:1-3, NA28)

Let us look at the essential quality of love as formulated in the Christian and Muslim understanding of God.

2. Love of YHWH and the love of Allah.

Christian conception of God's love
The very central revelation of the Christian Scriptures defines an understanding of a God that comes to us as a loving self-sacrificing entity personally involved with the world and creatures he created. Rowan Williams states;

> The mutual self-giving love that is the very life of God is made real for our sake in the self-giving love of Jesus.[28]

The beloved disciple John mentions that this God is, in his very essence, love (1 John 4:8), and that as a result of him being loving, he sacrificially loves us first so that we might experience eternal life through an act of his own self-giving (John 3:16). Theologian Timothy George mentions that;

> God's divinity does not consist in his ability to push things around, to make and break, to impose his will from the security of some heavenly remoteness, to sit in grandeur while all the world does his bidding. Far from staying above the world, he sends his own glory into it. Far from imposing, he invites and persuades. Far from demanding

---

[28] *A Common Word between Us and You*, (Amman: The Royal Aal Al-Bayt Institute for Islamic Thought, 2012), English Monograph Series, No. 20, 194.

service from men in order to enhance himself, he gives his life in service to men for their enhancement.[29]

We find ourselves in his love, simply because he first loved us, and gave himself to us (1 John 4:9-10). The point that needs to be considered is that the Christian conception of God reveals that love is essential to the inner working and nature of the Triune community (John 3:16, Eph 5:25, Rom 15:30). Peter Toon writes;

> Only a God who is Triune can be personal. Only the Holy Trinity can be love. Human love cannot possibly reflect the nature of God unless God is a Trinity of persons in union and communion. A Solitary Nomad cannot love and, since it cannot love, neither can it be a person. And if God is not personal, neither can we be-and if we are not persons, we cannot love.[30]

The gospels show a clear distinction between persons and at the Baptism the Disciple of Jesus, Matthew wrote:

> As soon as Jesus was baptized, He went up out of the water. Suddenly the heavens were opened, and he saw the Spirit of God descending like a dove and resting on Him. And a voice from heaven said, "This is My beloved Son, in whom I am well pleased!" (Matt 3:16-17).

We can clearly see that the Triune God is a dynamic loving community working together in accomplishing various initiatives. What is essential though is that there is clear dynamic of love evident within this community that order their very tasks at hand. Because God is clearly sufficient in himself, we know he expresses

---

[29] George, Timothy Ed., *God the Holy Trinity: Reflections on Christian Faith and Practice*, (Grand Rapids: Baker, 2007), 127.

[30] Toon, Peter, *Our Triune God: A Biblical Portrayal of the Trinity*, (Vancouver: Regent College Pub., 1996), 241.

who he is and what he does because of that inner working as a Triune community. Richard Swinburne argues for this Christian truth on priory grounds when he writes:

> God's "perfect goodness requires a first divine being to produce a second and in cooperation with the second to produce a third; but that there is no necessity to produce a fourth." "There is something profoundly imperfect and therefore inadequately divine in a solitary divine individual. If such an individual is love, he must share, and sharing with finite beings such as humans is not sharing all of one's nature and so is imperfect sharing. A divine individual's love has to be manifested in a sharing with another divine individual, and that (to keep the divine unity) means (in some sense) within the Godhead, that is, in mutual dependence and support.[31]

This is a fundamental difference in our understanding of the love of Yahweh and Allah. When we consider the *'one'* as the primary principle beyond being and thought in Islamic theology, the very conception of this deity has little or no metaphysical value because it has no definite meaning. That is why Arabic philosophers like Averroes grapple with this idea and surmise that Allah is a correlative to the universe because he needs the universe to display his attributes, and the universe needs Allah to uphold it. Other philosophers that concluded the same was Avicenna (influenced by Al-Farabi) who questioned the difference between essence (*mahiat*) and existence (*wajud*) and postulated that existing things coexists with its effect and is thereby the eternal abstract unity which is inescapably dependent on the temporal universe. An essential "solitary" demands agency to express whom he is and thereby makes the universe actual with him. Within a Triune

---

[31] Swinburne, Richard, *The Existence of God*, 2nd Ed., (New York: Clarendon Press, 2004), 344-345.

reality, we do not have dependence from the Creator on his creation because this God is a self-sufficient unity in himself. Bosserman writes;

> The Trinity safeguards the Creator-creature distinction by demanding that the latter must have been created (a) "out of nothing" and (b) with a temporal beginning (cf. Gen 1:1; Col 1:16; Rev 4:11). First, as a self-defined being, the Triune God is not reliant on a contrasting material universe to express Himself.[32]

The Christian concludes that the only true theism is Christian theism, and the greatest conceivable being is independent in himself and wholly personalistic from himself. What is the Islamic conception of love like?

Islamic conception of Allah's love

Daud Rahbar mentions that, "Unqualified divine love for humankind is an idea completely alien to the Quran."[33] Historically, there are variant perspectives in different movements of Islam on the way in which devotees could express their love towards the divine. The Ash'arites held that adherents of the Quran could be affectionate about the actions that bring them closer to Allah. The Hanbalites contends that Allah ought to be loved for his own sake, and others, for his sake. Sufism focuses more on an experiential pragmatism in loving Allah striving to be in his presence through various activities loving Allah for his own sake.[34] Muslims usually mentions that Allah is "*Al-Wadūd*" or the One who love those who does well, and bestows on them his

---

[32] Bosserman, *A Vindication of Divine Paradox*, 139-140.

[33] Rahbar, Daud, *God of justice: A Study of the Ethical Doctrine of the Quran*, (Leiden: Brill, 1960), 223-225.

[34] Abdin, Amira Shamma, 2004. "Love in Islam," *European Judaism*, 37.1, 92-93.

compassion. Surah Al-Buruj (85:14) says, "He (Allah) is the All-Forgiving, the All-Loving."

So what is problematic about the Islamic conception of the love of Allah? First, there is a difference in the individual's qualification for Allah's love. Surah Maryam (19:96) says,

> On those who believe and work deeds of righteousness, will (Allah) Most Gracious bestow love.

In stark contrast Paul writes to the Romans (5:8) and says,

> But God demonstrates his own love for us in this: While we were still sinners, Christ died for us.

The recipient that qualifies for the love of Allah has to sustain and fulfil the preconditions of Allah's laws before the individual can experience this mercy. In the Christian conception of God's love, he qualifies by the fact that God loves him from himself without any merit before the required pre-conditions. The Christian conception of God's ultimate love stems from the actuality that the greatest love is directed from him [God] that loves us from himself. John writes,

> "We love him because he first love us." (1 John 4:19)

God's love is not merited by what we do, but rather by who he is revealed to be in the Christian Scriptures. Allah in the Quran is in no way a reflection of his essential attributes because he attributes these to himself but he remains above them. Imad Shehadeh has noticed this central difficulty:

> For moral attributes to be active in God apart from creation [it] requires a relationship within God; otherwise, God would need to become dependent on creation to exercise

them... No adequate relationship can exist in one unipersonal being, and the triune relationship is others-love and not self-love. In fact, the glory of the Trinity is in the honor each person gives to the others. This love and humility not only overflowed in creating but also in Christ's death on the cross... the formal dominant historic Ash'arite position on the attributes of God... emphasizes that all moral attributes stem from God's powerful will (not his nature) so that they are accidental and not essential to his nature. Herein, God loves not because he is love but because he chooses to love and could choose not to. Similarly, God being "merciful and compassionate" in Islam describes only what he can do, not what he is. In Christianity, however, God's mercy and compassion are grounded in eternal relationships between persons in the perfect unity of God's being. Additionally, God's relationship to his people in the Bible is further described as that of a spouse, a lover, a father, a brother, a friend, etc.–concepts foreign to Islam, and possibly offensive. Love in Christianity is initiated by God, not man (1 John 4:10).[35]

As we have mentioned earlier, the problem with an absolute unity is that an ontologically pure unity equates to essential nothingness. It is important to note once more that in Islam, Allah stands aloof from any known attribute, which renders this divinity neither picturable nor conceivable. This is not a problem in Christian theism because a loving compound Triunity can completely be made known and be distinct in his moral attributes.

---

[35] Shehadeh, Imad, 2011. "Book Reviews: Allah: A Christian Response by Miroslav Volf," *Biblical Missiology*, http://biblicalmissiology.org/2011/10/10/book-review-allah-a-christian-response-by-miroslav-volf/. Accessed 02/21/2018.

In the absolute monotheism of Islam, the idea that God was "alone" before creation is inconceivable and foreign because love is essentially relational and thereby necessitates relationship. Any deity that existed eternally before time without relations that is seemingly captivated by his own "loneliness" cannot existentially deemed to be relational, personal, or loving and by his own lack of self-disclosure equates to nothingness. The Allah of the Quran is therefore simply expediently a solitary monad void of qualities we should see as a person. This is why it is the biblical contention that the Christian God is both essentially personal and loving and therefore the truest for of theism. What do we then make of the way in which we can think about our respective Gods?

3. The knowability of YHWH and the knowability of Allah.

Christian Conception of the knowability of God:
A clear distinct feature of Christian theism is the promise that God has made himself known in His Son Jesus Christ (John 1:18). The author of Hebrews (1:3) also mentions that Jesus is the "radiance of God's glory and the exact representation of his being." Thomas Schreiner says that the Son reflects God's glory and represents the nature and character of the one true God. Christ is the definition of God and Christianity finds the true picture of their God in the expressed person of Jesus Christ. Jesus exhausts the very definition of God through the revelation of his being. That is why Jesus answers Philip after he asked if Jesus could show them the Father, "Anyone who has seen me has seen the Father" (John 14:9). Reverberating Richard of St Victor's conception of a personal deity, Robert Letham writes:

> Only a God who is Triune can be personal. Only the Holy Trinity can be love. Human love cannot possibly reflect the nature of God unless God is a Trinity of persons in union and communion. A solitary nomad cannot love and, since it

cannot love, neither can it be a person. And if God is not personal, neither can we be-and if we are not persons, we cannot love. This marks a vast, immeasurable divide between those cultures that follow a monotheistic, unitary deity and those that are permeated by the Christian teaching on the Trinity. Trinitarian theology asserts that love is ultimate because God is love, because he is three persons in undivided loving communion. By contrast, Islam asserts that Allah is powerful and that his will is ultimate, before which submission (Islam) is required.[36]

The first distinction between the revelation of God in the Quran and the Bible is that God is intimately known through Jesus Christ. John (17:3) says,

"This is eternal life that they may know you, the only true God, and Jesus Christ whom you have sent."

Biblically we see that there is no knowledge of God where there is no true revelation of Jesus Christ (Eph 1:17, Col 2:2). The essential character of the God revealed in the Bible is love and love seeks to be made known (John 3:16, 1 John 4:7-9, 16). John MacArthur writes that the Christian God is not an unknown, impersonal force but he is a personal being with the full attributes of personality, volition, feeling, and intellect. God in Christianity is known through Jesus Christ and we are assured that he is qualitatively love which is essential to our understanding of his being (1 John 4:7).[37] In stark contrast, when we look at the God of the Bible and the God of the Quran this is a cardinal difference.

---

[36] Letham, Robert, *The Holy Trinity: In Scripture, History, Theology, and Worship*, (Philipsburg: Presbyterian & Reformed, 2004), 446.

[37] MacArthur, John F., *The Love of God: He Will Do Whatever It Takes to Make Us Holy*, (Dallas: Word Publishing Group, 1996), 165f.

Herman Bavinck remarks that if God does not reveal himself to his creatures, essentially knowledge of him is utterly unattainable. It is important to know that even though God is unique and incomprehensible there are communicable attributes like love, holiness, mercy, justice, goodness and grace that is essentially qualitative of him. He acts therefore consistent with his comprehensive attributes and the Christian can know their God because he is constant in his revealed nature.[38] Faith is therefore truly possible for the Christian conception of God because we can surely account for God's consistent self-revelation as revealed in his Son Jesus Christ (John 1:1-3, vv. 14, and 18). The Christian conception of God can be both knowable and unknowable without any form of contradiction because God is wholly transcendent but in Christ wholly immanent. He has nothing comparable to him in this world, but he is also Immanuel, God with us (Matt. 1:23). The God of Scripture is revealed as transcendent but also personal, he is known by his Son. As John affirmed:

> That which was from the beginning, which we have heard, which we have seen with our eyes, which we have looked upon, and our hands have handled, concerning the Word of life— the life was manifested, and we have seen, and bear witness, and declare to you that eternal life which was with the Father and was manifested to us— that which we have seen and heard we declare to you, that you also may have fellowship with us; and truly our fellowship is with the Father and with His Son Jesus Christ. (1 John 1:1-3)

Islam cannot provide a cogent perspective of God because they do not have a true conception of the person of Jesus Christ. Elsewhere I've noted the absolute certainty Christians can enjoy

---

[38] Bavinck, Herman, Trans. by Hendrickson, William, *The Doctrine of God*, (Carlisle: Banner of Truth, 2003), 41.

when we look at the revelation of Jesus Christ and his revelation of the Father.[39] Our Muslim friends might mention that Allah can be known through his 99 beautiful names, but as we will see in this last section, Allah is not identified by his distinct attributes but he is seemingly above them. He is beyond reason, realm, and revelation. This is the catastrophic state of Islamic theology in that there is no validation or disclosure of the unique God.

Islamic Conception of the knowability of Allah

In historical Islam, the Mu'tazilites denied all distinct and co-eternal attributes of Allah but the essence of Allah because for them it was against monotheism to have faith in anything primeval other than Allah's essence. Abdul-Hasan Ash'ari held that Allah's attributes are simply co-eternal with him and not distinct from his essence but the attributes are not Allah's very essence.[40] The Asharite position is the popular position and majority of Sunni Islam would hold that the essence of Allah is not in the word Allah. This very conception of Allah leads the devotee to a clear inability to grasp the very nature of Allah. Rami al Rifai, in his book *Imam al Ghazali on the Foundations of Aqeedah*, affirms that,

> All this too impossible (to imagine) in the mind. For whatever the mind conceives is definite in so far as it is limited by place, in the same way as substances are limited, or by substances, in the same way as their qualities are. But the impossibility of his [Allah's] being a substance or its quality has been established – consequently his being

---

[39] Boshoff, Rudolph P., 2018. "The Deity of Christ as Primer to Understand the Difference Between Yahweh and Allah," *Ad Lucem*, http://adlucem.co/deity-christ-primer-understand-difference-yahweh-allah-rudolph-p-boshoff/. Accessed 02/21/2018.

[40] Zafar, Muhammad, *Christio-Islamic Theologies*, (New Delhi: Adam Publishers, 1994), 110.

subject to a direction becomes impossible.[41]

That is why notable Islamic scholars affirm that Allah is ultimately inconceivable, which leads them to negative theology rather trying to describe what Allah is not! (i.e., 'Whatever the mind conceives Allah to be, he is not!'). It might therefore not be unfair to describe the very heart of Islamic devotion as a commission to submit to Allah. The heart of Islam is to surrender to Allah and to obey him rather than as a priority to know him. The very central means of the Islamic conception of Allah not being able to identify him by his attributes leads to a form of agnosticism that is perpetuated through a form of deism. This happens because the Muslims believe that Allah caused everything by extrinsic causality with no essential revelation of his essential attributes. Islamic scholar Jamal Elias mentions that,

> Human Beings can know God [Allah] through his attributes (such as mercy, justice, compassion, wrath, and so on), but the ultimate essence of God [Allah] remains unknown.[42]

It is important to note that Yahweh in the Bible is known by his effects where Allah is named from his effects but not known by them (Surah 6:12). The revelation of Allah is therefore extrinsic towards his creatures and not intrinsic towards himself because he is not identified by his actions but for his actions. From a Christian theistic perspective, this causes numerous problems. Ahmed Hulusi adds:

> Allah is samad... If we take an extensive look at the meaning of this word, we will see that Samad means the

---

[41] 2014. "Imam al Ghazali on the Foundations of Aqeedah," *Sunnah Muakada*, https://sunnahmuakada.wordpress.com/2014/01/18/imam-al-ghazali-on-the-foundations-of-aqeedah/. Accessed 02/21/2018.

[42] Elias, Jamal J., *Islam*, (Boston: Pearson, 1999), 62.

following: A whole without any void or emptiness, impermeable, nothing penetrates into it, nothing extends out from it, pure and only![43]

In Christian Theism, there are incommunicable attributes of God e.g., (infinity, eternality, sovereignty, omnipresence, omnipotence) that we cannot comprehend but there are also communicable attributes (e.g., holiness, love, truthfulness, wisdom) that the biblical God express that we can intimately know and recognize. It is important to note that Allah is not identified with his revealed attributes, as his attributes do not disclose his essential nature.

Sirajuddin Ali (AD 1173), author of the renowned book Emali, affirms that:

> The attributes of God [Allah] are not God [Allah] Himself. But neither are they distinct nor independent from His being. Rather, his attributes, as manifestations of his being and works, are eternal (*qadim*) and impersonal.

When the Quran mentions that Allah deceives or leads astray (Surah Ali 'Imran. 3.54; cf. Surah Al-Anfal 8.30), these actions do not impugn on who Allah essentially is, because he attributes to himself deception but is not identified by it. Samuel Zwemer is therefore not unfair in his appraisal of Allah when he comments:

> We will find in this study that orthodox Islam is at once deistic and pantheistic. Theologians and philosophers have pantheistic views of Allah, making Him the sole force in the universe; but the popular thought of Him (owing to the iron-weight of the doctrine of fatalism) is deistic. God [Allah] stands aloof from creation; only His power is felt;

---

[43] Hulusi, Ahmed, *Muhammad's Allah*, (Location Unknown: Self-Pub., 2012), 28.

men are like the pieces on a chessboard and He is the only player. Creation itself was not intended so much for the manifestation of God's [Allah's] glory or the outburst of His love, as for a sample of His power.[44]

Samuel Zwemer goes even further and says:

The worst form of monotheism in that it makes of God pure will, will divorced from reason and love." Islam, instead of being a progressive and completed idea, goes to a lower level than the religions it claims to supplant. "Mohammed teaches a God above us; Moses teaches a God above us and yet with us; Jesus Christ teaches God above us, God with us and God in us." God above us, not as an Oriental despot, but as a Heavenly Father. God with us, Emmanuel, in the mystery of His Incarnation, which is the stumbling block to the Moslem. God in us through His Spirit renewing the heart and controlling the will into a true Islam, or obedient subjection by a living faith.[45]

The very progressive revelation of the Old and New Testament demonstrates a God who longs to be amongst his people (Exod 29:45-46; Eze 37:26-28; Zech 2:8-10; John 1:14; 2 Cor 6:16). The sad reality is that when we look at the God of Islam, we are left with god that is seemingly removed from humanity and even worse, a god that is beyond comprehension and notice. Geisler and Saleeb affirm:

"For Islamic theology, God has willed and has acted in many ways, but these actions in no way reflect the divine

---

[44] Zwemer, Samuel M., *The Muslim Doctrine of God: An Essay on the Character & Attributes of Allah According to the Koran & Orthodox Tradition*, (New York: Young People's Missionary Movement, 1905), 69-70.

[45] Ibid., 76.

character behind them."[46]

The adherents of Islam can be truthful about who they worship, and the worship rendered to this being is purely a gamble with the unknown! Close friend John GilChrist writes,

> Many scholars of Islam in past centuries, when seeking to define the character of Allah, invariably concentrated on what he is not. Abu'l Hasan `Ali Al-Ash`ari, the famous theologian born in Basra in the third century after Muhammad's death, gave a very negative description of Allah in his Makalat al-Islamiyin. He said he had no body, nor object, nor volume. No place could encompass him [Allah]; no time could pass by him. Nothing that could be said of any of his creatures could be used to describe him. Nothing, either, that could be imagined in the mind or be conceived by fantasy resembles him. Eyes cannot see him, harm cannot touch him, nor can joy or pleasure reach him. Nothing moves him. Another early Muslim scholar perhaps summed up the Muslim position in saying that, whatever you might conceive Allah to be, he is not that![47]

In the book of Acts (17:22-23) Paul laments and call the Athenians to the knowledge of the One true God as revealed in the person and work of Jesus Christ. The central priority then for the Christian is to know God and to love him with all our mind, soul and strength (Deut 6:5, Matt 22:37; Luke 10:27). The Apostle John writes to the Samaritans (4:22-23) about the priority to know God and to Worship him:

> You worship what you do not know; we worship what we

---

[46] Geisler, Saleeb, *Answering Islam*, 143.

[47] Goldsmith, Martin, *Islam and Christian witness*, (Milton Keynes: Paternoster, 1991), 54.

do know... But a time is coming and has now come when the true worshipers will worship the Father in spirit and in truth, for the Father is seeking such as these to worship him.

After the Samaritans come to a full realization of the person of Jesus Christ, it confirms in verse 41-42:

Many more believed because of his word; and they were saying to the woman, "It is no longer because of what you said that we believe, for we have heard for ourselves, and know that this one is indeed the Savior of the world."

There is clearly a difference in intention when we read both the Quran and the Bible. The Christian Scriptures occupy itself with the full revelation and self-disclosure of the One God of Israel in the person of Jesus Christ. The Quran is seemingly void of this pursuit. Paul of Tarsus reveals this priority when he writes to the Church in Philippi (3:8):

More than that, I count all things as loss compared to the surpassing excellence of knowing Christ Jesus my Lord, for whom I have lost all things. I consider them rubbish that I may gain Christ.

Again, Paul shows that the central task of the Christian is to worship what they do know, and the best reference to the fact of this task is ultimately found in the person of Jesus Christ our Lord. When we look at the central perceptions of both Christian and Islamic theology, there seems to be a clear difference in perspective concerning the way Christian and Muslim articulate their faith. Christians view the full revelation of Jesus Christ as the foundational means to understand and know God. Muslims are not concerned with 'knowing' God but rather their submission to him. From a Christian perspective, we can see there is clear problems with a deity that is just known through his volition and pure will. Ultimately, we are not assured who the God of Islam is or even determine what he will do, as he is not what he does. Whereas the central purpose of the Christian Scriptures is to lead people to know their God and to obey him, the central purpose of the Islamic text if for Muslims to submit to their God and receive his favor as a result of their obedience. In the Islamic conception of Jesus, he is simply a prophet and servant from Allah but not the revelation of Allah. In Surah Maryam (19.30) it is said;

> [Jesus] said, 'Indeed, I am the servant of Allah. He has given me the Scripture and made me a prophet.

Biblically, Jesus is the very definition of God. In Paul's letter to Timothy (1, 3:16) we read:

> The mystery of godliness is great: He was manifested in the flesh, vindicated in the Spirit, seen by angels, preached among the nations, believed on in the world, taken up in glory.

The Apostle John (1, 5:19-20) writes:

> We know that the Son of God has come and has given us understanding so that we may know the true One. We are in the true One—that is, in is Son Jesus Christ. He is the true God and eternal life.

The Christian promise is one of proximity and promise where Jesus Christ manifest in the flesh to the glory of the Father by the Holy Spirit draws us into that loving relationship by which we can cry 'Abba Father.'

ANSWERING ATTACKS ON THE TRINITY FROM THE NEW URBAN ALTERNATIVE SPIRITUALITIES: THE TRIUNE NATURE OF GOD IN ANTE-NICENE AND EARLY AFRICAN CHRISTIANITY

Vocab Malone[1]

This chapter focuses on early Christian writings discussing and advocating forms of trinitarian monotheism. I use forms of trinitarian monotheism because each author expresses these concepts in their own way, using the language of their distinctive mind and culture, and sometimes trinitarian modes of thought are expressed but not fully unpacked as to their meaning. For example, there is a difference between a church writer writing a whole

---

[1] Vocab was born and raised in Columbus, Ohio. He holds an MA in Biblical Leadership (Phoenix Seminary) and is a DMin candidate (ABD, Talbot School of Theology). Vocab's ministry focus is urban apologetics and cultural worldview analysis. Vocab has done a number of debates and dialogues with Muslims, atheists, and "Hebrew Israelites." Vocab is an adoptive father who enjoys coffee, ComiCon life, and Old School nostalgia. He is the author of *Barack Obama vs. the Black Hebrew Israelites*.

treatise on the Trinity compared to a church writer writing two or three sentences on the Trinity. Both are valid examples because both are still writing on the Trinity in some way. While some actually do use a form of the word "Trinity" (trias/triad), others write on the three persons of the Trinity without using the word. But, often their terse language still matches or is at the least, not contradictory to the Christian doctrine of the Trinity. This is not to say these writers do not have shades of difference on some of their meanings or understanding—this is still the case today, even among the orthodox. For the purposes of this chapter, here is the definition of the Trinity from the 1689 London Baptist Confession:

> In this divine and infinite Being there are three subsistence's, the Father, the Word or Son, and Holy Spirit, of one substance, power and eternity, each having the whole divine essence, yet the essence undivided: the Father is of none, neither begotten nor proceeding, the Son is eternally begotten of the Father; the Holy Spirit proceeding from the Father and the Son; all infinite, without beginning, therefore but one God, who is not to be divided in nature and being, but distinguished by several, peculiar, relative properties and personal relations; which doctrine of the Trinity is the foundation of all our communion with God, and comfortable dependence on Him.[2]

A more concise definition is offered by theologian Larry Hart: "The Triune God is one God who exists eternally as three infinite, eternal, interpenetrating Persons: Father, Son, and Holy Spirit."[3] Of course, the ins and outs of trinitarianism are discussed in the rest of this volume, I only offer a brief definition to get us

---

[2] Chap. 2, § 3.
[3] Hart, Larry D., *Truth Aflame: Theology for the Church in Renewal*, (Grand Rapids: Zondervan, 2005), 128.

started.

Because of specific oddities of some attacks by new alternative urban spiritualities on the Trinity—the Trinity is a "white" doctrine invented at Nicaea—the bulk of my interaction will be with Ante-Nicene church fathers and then African church fathers (both before and after Nicaea). This will show two things:

(1) The doctrine of the Trinity precedes Nicaea.
(2) The doctrine of the Trinity is not a European invention.

Attacks from the New Urban Alternative Spiritualities

Attacks on the Christian doctrine of the Trinity never seem to go out of style. Muslims, Jehovah's Witnesses, unitarians, Mormons, Oneness Pentecostals, and atheists attack the doctrine. It was popular to attack the Trinity in the ancient world. Today, it is still popular to attack the Trinity on the Internet. Cult members at the door attack the Trinity. Academics at the lectern attack the Trinity. Adherents to the new urban alternative spiritualities attack the Trinity. Since it's a focal point of this chapter, the phrase new alternative urban spiritualities requires some unpacking.

Some specialists emphasize "the sectarian nature of Black religious groups:" "they all exist in a state of tension with the larger society. While religious sects generally find themselves in conflict with some aspect of the larger society, racial status contributes an additional element to this tension that distinguishes black from white sectarian groups."[4] This comes from a book titled *Black Spiritual Movement: A Religious Response to Racism*. Note the subtitle. It essentially means there is a strong "reactionary" element to some of the new alternative urban spiritualities. Baer says as much:

---

[4] Baer, Hans A., *Black Spiritual Movement: A Religious Response to Racism*, (Knoxville: The University of Tennessee Press, 2001), 8.

Lower-class blacks ... perhaps because of their greater sense of powerlessness, have been particularly creative in developing strategies that attempt to instill dignity and meaning in their often seemingly hopeless lives in a racist and stratified society.[5]

Just as it is a bit unorthodox to begin a discussion on the Trinity in ethnography, it is only slightly less orthodox to briefly discuss what scholars call "New Religious Movements," abbreviated as NRMs in the field. Nonetheless, this introductory discussion is needed because it sets the stage for the rest of the chapter. I am using the phrase "new alternative urban spiritualities," a type or species of NRM. The concept of "new" is not without its challenges (even more wrought with more potential land mines is the word "urban!"):

> The description of a religious movement as new only begs further questions. Novelty can be in the eye of the beholder, or in the mind of someone claiming to be innovative, or both or in only one. That is to say that religious movements are judged to be new only in particular contexts and by certain audiences. They may claim, for example, to retrieve and correctly represent proper past practice, which has somehow been neglected or forgotten. But their opponents might view the same claims as dangerous and deviant inventions. New religions themselves often manifest a pronounced ambivalence about their own novelty.[6]

NRM's, of which the new alternative urban spiritualities may be a subclass, "strive to present themselves as both new and

---

[5] Ibid.

[6] Gallagher, Eugene V., *The New Religious Movements Experience in America*, (Westport: Greenwood Press, 2004), 15.

old, as both unprecedented and familiar. From their perspective, a new revelation necessitates the reconceptualization of all of history."[7]

My friend Ernest Cleo Grant has written a series of very helpful articles for *Christianity Today* dealing with apologetics as it relates to the "new alternative urban spiritualities." This will be the last generalized section before we outline some specific attacks by specific groups, but these words are extremely important for the reader to get a proper "feel" for the context in which this chapter operates. In discussing the current syncretism found in many of the "new alternative urban spiritualities," Ernest uses the entertainer Nick Cannon as a test case. It's three paragraphs but please do not skip them!

> While syncretism occurs in every context, it takes a different shape in the inner city. Urban religious syncretism is often a fusion of Egyptian Mysticism (often learned from YouTube videos), ahistorical documentaries (i.e. Hidden Colors and Christ in Egypt: The Horus-Jesus Connection), urban folk religions (i.e., Moorish Science Temple, Nation of Islam, Black Hebrew Israelites, etc.), misunderstood Christian doctrine, unbiblical pan-African rhetoric, and countless other falsehoods.

> Before falling back to sleep, I thought about the ever-evolving, pluralistic urban context and the similarities between Cannon's philosophy of religion and the religious pundits that proselytize their beliefs on the street corners of the inner cities of America. Comparatively speaking, Cannon's rhetoric is very similar to the doctrines of those who deny the historical Christ in the Afrocentric movement, whom I've engaged in the urban/inner-city

---

[7] Ibid., 16.

context. Like Cannon, they combine complex, often contradictory, spiritual elements and blend religious practices to form personal, pseudo-indigenous religions that suit their lifestyles and passions.

While urban religious syncretism can take a plethora of forms, no matter the form, it's disheartening because it compromises the tenants and integrity of the gospel. Urban religious syncretism discards core doctrines—such as the divinity of Christ, penal substitution, and the Trinity, among other things—to form a new gospel that is tailor-made to be inoffensive, unobtrusive, and ultimately ineffective. Consequently, unwitting and incognizant brothers and sisters have been drawn away from the gospel of Christ by doctrines that sound true, but only borrow authority from other religions and distort the gospel (Gal. 1:6–9).[8]

As Ernest notes in another CT piece, Black Hebrew Israelism is an example of a new urban alternative spirituality. Black Hebrew Israelism is growing in numbers and influence—they are also anti-trinitarian. Moses Farrar, a Tanakh-Only "Hebrew Israelite" author writes,

Christianity did not totally abolish all its idolatrous ways, and its true founders, Paul and Emperor Constantine, set forth 'the Doctrine of the Trinity'—God the Father, God the Son, and God the Holy Ghost. Until this very day almost all of

---

[8] Grant, Ernest Cleo, 2017. "Urban Mix-and-Match Religion Didn't Start with Nick Cannon: Why this 'new spirituality' is really just old-fashioned syncretism," *Christianity Today*, https://www.christianitytoday.com/ct/2017/february-web-only/roots-of-urban-religious-syncretism-nick-cannon.html. Accessed 5/14/2018.

Christendom engages in the worship of Jesus Christ."[9]

Here, Farrar is writing about the first 300 years of Christian development. The most shocking and accidentally humorous part of this quote is where Farrar calls Paul and Constantine the founders of Christianity. Emperor Nero executed Paul in 67 AD and Constantine became the sole Roman Emperor in 324 AD. How then, can these two men, separated by more than 250 years, be the founders of Christianity? Specifically, how could they in any meaningful way "set forth the Doctrine of the Trinity"? Did Paul invent the Trinity doctrine and then it was laid down until Constantine picked it back up? Did Paul come up with it, tricked everyone into believing it, and then later Constantine forced it upon everyone?

I am guessing what Farrar's argument is because he never lays out his case, nor does he give any documented evidence for his claim. Why then would I even mention such an unscholarly claim? I believe we should not only dispel the myths of academics but also lay arguments. Many "lay arguments" are repeated uncritically and then influence others. The sentiments of the aforementioned book by Farrar (and others) have been turned into Internet memes which attack the Trinity. Bad scholarship amplified through the megaphone of the Internet means more people hear these false claims—and often without refutation. One reason for this is very few scholars take these claims seriously. In this chapter, I aim to provide some refutation to a few bad ideas.

Black Hebrew Israelites Attack the Trinity

Black Hebrew Israelism is a religious movement consisting mainly of people of African-descent living in the Western

---

[9] Farrar, Moses, *Christianity: A False, Man-made Religion! The Hebrew Israelite Way: Ordained By The Creator*, (Elmont: African Tree Press, 2016), Kindle, 13.

hemisphere who believe they are the true descendants of the tribes of Israel over and against other "claimants" (their favorite targets are Ashkenazi Jews, whom they usually believe to be descendants of converts at best or outright frauds at worst). It is wildly diverse in beliefs and structures, but the central unifying thesis is each adherent believes they are in some way a blood descendant of Jacob. I have written an introductory book on their history and doctrine.[10] In my time studying their sources, I have never heard of any adherent affirming belief in the Trinity. I have seen them attack the doctrine though—a lot.

Some Black Hebrew Israelites ascribe nefarious sources towards the spread of the doctrine of the Trinity. As bizarre as it may sound, some Black Hebrew Israelite teachers accuse the US government of promulgating the doctrine of the Trinity. The teachers of the Israelite School of Biblical History and Practical Knowledge (ISBHPK), in a video titled *Trinity Exposed!* state the following about the Trinity:

> If we don't start putting a separation between all these new things, these engrafted things that these people are bringing into the Knowledge... they're not going to know... the difference. And... how diluted it's getting. And like I said, you know, I'm chalking it up as the Devil, I'm chalking it up as the Wicked One because it can't be our brothers. There's no way it could be our brothers bringing up this madness. It's got to be the Devil engrafting in the FBI and dividing. Because our brothers, our true brothers in Christ—they would know: God is not the author of confusion. You didn't learn that, why are you teaching that? Why are you coming up with these doctrines that

---

[10] Malone, Vocab, *Barack Obama vs The Black Hebrew Israelites: Introduction to the History & Beliefs of 1West Hebrew Israelism*, (Scottsdale: BookPatch, 2017).

don't got nothing to do with what the Bible is saying?[11]

Maybe it's true? Maybe the FBI *is* the ultimate promulgator of the Trinity doctrine in the black community! After all, there are three letters in the acronym FBI, aren't there? What, you think that's a coincidence? No, we all know the wicked government never does anything by accident... it's part of a plan to make you believe in the Trinity. They try to get you to start thinking in threes. U-S-A. Now that I think of it, maybe the CIA is involved, too!

Hopefully, you've caught on that the above paragraph is satire. If not, I assure you it is satire. I am not claiming all adherents to Hebrew Israelism think this way. But I am pointing out via lampooning that many of the new alternative urban spiritualities, Hebrew Israelism included, operate on the assumption of anti-establishmentarianism. I believe this axiom is one reason for their growth, as more people think in this vein and are therefore more open to what would traditionally be considered outlandish conspiracy theories. To be sure, we live in an age of epistemological fog.

Is the Trinity...White?

This next one is the least coherent and most bigoted Black Hebrew Israelite attack on the Trinity I will share. Please note, I am reproducing the author's work exactly as he wrote it in his book; mistakes, typos, caps lock, and all:

IT WAS THE SATANIC SODOMITE DOMINATED EDOMITE-(CAUCASIAN) CONTROLLED ROMAN CATHOLIC CHURCH THAT CREATED THE FALSE HOMOSEXUAL (TRINITY) OF THE HOLY GOD HEAD

---

[11] 2014. "Trinity Exposed,"
Israelite School of Biblical History and Practical Knowledge,
https://youtu.be/fScK5-DFZPY. Accessed 3/5/18.

BEING 3 MALE FIGURES. THIS IS BLASPHEMY
AGAINST THE MOST HIGH AS HIS-(GOD
ALMIGHTY) GREAT IMAGE IS MALE, FEMALE AND
CHILD-(SON), YASHAYA CHRIST.[12]

Certainly, there is a lot there. I want to focus on the claim
that it was the "Caucasian controlled" church "that created" the
doctrine of the Trinity. Some Black Hebrew Israelites spread the
idea that Christians ripped off pagan ideas for the Trinity. For
example, one popular meme lays the Trinity at the sandals of
Nimrod. Other Black Hebrew Israelites indicate the Trinity is a
Roman, even "white" doctrine: the "Caucasian controlled" church
"created" the doctrine of the Trinity. When a 1West "Hebrew
Israelite" uses the slur "Edomite," it is code word for the so-called
white man, who is actually a red man like Esau, his father. A Black
Hebrew Israelite believes the children of Esau are Edomites and
Europeans are the modern-day descendants of the Edomites! In
their worldview, Edomites are "the devil of whom the Bible
speaks." Black Hebrew Israelites are not the only ones who paint
the doctrine of the Trinity in ethnic terms.

Some Afrocentric or "Conscious" authors do the same.
There are many varieties of Afrocentrism, including the Moors,
Egyptology, Kemetic Science, Five Percenters, and conscious
community adherents. Some of these groups emphasize the
connection of black peoples to Egypt or Africa or both. Others
desire to begin a new spirituality (which they see as a continuation)
based on their perception of the (supposed) ancient Egyptian (or
African) worldview, including a reconstructed version of their
religion. These groups engage in polemics against Christianity
which involve leveling charges of extreme borrowing or outright
rip-offs of other myths and/or true (?) ancient African/Egyptian

---

[12] Willis, J.R., *THE PROPHECIES: The Book of the Hebrew
Israelites*, (Y.C.I.K Productions Ltd., 2017), Kindle, loc. 5163-5165.

beliefs and practices. Let's look at one Afrocentric author and see what we find. In his 820-page book, The *Genesis of the Bible*, Shaka Saye Bambata Dolo writes several fallacious statements on the Trinity, many with a strange preoccupation with ethnicity or nationality (typos are original):

> One must understand that, the concept of the Trinity or the dogma of the Roman Cathelism, was established in Western Christianity around 325 A. D., by Emperor Constantine of the Greek Empire. There is no Biblical, Historical, and Cultural foundation for the Doctrine of the Holy Trinity. That means, Jesus Christ, as the Divine Son of God, and members of the Holy Trinity, is a false Doctrine without historical and cultural foundation.[13]

In the above quote, we see the charge repeated the that Trinity was "established" around 325 AD. Bambata Dolo claims "there is no Biblical, Historical, and Cultural foundation for the Doctrine of the Holy Trinity." This chapter demonstrates the opposite: there is indeed a historical foundation for the doctrine of the Trinity (the rest of this book establishes the biblical foundation for the doctrine of the Trinity). As far as a "cultural foundation," it is ambiguous what Bambata Dolo means, but his statement indicates the Trinity is a "foreign" concept of God for African peoples and therefore false.

> The people of Afrika do not believe in the teaching of the Trinity in which the Father, Son, and the Holy Ghost, are three distinct persons of a singular being who is God. The father and the son are not separate beings with separate consciousness. The Holy Ghost is not a conscious being,

---

[13] Bambata Dolo, Shaka Saye, *The Genesis of the Bible*. (Bloomington: AuthorHouse, 2012) Kindle, 227.

but the power of God in action.[14]

"The people of Afrika do not believe in the teaching of the Trinity..."? African people do not believe in the Trinity? When? In the first century? Now? The North African church was very important in the early church. Later, I will show African church men such as Tertullian and Origen who certainly believed in the Trinity. A quick visit to the modern Ethiopian Orthodox Church website indicates a strong belief in the Trinity.[15] What does it mean to say Africans do not believe in the Trinity? How can one even say what the people of one massive continent believe?

> As I said, "The Nicene Creed" laid down the foundation for Western Christianity and the concept of the Holy Trinity. The Nicene Council in 325 A.D. Laid down the foundation of Western Christianity as a white Religion, of Polytheism, consisting of three Gods, God, the Father, God, the Son, and God, the Holy Spirit, as opposed to the Afrikan Religion of Monotheism in which there is only One God who expresses Himself in all of His creations.[16]

The third quote indicates a major misunderstanding of the early church and what happened at the Council of Nicaea. Let us focus on the most racist and ridiculous part: "The Nicene Council ... laid down the foundation of Western Christianity as a white religion..." A ... "white religion?" What is meant by this? In what way was Nicaea or Christianity "white?"

This quote deserves a brief refutation before we move onto

---

[14] Ibid., 92.

[15] 2003. "The Faith of the Church," *The Ethiopian Orthodox Tewahedo Church Faith and Order*, http://www.ethiopianorthodox.org/english/dogma/faith.html#trinity. Accessed 3/5/18.

[16] Bambata Dolo, *The Genesis of the Bible*, 611.

the next quote. Many Bishops from non-Western churches were at Nicaea. In fact, Egypt was the epicenter of the whole Arian controversy (for which the council was called). After Nicaea examined Arianism in light of Scripture and rightfully saw it to be an unbiblical teaching on the nature of Christ, letters were sent out to various churches. Here are two excerpts from the letter sent from the Council of Nicaea to Alexandria and Egypt:

> To the holy, by the grace of God, and great church of the Alexandrians, and to our beloved brethren throughout Egypt, Libya, and Pentapolis, the bishops assembled at Nicea, constituting the great and holy synod, send greeting in the Lord.

Notice the church in Alexandria and all of Egypt is mentioned, as well as Libya and Pentapolis (now northeastern modern Libya). Furthermore, in the quote below you will see the Council recognizing Egypt and Bishop Alexander's significance:

> These are the things which especially affect Egypt and the most holy church of the Alexandrians. If any other canon or ordinance has been established, our lord and most-honored fellow-minister and brother Alexander, being present with us, will on his return to you enter into more minute details, inasmuch as he has been a participant in whatever is transacted and has had the principal direction of it.[17]

The primary source documents do not lead us to believe there was anything "white" about the early church, Nicaea, or the doctrine of the Trinity. Bambata Dolo has four more quotes I want to reproduce and interact with here:

---

[17] *Ecclesiastical History of Socrates Scholasticus* I:9.

The Afrikan Christians questioned the divinity of a man born by a woman, being defined as God, or equal to God, God, the Father, God the Son, and God, the Holy Spirit. This doctrine came to be known as "the Doctrine of the Holy Trinity" in Western Christianity.[18]

The problem with many books like these is they make sweeping claims about historical events without proper documentation. Church history is not in the top #trending topics on Twitter. Needless to say, not many people, whether Christian or not, are familiar with early church history, especially in specific regions such as Africa. What is the truth? In short:

Yet from the start of African Christianity, the Trinity was an African Christian doctrine. The Ethiopian church accepted the same doctrines as the North African, Greek, and Roman churches, doctrines formally recognized at Nicaea (A.D. 325), Constantinople (381) and Ephesus (431). East African Christians maintained close relationships with Egyptian and Syrian Christianity and functioned as part of the Eastern church.[19]

Furthermore:

North African theologians like Tertullian and Athanasius were among the foremost defenders of the orthodox faith in early Christianity (though many Gnostics and Arians also taught in that region). Ethiopian Christians continued to praise Father, son, and Holy Spirit. [20]

---

[18] Bambata Dolo, *The Genesis of the Bible*, 714.

[19] Keener, Craig S., Usry, Glenn, *Defending Black Faith: Answers to Tough Questions About African-American Christianity.* (Downers Grove: IVP, 1997), 51.

[20] Ibid., 182. E.g., Emperor Amda Tseyon, in Pankhurst 1967: 20,

The Trinity was never a white or Western doctrine; it was not something one rejected because they were black or African; rather, the doctrine of the Trinity is and was something an ancient Christian believed in if they believed in the Old and New Testaments as Sacred Writ. Continuing with Bambata Dolo:

> The Western Christians concept of the Holy Trinity is therefore, the concept of Polytheism, as opposed to the Afrikan Monotheism of the Pharaoh, Akhenaten of ancient Egypt, North Afrika.[21]

This claim not only contradicts the evidence, it contradicts other Afrocentric writers! Describing Egyptian religion as monotheistic is inaccurate and the phrase "Afrikan Monotheism of the Pharaoh Akhenaten" is problematic, to say the least. Akhenaten's temporary reforms were more akin to monolatry or henotheism, not monotheism proper. He was identified as a "heretic" by the ancient Egyptians themselves, and his reforms were turned back after his reign ceased. To use Pharaoh Akhenaten as a spring board into the dubious phrase "Afrikan Monotheism" is shamefully irresponsible. Even if Pharaoh Akhenaten was a true monotheist, the author is plucking one anomaly out of a sea of Egyptian polytheism.

The writer claims the concept of the Trinity is polytheistic. Trinitarianism is by definition a species of monotheism—it is not tritheism, it is not polytheistic, it is a form of monotheism. A core conviction of trinitarianism is that there is only one God and the one true God is a Triune God.

The concept of The Western Christian Holy Trinity, is a

25.

[21] Bambata Dolo, *The Genesis of the Bible*, 716.

false Doctrine created by man, and not by God. It is found nowhere in the original manuscripts from Afrika.[22]

What is this writer's authority to tell us the Trinity is a man-made doctrine? What are "the original manuscripts from Afrika"?

The Nicene Council created three Godheads in 325 A. D. in Western Christianity, a myth, Professor Aries, who was a Bishop in North Afrika, argued his objection to the Europeans' Creed of the Trinity...[23]

Three "Godheads?" Since when was Arius a professor? Well, I guess he did profess heresy. The main opponent of Arius was an actual African bishop, Alexander of Alexandria. The main defender of Nicene orthodoxy was Alexander's successor, Athanasius of Alexandria. Alexandria is in Egypt, and Egypt is in Africa, not Europe. Even Nicaea itself was in Asia Minor, modern day Iznik in Turkey. Again, not Europe. As the kids say, IJS LOL ("I'm just sayin" and "laugh out loud").

Is the Trinity...African?

In contrast to the Black Hebrew Israelites who sometimes say the Trinity is a European invention, some Afrocentric authors claim the Trinity is African. Afrocentric writers influence many subgroups (Kemets, Moors, Nation of Islam, Five Percenters and even certain Black Hebrew Israelites) online and in urban communities. Two such Afrocentric writers are Diop and Boyd, both of whom claim African spirituality and thought are the background for Trinity.[24] Writers like these (and their followers) go

---

[22] Ibid., 726.
[23] Ibid., 729.
[24] Diop, Cheikh Anta, *The African Origin of Civilization: Myth or*

searching though polytheistic pantheons which had three primary deities (others had two, others had more) and claim parallel faster than The Flash when he's generating lightning. To use an illustration, imagine picking only three puppies out of the 101 Dalmatians, setting them in a separate group, and then declaring, "CERBERUS"! However, none of these pantheons had only three deities, though. I can do no better than long quote Keener and Usry's note:

> Ancient Egyptian literature emphasized a number of gods, not just a triad, and writers select three in particular to make the parallel, not because Egyptians typically thought only of three; cf., e.g., *Book of the Dead* 1974:5 (spell 1), 119 (spell 142, part S-4). Persians had also modified Zoroaster's one Ahura Mazda by adding the goddess Anahita and the popular god Mithra (Olmstead 1959: 423), but this temptation to add a mother-goddess is not part of the early Christian Trinity (although one was added in some later sectarian movements). The Persian addition of Anahita eventually accommodated other Persian views still more fully, making Ahura Mazda "again an eternal monarch with a harem full of mother-goddesses" (Olmstead 1959: 475); even during the stage where three main deities were prominent, many other deities remained alongside them (Olmstead 1959: 444). And in contrast to Egyptian formulas in which deities blended into one another (e.g., *Papyri Demoticae Magicae* 14.349, where one is both Ra and son of Ra), the New Testament never confuses or mingles Father and Son.[25]

Reality, trans. Cook, Mercer, (Chicago: Lawrence Hill Books, 1974), 194. Paul C. Boyd *A Biblical and Historical Account*. Vol. 1 of the *African Origin of Christianity*, (London: Karia Press, 1991), 57.

[25] Keener Usry, *Defending Black Faith*,182.

Logically, these arguments from supposed prior parallels fail anyway. Imagine there was some culture we discovered which had an authentic "pagan Trinity," this does not mean the biblical teaching is therefore false. It is not impossible that another religion taught something true! Yet, it is highly unlikely, as the Triune nature of God seems to be revealed specifically from special revelation.

Brief Bullet Points on the Biblical Basis for the Trinity
    The bulk of this chapter focuses on the discussion and/or affirmation of the Trinity within Ante-Nicene Christianity with a special emphasis on what early African-based Christians wrote on the doctrine of the Trinity. Prior to that, I am including a brief sketch of the biblical basis for the Trinity. Here are the foundational ideas drawn from Scripture which lead us to affirm our God is Triune:

- Monotheism: Acts 17:24-29; 1 Cor 8:4-6; Gal 3:20.

- The person and deity of the Father: 1 Cor 8:6; Gal 1:3; 1 Thess 3:11; 1 Tim 2:5-6; 2 Tim 4:1; 2 John 3.3

- Jesus Christ is the unique Son of God: Matt 16:16; Rom1:2-4; Heb 1:1-3.

- The person and deity of the Son: Mark 2:7; John 1:1, 18; 8:58; 20:28; Col 2:9; Titus 2:13; Heb 1:8-10.

- The person and deity of the Holy Spirit: John 7:39, 14-16; Rom 8:9, 14; 2 Cor 3:17-18.

- One God who is three distinct persons—Trinity: Matt 28:19; Eph 4:4-6; 1 Cor 12:4-6; 2 Cor 13:14; 1 Peter 1:2.

Trinitarian Rumblings in the Apostolic Ante-Nicene Era

Discussions of the relationship between the Father, Son, and Spirit are replete in Ante-Nicene church letters and liturgy. One does not have to dig or stretch. This is not to deny any development as new vocabulary emerged and sophistication increased. But the foundation was Scriptural. "The early church affirmed belief in one and only one God," affirms church historian Gregg Allison, and yet "the early church developed a 'Trinitarian' consciousness, noting the relationships between the Father, the Son, and the Holy Spirit."[26]

Although later I highlight non-European (surely an anachronism) based authors due to the specific nature of this chapter, there are some early Christian authors I would be remiss to not include. The reason? If the doctrine of the Trinity was invented at Nicaea, we should not discover any Triune talk prior to Nicaea, would we? Yet, we do. Plenty. Here are some:

Clement of Rome (died circa 99 AD)

From Clement's writings, we can discern some of his theology. It is clear, for example, he believes that the Father, the Son, and the Holy Spirit are distinct persons. Clement differentiates between the three persons in several passages: "Have we not one God, and one Christ, and one Spirit of grace poured upon us"?[27] Here is another example of a clearly Trinitarian passage found in Clement:

For as God lives, and the Lord Jesus Christ lives, and the

---

[26] Allison, Gregg R., *Historical Theology: An Introduction to Christian Doctrine* (Grand Rapids: Zondervan, 2011), 232.

[27] *1 Clement*, 46, 6.

Holy Spirit, who are the faith and hope of the chosen ones—the one who in humility of mind, with extended gentleness, without regret has done the ordinances and commandments given by God, this one will be enrolled and given a name among the number of the saved through Jesus Christ, through whom is the glory unto him for ever and ever, amen.[28]

Ignatius of Antioch (died circa 107 AD)

Ignatius holds to the virgin conception and refers to Jesus as "our God." He writes of the three persons as distinct and yet all playing a role in the advent of Christ.

For our God, Jesus the Christ, was conceived by Mary according to a dispensation of God, from the seed of David, yes, but of the Holy Spirit as well.[29]

In yet another trinitarian passage, Ignatius notes the unified work of all three persons regarding salvific activity:

You being stones of a temple, prepared before as a building of God the Father, being raised up to the heights through the mechanism of Jesus Christ, which is the cross, and using as a rope the Holy Spirit ...[30]

Athenagoras of Athens (133-190 AD)

Athenagoras is another apologist who needs to be included because he is considered the first writer to offer a rational apologetic for the doctrine of the Trinity. For example, he writes of "God the Father, God the Son, and the Holy Spirit" in his *Embassy*

---

[28] *1 Clement*, 58.

[29] *Ephesians* 18.

[30] *Ephesians* 9.

for the Christians (177 AD). He insists Christians "proclaim both their powers in their unity and their diversity in rank" (6.1) and the three are "united in power yet distinguished in rank" (10.5).[31] His writings also include a defense for the Christian doctrine of the unity of God.

Irenaeus of Lyon (born circa 120 AD, died circa 200 AD)
    Originally from Smyrna, he studied at Rome and then became Bishop of Lyon. In his treatise entitled *Demonstration of Apostolic Preaching*, Irenaeus includes contemporaneous catechetical instruction, which includes the following phrases:

- God the Father, not made, not material, invisible; one God, the Creator of all things…
- The Word of God, Son of God, Christ Jesus our Lord.
- The Holy Spirit, through whom the prophets prophesied, and the fathers learned the things of God, and the righteous were led into the way of righteousness.

Each person is introduced with the formulaic phrase: "this is the first/second/third point of our faith". Even the structure is threefold. One author summarizes Irenaeus' theology of God this way:

> For Irenaeus the Son is fully divine (Dem. 7), as is the Spirit (Her. 5.12.2). Thus Irenaeus progressed beyond the Apologists in a fuller recognition of the place of the Spirit in his idea of economy. Still he is clearly a second-century theologian as his picture of the Trinity discloses.[32]

---

[31] Grant, Robert M., *Greek Apologists of the Second Century* (Philadelphia: The Westminster Press, 1988), 109.
[32] Rusch, William G., *The Trinitarian Controversy,* Sources of Early

Jason (flourished circa 140-160 AD)

The body of literature designated as *Contra Iudaeos* is primarily filled with Christians arguing the Messiahship of Jesus based on fulfillment of Old Testament prophecy. Other topics demarcating the differences between Christianity and Judaism are discussed in this literature, sometimes via dialogues.

Within this genre of Christian literature lies a lesser known Latin translation of a Greek original, *The Dialogue of Jason and Papiscus.*[33] The work is commonly dated around 140 AD and was possibly composed by Aristo of Pella.[34] The full text is not extant, but we possess enough information to know the featured Christian is Jewish.[35] Celsus Africanus described the non-Christian Jew in the dialogue, Papiscus, as an Alexandrian.

There are a few references to this work by early Christian writers (Tertullian, Jerome, and Bishop Vigilius) but only a few excerpts remain extant. This author and work are included not as evidence for early belief in the Trinity. This inclusion is to show

---

Christian Thought, (Philadelphia: Fortress Press, 1980), 7.

[33] Clement of Alexandria believed the Jason of *The Dialogue of Jason and Papiscus* is the same Jason of Thessalonica in Acts 17:1-9. Clement's statement about this is said to come from his now lost *Hypotyposeis*. This is according to John of Scythopolis' *Notes on the Mystic Theology of the Areopagite*. John of Scythopolis is sometimes mistakenly referred to as Maximus the Confessor in older scholarship. For more information, see Tolley, Harry, 2012. "Clement of Alexandria's Reference to Luke the Evangelist as author of The Dialogue of Jason and Papiscus," *The Journal of Theological Studies*, 63.2 and Varner, William, *On the Trail of Trypho: Two Fragmentary Jewish-Christian Dialgoues from the Ancient Church*, (Leiden: Brill, 2012) 553-565.

[34] John of Scythopolis, writing in the sixth century, attributes the work to Aristo of Pella.

[35] Celsus Africanus calls Jason a *Hebraeus Christianus* in his *Letter to Viglius Concerning Jewish Unbelief* 8.

that Jewish Christians were still part of the early church and even arguing for things like the deity of Christ against other (non-Christian) Jews. If Christianity was "Europeanized" or "whitewashed," there should be a trail of evidence of when this happened. Jason is not a Gentile and yet, here he is, doing evangelistic apologetics!

Justin Martyr (died circa 163-167 AD)

A man born in Samaria at Flavia Neapolis (Shechem). His parents were Greek-speaking Romans and he called himself a Samaritan in his *Dialogue* (120.6). In his *1 Apol.* 13.3 and 60.6-7, Justin explicitly spoke of three divine persons. Also, Justin characterized the Matthean baptismal formula this way:

> In the name of God, the Father and Lord of the Universe, and of our Savior Jesus Christ, and of the Holy Spirit, they then receive the washing with water.[36]

Theophilus of Anitoch (died circa 183-185 AD)

From what we know, the Greek apologist Theophilus was the first Christian writer to use *trias* (τριάς), translated as "triad" in his commentary on Genesis 1-3:

> In like manner also the three days which were before the luminaries, are types of the Trinity, of God, and His Word, and His wisdom. And the fourth is the type of man, who needs light, that so there may be God, the Word, wisdom, man.[37]

Sabellius the Libyan (flourished circa 215 AD)

As the early church strived to tease out the implications of

---

[36] Justin Martyr, *First Apology*, 61.

[37] Theophilus, *Apologia ad Autolycum*, Book II, Chapter 15.

Scriptural teaching on the three persons of God, heresies arose. Sabellius was an African thinker who tried to define God as three modes (sometimes called aspects or energies). This line of thinking was rightfully condemned at Nicaea (and before that by men like Bishop Alexander of Alexandria).

The reason I include Sabellius here is *not* because he was orthodox. I include Sabellius because he was from the African continent and even his heresy is closer to orthodoxy than most Black Hebrew Israelites. Christian writer Epiphanius quoted followers of Sabellius asking this question: "Do we have one God or three"?[38] Sabellius himself was quoted saying this: "As there are 'diversities of gifts, but the same Spirit,' so also the Father is the same, but is expanded into Son and Spirit."[39] A later Sabellian, Marcellus, argued against the orthodox formulation, protesting that "it is impossible for three existing hypostases to be united by a monad unless previously the trinity has its origin from the monad."[40] At least Sabellius recognized the category of three, even if he attempted to define it incorrectly. It is also noteworthy that when most Black Hebrew Israelites define the Trinity, they do so usually according to Sabellianism, not orthodox trinitarianism.[41]

Novatian of Rome (200-258 AD)

Novatian wrote the first treatise on the Trinity, aptly titled, *On the Trinity*. In this work, Novatian affirmed the eternality of the Son (16; 31).

Dionysius of Alexandria (active circa 230-265 AD)

Dionysius of Alexandria, in an exchange with Dionysius of

---

[38] Epiphanius, *Adversus Haereses* 62.2.6 (GCS 31:391).

[39] Ps. Ath. *Ar.* 4.25 (PG 26:505).

[40] Marcellus, fragment 66 (GCS 14:197).

[41] Here is one example of many: "The Christian Doctrine of the Trinity is a Lie!!! Christ is not God," *ISUPK Texas*, https://youtu.be/ZaLTUSwMYDk. Accessed 3/22/18.

Rome, insisted on three distinct *hypostases* (the etymological equivalent of the Greek *hypostasis* was the Latin *substantia*).[42] This was viewed as a refutation for the heresy of Sabellian Monarchianism that took place around 260 AD. Athanasius of Alexandria[43] wrote about these exchanges, defending Dionysius of Alexandria against the charge of Arianism.

A Brief Word on Ante-Nicene African Christianity

The first Christian catechetical school was in Alexandria, Egypt, founded around 179-180 AD. The first teacher at the catechetical school of Alexandria was Pantaenus (died *circa* 216 AD). He was a convert from Stoicism. His most well-known student, Clement of Alexandria, dubbed him the "Sicilian bee."[44] It seems likely that he was from Sicily, Italy.

This chapter deals with biblical Christian doctrine and early church history with a focus on the geographical region of North Africa. It must be noted we do not know for certain the ethnic identity or physical features of most early Christians, including the writers mentioned here. In most discussions on church history, this would be considered a non-question, but due to the specific attacks focusing partially on ethnicity from the urban cults, it is prudent to briefly discuss it here. For example, we know for a fact that early Christianity was incredibly diverse. A snapshot into Clement of Alexandria's life is illustrative of this truth.

Clement of Alexandria (150-215 AD)

Clement (Titus Flavius Clemens) was an Athenian. Yet he wound up teaching Christians from all over at a school in Egypt. He describes his journey to find Christ this way, "having traced

---

[42] Rusch, William G., *The Trinitarian Controversy,* Sources of Early Christian Thought, (Philadelphia: Fortress Press, 1980), 16.

[43] *On the Opinion of Dionysius* (*De Sententi Dionysii*).

[44] Clement of Alexandria, *Stromata*, 1.1.

him out concealed in Egypt, I found rest."[45] His teacher at the Alexandrian school was Pantaenus. Pantaenus left the Alexandrian school to be a missionary to India around 189-190 AD. Eusebius writes that Pantaenus met Jewish Christians who read Hebrew—in India.[46]

In the beginning of Clement's *Stromata*, he tells readers he is partially writing so he won't forget what he was taught. Then he mentions some of the Christian mentors who poured knowledge into him. He speaks of "animated discourses which I was privileged to hear, and of blessed and truly remarkable men." Then, he speaks briefly about these remarkable men and mentions their places of origin: "Of these the one, in Greece, an Ionic; the other in Magan Graecia: the first of these from Coele-Syria, the second from Egypt, and others in the East. The one was born in the land of Assyria, and the other a Hebrew in Palestine."[47] This means he had mentors from (modern day) Greece (an Ionic), Southern Italy (Magan Graecia), Syria (Coele-Syria, which also included parts of modern Lebanon and Israel), Egypt, Iraq (Assyria), and Jewish (Hebrew in Palestine). What a truly diverse array of characters! Additionally, we know Clement left Alexandria and headed to Jerusalem, Israel, until his death around 215 AD.

Tertullian (born circa 155-160 AD, died circa 220-240 AD)

Tertullian, possibly the son of a Roman soldier, was said to have been born around 160 AD, and was thought to have died after a long life. Traditionally, it was thought he practiced law in Rome.[48] There is evidence the biographical material handed down to us by Eusebius and Jerome is accurate but these traditional biographical details have been called into question by some

---

[45] Clement, *Stromata*, 1.1.

[46] Eusebius, *Ecclesiastical History*, V, 10.

[47] Clement, *Stromata*, 1.1.

[48] Some scholars now argue he was not a legal expert (*jurist*) but rather a trained rhetorician who argued cases (*advocate*).

classical scholars.[49] Regardless, Tertullian left paganism, converted to Christianity, and may have become a presbyter in Carthage (near modern Tunis) in what is now Tunisia in North Africa.

Tertullian was the first Christian author (whose work we have) who wrote a treatise about the Trinity. His work on the Trinity laid the groundwork for almost all subsequent discussions on the Trinity. His well-known definition of the doctrine of the Trinity is as follows:

> All of them are One, by unity of substance; while we still keep the mystery of the distribution which spreads the Unity into a Trinity, placing in their order the three persons—the Father, the Son, and the Holy Spirit. But they are three, not in state, but in degree; not in substance, but in form; not in power, but in appearance; yet of one substance, and of one state, and of one power, inasmuch as he is one God, from whom these degrees and forms and appearances are understood, under the name of the Father, and of the Son, and of the Holy Spirit. [50]

Tertullian, writing in Latin, applied the word *trinitas* to God for the first time (from what we know). Tertullian is also the first early Christian writer to speak of the members of the Trinity as "persons." According to Charles Lowry, the established technical usage of *person* is "a permanent, individual mode or manner of Divine existence" and *substance* is usually defined as "a concrete being, including both the sum of attributes and the unique principle of individuality."[51] Ostensibly, the Latin word *persona*

---

[49] Barnes, Timothy David, *Tertullian: A Historical and Literary Study*, (London: Oxford, 1985) and Rankin, David Ivan, 1997. "Was Tertullian a Jurist?" *Studia Patristica*, 31, 335-342.

[50] *Against Praxeas 2.*

[51] Lowry Charles W., *The Trinity and Christian Devotion*, (New York: Harper and Brothers, 1946), 81-82.

contains fewer potential misunderstandings than our English word *person*. Gordon Fee explains: "Our term 'Person' causes all kinds of difficulties, partly because it stems from a Latin word that does not carry all the baggage that our word does."[52] 'Trinity,' 'person,' 'substance:' we still use these words and concepts, as they probably are the best English words to capture the biblical concept and teaching, we just have to exercise due diligence and explain what we mean—and do not mean—when we employ them. Leaving English and returning to Tertullian, he was also the first (from what we know) to speak of the their (Father, Son, Spirit) unity as "substance."[53]

Christian theologians still rightfully use this terminology today. *Substance* (*substantia* in Latin) refers to the essential

---

[52] Fee, Gordon D. *Paul, the Spirit, and the People of God*, (Peabody: Hendrickson, 1996), 47.

[53] The term "substance" (Latin: *substantia* or Greek: *ousia*) is tricky. It is traditionally used to refer to both the essence of a thing or a particular thing. Joe and Mary and Tom all share the human essence and, share the same substance; but Joe, Mary, and Tom are also three discrete substances. Humanness is their essence, or secondary substance; whereas Joe, Mary, and Tom are particular humans, which are primary substances. Trinitarian thinkers often bounce between these concepts, or blur them, in order to speak of the Trinity.

In Tertullian, the essence is, in fact, the Father. The Son and Spirit have the Father in them as that essence; just as you and I share humanness. In our modern way of thinking, we consider that you and I just have a sort of similarity, but in the ancient way of thinking, you and I literally have the same metaphysical "stuff"—namely humanness—in us. Imagine a fluid that flows through both of us, making us humans. That's the human essence. By the same token, for Tertullian, the Father flows through the Son and Spirit, who we experience in our world. So that's why Jesus says, "When you've seen me you've seen the Father." It would be like me saying, "When you've seen me, you've seen humanness." I exemplify it.

I am indebted to Moody Bible Inst. Professor Sanjay Merchant for providing the "essence" of this explanatory footnote.

qualities of a thing. The thing must have these qualities for it to be what it is; if it does not have these qualities, then it would not be what it is. When Christians explain that the three persons of the Trinity share one substance, they mean that the three persons share the same essential qualities. The three persons are of the same kind; they are all God. Tertullian indicates this is a paradoxical complexity to the Bible's teaching on the Triune nature of God: he shows some ways in which Father, Son, and Spirit are three (degree, form, appearance), and other ways in which they are one (substance, state, power).

It must always be remembered that trinitarianism is monotheism. This means Christians intend, by definition, to speak of one *and only one* God. True, trinitarianism is not *unitarian* monotheism; but rather *trinitarian* monotheism. To put it plainly: do not let the fact that Christians speak of three persons (because they believe it is biblically necessitated) cause anyone to forget that Christians (as trinitarian monotheists) are still only speaking of one God.

Remembering this truth, we should recognize another shade of meaning of "substance"—as having a legal meaning equivalent to "property." When Tertullian writes the three persons share "substance," he suggests a very intimate relationship between Father, Son, and Holy Spirit. The one being who is God is comprised of three persons—and these three persons share everything in common: "of one substance, and of one state, and of one power, inasmuch as he is one God." After Nicaea, the Cappadocian Fathers explained how the principle of the three sharing everything in common extended to their work.[54]

Tertullian was a bold thinker. This can be seen in the imagery he draws from to argue for the possibility of the Trinity:

---

[54] Toon, Peter, Spiceland, James D. Eds., *One God in Trinity: An Analysis of the Primary Dogma of Christianity*, (Westchester: Cornerstone Books, 1980), 58.

I should not hesitate to call the tree the son or offspring of the root, and the river the son of the fountain, and the ray the son of the sun; because every original source is a parent, and everything which comes from the origin is an offspring. And this is even more true of the word of God, who is actually called Son as his own name. But still the tree is not severed from the root, nor the river from the fountain, nor the ray from the sun; nor, indeed, is the Word separated from God. ... Now the Spirit is third from God and the Son; just as the fruit of the tree is third from the root, or as the stream out of the river is third from the fountain, or as the apex of the ray is third from the sun. But nothing is different in character from its original source. In the same way, the Trinity, flowing down from the Father through intertwined and connected steps, does not at all disturb the monarchy.[55]

Tertullian uses "monarchy" to describe the unity of the rule of Father, Son, and Spirit, for Yahweh is King. Tertullian also uses examples in creation where three things are observed as being distinct and yet unified. The tree is joined to the root, the fountain is inseparable from the river. Likewise, with the Word. He extends the imagery even further when he adds the additional ideas of fruit and stream, respectively. Likewise, with the Spirit.

Tertullian also uses the sun being the origin of the light ray as an analogy for the Father being the point of origin for the Son and Spirit's divinity. In Tertullian's thought, the Son and Spirit are divine because they "originate" from the Father. When seen in early Christian writers (for example, Justin Martyr and Origen), this is sometimes called "Logos theology."

Looking back throughout church history, this idea has been

---

[55] *Against Praxeas 8.*

present in several discussions on the Trinity. "Before Nicaea," writes Robert Grant, "Christian theology was almost universally subordinationist. Theology almost universally taught that the Son was subordinate to the Father"....[56] After Nicaea, it is a minority view, however, and is sometimes referred to as "subordinationism". *Subordinationism* can contain the idea that the Son is subordinate or secondary to the Father in some way. Western "Christendom" has sometimes viewed Eastern Orthodox Christology as a form of subordinationism, although the *Revised Catechism of the Orthodox Faith* denies this charge (Question 95). Within modern day evangelicalism, recent debates have centered on the Eternal Subordination of the Son. This debate has been complicated by the potentially related matters of complementarianism and egalitarianism. To be fair, advocates for the Eternal Subordination of the Son state their view should be distinguished from subordinationism.[57]

The reason I mention the above is to show that Christians have had to reflect in a mature and balanced way upon the biblical texts (especially ones which speak of the nature of the relationship between the Son and the Father) in order to accurately portray the teaching of Scripture as well as some possible logical outcomes from these texts. Of course, it is unfair to put all those modern categories and questions upon Tertullian (or any other early Christian writer), however, as he was fighting different battles and using "fresh" words before they were filled up with subsequent meanings. In fact, Tertullian's stated goal in *Against Praxeas* was to dispel patripassianism and give the Paraclete his proper place.

Origen of Alexandria "The Iron Man" (born circa 185/6, died 251 AD)

---

[56] Grant, Robert M. *Gods and the One God*, (Philadelphia, PA: Westminster Press, 1986), 160.

[57] Kovach, Stephen D., Schemm Jr., Peter R., 1999. "A Defense of the Doctrine of the Eternal Subordination of the Son," *JETS*, 42.

Origen was born in Alexandria, Egypt to a Christian father named Leonides. In accordance with his name sake ("Bold Lion"), Origen's father was imprisoned and executed when the North African church was persecuted under Septimius Severus. To make matters worse, the government seized the family's property. This experience likely influenced Origen's thinking regarding pagan philosophy. While Origen was well versed in pagan thought, he saw it as antithetical to the Christian faith.

It is ironically evident that Origen (like all of us) never fully shook his cultural environs when he approached theology (he was influenced by Platonism, for example). Yet, Origen's thought displays a cautious attitude towards Greek philosophy. Evidence of this attitude is when Origen, now a young Christian instructor, sold all his books in order to study only the Scripture. Origen fasted frequently and embraced ascetic ideas.

Persecution flared up again, and some of his students in Alexandria were martyred. At times, he strove to become a martyr himself (he came close as a teenager until his mother intervened), at other times in his career, he was attacked and hunted by mobs and soldiers and had to flee from house to house. Through all this, he displayed extreme bravery and courage, hence, his nickname: *Origen Admantius* (implying he could not be broken). Origen even learned Hebrew from Jewish rabbis, something Christians of the era.

Eventually, Origen was tortured under Decius: He was stretched in stocks and burned with torture instruments. He was released and (as a result of the torture) died soon after in Tyre at 70 years old. This biographical information is included for the internet naysayers who claim Christians who advocated for the deity of Christ or the Trinity did so as agents of the Roman government.

If he's read in context, it's clear Origen recognized some of the challenges in understanding and articulating pneumatology and yet plainly stated, "The apostles handed down the tradition that the Holy Spirit is associated with the Father and the Son in honor and rank."[58] This did not stop the brilliant Origen from Trinitarian speculation, as he speculated about the Father being the fount of ontology, the Son being the fount of rational thought, and the Holy Spirit being the fount of holiness.[59]

One author observes that "Origen's insight into the Christian understanding of God was of such a caliber that it was to have a lasting impact." Rusch has noted:

> Origen's greatest contribution—and here he decidedly moved beyond all his predecessors—was the teaching that the three (Father, Son and Holy Spirit) are of the eternal mode of God's being and not just determined or evoked by the needs of the economy.[60]

Relevant Irrelevant Funeral Drawings of Ancient Egyptians
Very rarely do we find extensive physical descriptions of early church fathers which would give us strong clues as to their ethnic background. Very rarely do we find direct and irrefutable evidence as to their ethnic lineage, either. However, we do have some idea of what some Egyptians from the first to third centuries looked like. Funerary portraits from 1st – 3rd century Roman Egypt display a diverse array of skin shades present in Egypt. Most could be described as light brown, muddy brown, or olive; some could be described as dark or black.

Normally, this information would be irrelevant to a discussion on the Trinity (technically, it still is irrelevant). But since some modern-day urban religions essentially distrust any information coming from fair-skinned people (thereby committing the genetic fallacy—pun intended), I am pointing this out since several the early Christians under discussion in this chapter are

---

[58] Origen, *On First Principles* (preface 4).
[59] Origen, *First Principles* (1.3.5-8).
[60] Rusch, William G., *The Trinitarian Controversy,* Sources of Early Christian Thought, (Philadelphia: Fortress Press, 1980), 15.

Egyptian or North African. The point: the Fayum mummy portraits give us some idea what the average person in this region in this era looked like, and they do not (generally speaking) look like stereotypical white Western Europeans.

Post-Nicene African Christians on the Trinity: Athanasius & Augustine

Athanasius (295-373 AD)

Athanasius was a North African from Alexandria, Egypt. He is associated with defending the deity of Christ over and against the errors of the Arians,[61] which is true enough. However, the common depiction of the victorious Athanasius facing off against Arius during the Council of Nicaea in front of the watching bishops isn't exactly correct. The more I've investigated this, it seems Athanasius was only a minor player at Nicaea. For example, Athanasius was an assistant to the main bishop involved with the initial Arian controversy, Alexander of Alexandria. This was the case until Alexander died in 328 AD, and then Athanasius

---

[61] In a dialogue I once had with a well-known Black Hebrew Israelite leader of the Sicarii camp, I was told that his group was more closely aligned to Arianism. Yet, even the heretical Arians were much closer to orthodoxy than the Sicarii, or any Black Hebrew Israelite camp. To see just how far off these groups are (Sicarii in particular), see two debates where they ridicule the deity of Christ and the concept of the Trinity: "Kdub & Brotha J vs Sicarii on the Nature of Christ (Is Jesus God)" and "Guerilla Hebrew vs. Ex IUIC Member Turned Christian on Trinity" (both videos can be found on YouTube, https://youtu.be/kQidV1CmGt4 and https://youtu.be/2QFR4OEFwaw, respectively. Accessed 5/5/2018). For example, some Arian groups were said to still baptize in the name of the Father and of the Son and of the Holy Spirit! See Gr. Naz. *Or.* 40.42 (PG 36: 417-20); Cyr. *Inc unigen.* (SC 97: 276). It is even reported some Arian groups utilized a revised version of the *Gloria Patri*: "Glory be to the Father through the Son in the Holy Spirit". How subtle is that? (This is according to *Didym. Trin.* 3.23 (PG 39: 928-29).

succeeded him as bishop of Alexandria. Only until after the Council of Nicaea, does Athanasius proceeded to vigorously fight in person and pen against Arianism. He was not a champion at Nicaea, per se, rather, he was the champion of Nicene orthodoxy…after Nicaea.[62]

He was alive, of course, before the Council of Nicaea in 325. Thus, in that sense he was Ante-Nicene. But we don't know much about him until after Nicaea, for that is when he became well known. Yet, in support of the rebuttal to various cults and religious groups which posit the Trinity was invented at Nicaea and/or a European/white doctrine, I quote Athanasius:

> The holy and blessed Triad is indivisible and one in Itself. When mention is made of the Father, the Word is also included, as also the Spirit Who is in the Son. If the Son is named, the Father is in the Son, and the Spirit is not outside the Word. For there is a single grace which is fulfilled from the Father through the Son in the Holy Spirit.

And again:

> There is then a Triad, holy and complete, confessed to be God in Father, Son and Holy Spirit, having nothing foreign or external mixed with it, nor composed of one that creates and one that is originated, but all creative; and it is consistent and in nature indivisible, and its activity is one. The Father does all things through the Word in the Holy Spirit. Thus, the unity of the holy Triad is preserved.[63]

---

[62] See Anatolios, Khaled, *The Early Church Fathers: Athanasius*, (New York: Routledge, 2004), 5ff.

[63] Athanasius, *Ad. Serapion* 1.28.

Augustine of Hippo (354-430 AD)

Augustine was born in North Africa, in a small town called Tagaste (or "Thagaste", now called Souk Ahras), a Numidian village in modern day Algeria. In *On the Trinity*, Augustine showed the doctrine of the Trinity from the Scriptures, including the Old Testament. He also argued the Trinity was the answer to metaphysical questions about motion and ontology.

Augustine developed a "quasi-identity" (see appendix) model of the Trinity in the late 4th and early 5th centuries that entirely avoids tritheism, which is the heretical doctrine that the divine persons are discrete gods. Augustine likened the Father to a personal being with the abilities to reason by means of his Son and love by means of his Spirit. There is no divine essence in Augustine's theology, per se. The Father is the divine particular, whereas the Son is like his relational trope of knowledge and the Spirit his relational trope of love. How, then, are the Father, Son, and Spirit individuals? Augustine was determined to avoid modalism, which is the heretical doctrine that the Father, Son, and Spirit are the same person under different names.

To help understand Augustine's model, first consider your self-concept. Although you know nearly everything about yourself, you do not know yourself completely. God the Father, however, knows himself perfectly. In fact, his self-concept, Augustine conjectured, is "evolved up" so as to constitute another person within God, like the "other person" when you talk to yourself. In God, the other person is not imaginary, but real. Similarly, God's love is evolved up in the person of the Spirit, such that his knowledge and love are eternally distinct, like friends rather than properties. Augustine broke Aristotle's categories by suggesting that the Son and Spirit are "subsistent relations:" self-referential relations that are also substances.[64]

---

[64] I am here indebted to Dr. Merchant for a helpful outline of Augustine's trinitarian model.

Conclusion

The real place to look for the background of the Trinity is not in Africa or Europe or any other patch of soil with a portion of people; no, the real place to look for the background of the Trinity is in the pages of Scripture.

Appendix: Early Models of the Trinity

Sanjay Merchant is a friend of mine as well as a philosophy and theology professor at Moody Bible Institute. After looking over this chapter, he provided me with an appendix which briefly introduces some of the early models of the Trinity.

Scripture teaches that (1) the Father is God, (2) the Son is God, (3) the Holy Spirit is God, (4) the Father is neither the Son nor Holy Spirit, (5) the Son is neither the Father nor Holy Spirit, (6) the Holy Spirit is neither the Father nor the Son, and (7) there is only one God. Teachings 1 through 3 indicate that the Father, Son, and Spirit are equally and fully divine. None is greater or lesser than another. Teachings 4 through 6 indicate that the Father, Son, and Spirit are individuals; that is, the Son is not simply the Father in another form, and so on. Finally, teaching 7 indicates that there is only one divine being. In response to the scriptural implication that the deity and individuation of the divine persons is consistent with monotheism, early theologians proposed doctrines of the Trinity so that Christians might simultaneously affirm teachings 1 through 7.

Theologians utilized philosophy, particularly Aristotle's categories, to provide a framework for the Trinity. Recall that Aristotle distinguished between particular things—like Peter, James, and John—and essences—like humanness, which Peter, James, and John share. While the apostles are equally, fully, and indistinguishably human, they are discrete beings—specifically, three men—individuated by unique tropes, including both physical

322

features and psychological dispositions. John is, say, 6 feet tall and Peter is 5 foot 9; or that Peter is irritable, and James is unfailingly patient.

The apostles, who share humanness, are discrete humans because of their unshared accidents, or tropes.

According to the earliest "quasi-creational model" of the Trinity, developed in the 3rd and early 4th centuries, the Father is similar to an essence— "Godness" or "divinity"—that the Son and Spirit instantiate as particulars. Tertullian and Athanasius compared the Father to the sun, emitting the Son like light—God's visible representation—and the Spirit like heat—God's felt presence. Just as we see and feel the sun by its light and heat, the Son and Spirit reveal the invisible God. Thus, the divine persons are as individuals as the sun, its radiance, and its calidity while remaining one thing. Where, after all does the sun end and the sunlight begin? And when has the sun existed without its light and heat? God is always Father, radiating or into the world through his Son and Spirit. Early theologians called these two modes of radiation "processions."

There are, however, two weaknesses of the quasi-creational model. First, the Son and Spirit, who derive from God the Father, are seemingly less than fully divine. Arius of Alexandria taught that the Father, who is the only God, created the Son and Spirit, contrary to teachings 2 and 3. Quasi-creational trinitarians rejected Arianism—after all, the sun does not create its light and heat—but struggled to articulate the fully deity of the Son and Spirit. How are the divinities of the Father, Son, and Spirit equal? Second, the Father is seemingly impersonal, like a divine stuff that the personal Son and Spirit possess. For these reasons, later theologians offered alternative theories of the Trinity.

According to the "quasi-generic" model of the late 4th century, the divine persons are particulars who share divinity, like Peter, James, and John share humanness. The New Testament depicts the Father, Son, and Spirit as equal and distinct persons.

But how are they, literally, one being as per teaching 7? Platonists count four discrete things between the form of divinity and the divine person. Aristotelians count three things, conjecturing that the divine essence flows through the divine persons like a shared liquid. Christians count one thing: God. The Cappadocian Fathers suggested that the Father, Son, and Spirit flow into one another, like statues of gold melting into one another, or torches coming together to form one light. Later theologians would call this concept "perichoresis."

THE AXIOM OF UNIPERSONALITY: EXAMINING UNITARIAN ARGUMENTS AGAINST THE TRINITY

Hiram R. Diaz III

What is The Axiom of Unipersonality?

When addressing the arguments of enemies of the Christian faith, it is necessary for us to examine their underlying presuppositions. This will help us understand how such arguments are constructed so that we can thoroughly deconstruct them, demonstrate their incoherence, and call those who propose them to repentance. This is the case whether our opponents are atheists, Muslims, or unitarian monotheists claiming to be Christians. By exposing the foundational presuppositions of our opponents' arguments, we are demonstrating that the conclusions arrived at via arguing from false presuppositions are false. Oftentimes the arguments of Christ's enemies simply unravel at the seams, for they rest upon false presuppositions.

Unitarian arguments against the doctrine of the Trinity, for instance, rest upon what can be called the axiom of unipersonality. The axiom states: "If x is an individual personal being then x is necessarily unipersonal." From this axiom, the unipersonality of God is deduced. The reasoning takes the following form:

1. If God is an individual personal being, then God is necessarily unipersonal.
2. God is an individual personal being.
3. Therefore, God is necessarily unipersonal.

The unitarian monotheist, building upon his deduced conclusion, subsequently presents a transitive argument against God's tripersonality. Robert L. Dabney summarizes the transitive argument as follows:

> ...let a. b. c. represent the persons, and x, the Godhead ; then a=x : b=x : c=x. Add, and we have a+b+c=3 x=x,) in the same sense...[1]

We can restate the argument as follows:

> If *a* is God and *b* is God and *c* is God, then *a=b=c*.
> trinitarians believe that *a* and *b* and *c* are God.
> Therefore, they believe that *a=b=c*.

God's unipersonality having been deduced from the axiom of unipersonality, the unitarian then attempts to deductively demonstrate that the doctrine of trinity incoherently posits that the three divine persons of the Godhead are distinct while simultaneously implying that they are really one and the same *person*.

Yet is the axiom of unipersonality revealed in Scripture? Is it even conformable to the overall teaching of Scripture? Is it true? If it is not, then should we accept the conclusion of the transitivity argument which is built upon it? The following article aims to show that the axiom of unipersonality, which functions as the foundational presupposition of nearly all unitarian arguments

---

[1] *Systematic Theology*, (Carlisle: Banner of Truth, 1985), 177-178.

against the tripersonality of God, is neither biblically derived nor conformable to the overall teaching of the Bible. In fact, implicit to the axiom of unipersonality is the assumption that God and his creatures comprise a univocal ontological order which can be called theistic metaphysical monism, or pantheism. Consequently, the axiom of unipersonality, as well the conclusions drawn from arguments using it, must be rejected as false.

The Creator/Creature Distinction

As explained above, the axiom of unipersonality states that if x is a personal individual being then x is necessarily unipersonal. What this implies is that all individual personal beings, including God, belong to a univocal ontological order. Post hoc argumentation meant to support to the axiom of unipersonality typically consists of appeals to the non-existence, among humans, of individual plural-personal beings, as well as Scriptural prooftexts seemingly suggesting that God, because he is an individual personal being, is unipersonal.[2] As James E. Dolezal notes, however, Scripture does not teach that "God and creatures are correlatives within a univocal [ontological] order."[3] Rather, as Creator "God is the sufficient reason for the world's existence and thus cannot be evaluated as if he stood together with it in the same order of being."[4] What obtains between the individual personal being of God and that of man is not a relation of structural identity, as the axiom of unipersonality implies, but one of analogy. Louis Berkhof explains:

> ...since man is created in the image of God, we learn to understand something of the personal life of God from the contemplation of personality as we know it in man. [Yet]

---

[2] This is a favorite argument of unitarian Anthony Buzzard.

[3] *God Without Parts: Divine Simplicity and the Metaphysics of God's Absoluteness*, (Eugene: Pickwick, 2011), xv.

[4] *God Without Parts*, xvi.

we should be careful... not to set up man's personality as a standard by which the personality of God must be measured. [For] the one outstanding difference between the two is that man is uni-personal, while God is tri-personal.[5]

Oddly enough, while most unitarians will readily acknowledge that much of Scripture's descriptive language about God must be understood analogically,[6] they are seemingly unable to keep this in mind when discussing the personal nature of God, consequently declaring the notion of individual plural-personality to be a logical impossibility.[7]

Yet man's inability to conceive of another kind of individual personal being (namely, individual tri-personal being) says nothing about whether or not God himself can be or is tri-personal. What can be known of God must be revealed by him in a manner that is accessible to the minds of men. He does this by accommodating himself to human limitations, a point which is given emphasis throughout the Scriptures via their use of anthropomorphic and anthropopathic language. God's seeming unipersonality, in other words, must be analyzed not according to the heuristic axioms of sinful men but the teaching of Scripture regarding the nature of God as ontologically distinct from all of his creation. Theology proper does not begin with an external source of information regarding the ontology of God and that of his creatures. Theology proper begins with, and is derived from, the Scriptures alone. And what is taught throughout the whole of the Bible is that there is no univocal ontological order which God and his creatures jointly occupy. There are two distinct ontological orders. The first is the Creator's ontological order, of which we

---

[5] *Systematic Theology*, (Grand Rapids: Eerdmans, 1996), 84.

[6] I.e. related, but differing meanings. I am not here employing Cornelius van Til's more radical doctrine of analogy, but that of Aquinas.

[7] This is also an instance of begging the question.

have analogies and can only faintly grasp. The second is the creature's ontological order, to which all created things belong.

Ontological Univocalism is Metaphysical Monism

In contradistinction to the Bible's clearly defined metaphysical dualism (here, meaning the dual ontological orders of Creator and creation) the axiom of unipersonality implies a monist metaphysics in which God and everything else form a single ontological unit. The fruit of this is not a full-blown pantheism, as is found in the Bhagavad Gita for instance, but something more akin to the graduated monism of Neoplatonism. Counterintuitively, it is the axiom meant to guard against supposedly false teachings about God (i.e. the Incarnation, the Trinity, *et al.*) which creaturizes God, erases his *sui generis* ontological status, and makes true monotheism impossible, seeing as all that exists would constitute a part of God.

The unitarian monotheist may wish to deny the axiom. This is a good idea, for it would (1.) deny that God and creatures are correlatives within a univocal ontological order, (2.) uphold the Creator-Creature distinction, and, thereby, (3.) eliminate the possibility of metaphysical monism. However, a denial of the axiom of unipersonality would simultaneously (1.) refute the belief that all individual personal beings are necessarily unipersonal, and (2.) reopen the possibility that unipersonality is impossible for God, seeing as he is ontologically other.[8] Abandoning the axiom of

---

[8]There have been, in fact, theologians who have argued that unipersonalism would be impossible for God, given that God's attributes are personal. For example, in his *Dogmatic Theology Vol I*, (New York: Scribner, 1889), 184-186, W.G.T. Shedd argues:

> "A subject [viz. God] without an object could not know. What is there to be known? Could not love. What is there to be loved? Could not rejoice. What is there to rejoice over?
>
> And the object cannot be the created universe. The infinite and

unipersonality would be undesirable for the unitarian, moreover, for it would render the transitive argument against God's tripersonality unsound and, therefore, false.

Theistic Metaphysical Monism Implies Pantheism: Some Concluding Remarks

Consistent unitarian monotheism, built on the assumed axiom of unipersonality, reduces God to merely another member of the

---

eternal object of God's infinite and eternal knowledge, love, and joy, cannot be His creation because this is neither eternal nor infinite. There was a time when the universe was not and if God's self-consciousness depended upon the universe, there was a time when He was neither self-conscious nor blessed. The objective God for the subjective God, therefore, must be very God of very God, begotten not made, the eternal Son of the eternal Father.

...In the Christian scheme of the Trinity, the media to self-consciousness are all within the divine essence, and are wholly separate from, and independent of, the finite universe of mind and matter. The divine nature has all the requisites to personality in its own trinal constitution. God makes use of His own eternal and primary essence, and not the secondary substance of the world, as the object from which to distinguish Himself, and thereby be self-knowing and self-communing. God distinguishes Himself from Himself, not from something that is not Himself. This latter [i.e. something that is not God, viz. anything that He has created] would yield consciousness only, not self-consciousness.

...The divine self-contemplation is the beholding and loving of one divine person by another divine person, and not God's beholding of the universe and loving and communing with it.... 'The first love of God the Father to the Son is that which we call ad intra, where the divine persons are the objects of each other's actings. The Father knows the Son, and the Son knows the Father; the Father loves the Son, and the son loves the Father; and so consequently of the Holy Ghost, the medium of all these actings' Owen, *Sacramental Discourse*, XXII.'"

ontological order comprised of everything. Lower creatures may be separated from him by a very large series of gradations, but they are not outside of him. Additionally, there are no perceptions, experiences, thoughts, words, or deeds that are attributable to either God alone or any part of his creation alone, for this would imply an ontological separation between Creator and Creature, and thereby eliminate the unitarian's axiom of unipersonality, reopening the possibility that unipersonalism is an impossibility for God, seeing as he would be ontologically "other," and demonstrating the unsoundness of the transitivity argument against God's tripersonality.

In summary, we have argued the following points.

1. If the axiom of unipersonality obtains, then the Creator-Creature distinction does not obtain.
2. If the Creator-Creature distinction does not obtain, then theistic metaphysical monism obtains.
3. If theistic metaphysical monism obtains, then monotheism does not obtain.
4. If theistic metaphysical monism obtains and monotheism does not, then pantheism obtains.

Ironically, the unitarian monotheist's axiom of unipersonality leads to pantheism. That is to say, the surface level creaturization of Yahweh observable in the axiom of unipersonality culminates in the full creaturization of Yahweh—he becomes not one thing among many but everything. Not only this, however, all that exists, everything, becomes him. Unitarian monotheists are left with a bipolar idolatry in which, on the one hand, the Creator is creaturized and, on the other hand, the Creation is deified.

In his wicked attempt to deny that God became a man in the incarnation of Christ, the unitarian implies that every *thing* is an incarnation of God. This should serve as a reminder to the reader that true monotheism is not arrived at via philosophical reflection but through the Scriptures alone. Man has been created in the image of God, given innate, intuitive knowledge of the fact of God's existence and attributes, but he has suppressed the truth in unrighteousness.[9] His mind is warped and cannot reason correctly about God and, thus, makes God and the creation a divine monad that has more in common with the speculative doctrines of the Neoplatonists than it does with the teaching of the Bible. May all who hold such a view be granted repentance for their idolatry. And may God the Father and the Son and the Holy Spirit be glorified.

---

[9] See Rom 1:18-32.

JESUS WAS A TRINITARIAN

Hiram R. Diaz III

Introduction

A precursory familiarity with unitarian[1] arguments against the deity of Christ will no doubt acquaint one with the following syllogism.

All Jews were strict monotheists.
Jesus was a Jew.
Therefore, Jesus was a strict monotheist.

This argument correctly identifies the Jews as monotheists, Jesus as a Jew, and, therefore, Jesus as a monotheist. Insofar as it does these things, it is not problematic. However, the argument uses the undefined modifier "strict" when describing monotheism, indicating that the kind of monotheism it is referring to is distinct from other forms of monotheism, especially trinitarian monotheism. Thus, it follows that *strict monotheism,* as the

---

[1] "Unitarian" in this chapter refers to any believer in unipersonal monotheism.

unitarian is using the phrase, is taken to mean *unipersonal monotheism* (hereafter, U^{mt})[2]. This presuppositional commitment to U^{mt} is what we have called the axiom of unipersonality,[3] the belief that "If x is an individual personal being, then x is necessarily unipersonal." With the axiom in place, the unitarian argues that since monotheism *is* U^{mt}, and Jesus was a monotheist, then it follows that he was a U^{mt}. A better reformulation of the above argument, then, would be the following —

> All Jews were U^{mt}.
> Jesus was a Jew.
> Therefore, Jesus was a U^{mt}.

This effectively draws a line between U^{mt} and whatever is $\neg(U^{mt})$, even those forms of $\neg(U^{mt})$ that are, in fact, monotheistic—such as trinitarianism. This is a deceptive move made by unitarians which attempts to force trinitarians to either identify Christ as a unitarian or a polytheist. And the deceptive nature of this argumentation is only heightened when an appeal is made to Scripture by the unitarian, for by emphasizing the Scripture's repeated stress on the ontological singularity of God (i.e. monotheism), he circularly argues that these are all proof of U^{mt}.

Perhaps the most used proof-text in this regard is Mark 12:28-34, wherein the Lord Jesus affirms the *Shema* of Deuteronomy 6:4-5, and further identifies his interlocutor's reaffirmation of the *Shema* as being a wise answer. Because Christ affirms this monotheistic creed and, more than this, reaffirms the creed as articulated by a Jewish interlocutor, and does not correct the scribe

---

[2] U^{mt} will signify either unitarian monotheism or unitarian monotheist depending on the context in which it appears.

[3] See *The Axiom of Unipersonality: Examining Unitarian Arguments Against God's Tripersonality* in this volume.

for his *strict* monotheism (the unitarian assumes), then it follows that Jesus was also a U^{mt}. The argument has a prima facie punch, but once the underlying assumptions made by the unitarian are revealed, and once the text of Scripture is read closely on its own terms, it quickly becomes apparent that the unitarian's argument is logically incoherent and biblically unjustifiable.

This chapter will make two broad argumentative moves. Firstly, it will refute the unitarian belief that being-person numerical identity is a necessary assumption, arguing that this is neither a necessity of logic nor of ontology. This will be further augmented by reference to the analogy of man, in which it is argued that the only analogy of God's personal-being that we have available to us in Scripture is the individual personal-being of man, and this individual personal-being of man is never completely isolated. Humans, rather, are revealed to be members of a plurality of either actual or virtual persons who are in communicative exchanges with one another. Following this, a brief examination of the divine singular-plural self-reference dialectic will be presented, in which it will be shown that the Godhead uses singular and plural personal pronouns interchangeably in Scripture.

Secondly, this chapter will offer a close reading of Mark 12:28-34, in its larger context, in which it will be demonstrated that neither Jesus' affirmation of the *Shema*, nor his affirmation of the wisdom of the scribe he interacts with, are affirmations of U^{mt}. Having already touched upon the axiom of unipersonality and its relation to the unitarian's argument that Jesus was a U^{mt}, the remainder of this chapter will further analyze the unitarian's misappropriation of Mark 12:28-34 in defense of U^{mt}. Negatively, it will be argued that the unitarian's interpretation of this passage is not merely incorrect, but impossible. Positively, it will be argued that the passage in question actually presents Jesus as a trinitarian monotheist.

§ I. *Being-Person Numerical Identity is Not a Necessary Assumption*

As we begin our study, we must note that the axiom of unipersonality implies being-person numerical identity. If every individual personal being is necessarily unipersonal, in other words, it follows that being-person numerical identity is a necessary assumption we must make when considering the nature of individual personal being. Yet this is contradicted by the phrase "personal being" itself, which implies a logical distinction between a being and the *personal* way in which it exists. While all personal-beings are beings, not all beings are personal. There is, therefore, a necessary logical distinction that must be made between a *being* and its *personhood* (i.e. that being's *uni-* or *multi-*personal nature). That a being is singular does not in any way suggest, insinuate, or imply that it is, for that reason, *uni-*personal. Commonsense based objections to the idea that there can exist an individual personal-being who is multipersonal are simply erroneous; being-person numerical identity is not a necessary assumption we must make when considering the nature of individual personal-being.

Nevertheless, although it is clear that the existence of a multipersonal individual personal-being is not logically impossible, some may object that since the only available way of understanding the nature of individual personal-being is by means of created analogues (i.e. created individual personal-beings), and these analogues exhibit being-person numerical identity, then it is more likely the case that God, the archetypal individual personal-being, is also unipersonal. This objection is impotent, in the first place, seeing as it rests upon an assumption that is false, namely that all individual personal-beings are analogues of God's individual personal-being. Scripturally, this is not the case. Human beings, and humans alone, are the image and likeness[4] and glory of

---

[4] See Gen 1:26; 5:1; James 3:9.

God.[5] Neither the elect angels, nor the angels who sinned were or are analogues of God.

Secondly, Scripturally we know that man is never actually completely isolated.[6] There are no individual human personal-beings who can actually model personal-being in complete isolation from other actual persons. Seeing as God did not acquire personhood through his act of creating personal beings in his image, moreover, it follows that if the individual personal-being of humans is the only analogue we have of God's individual personal-being, then the inextricable position man's individual personal-being occupies in a network of other personal-beings[7] can only serve to demonstrate that God's individual personal-being cannot be understood to be unipersonal. God existed as a personal-being prior to creating man in his image and likeness. What is more, the plurality of persons in God, we note, must be actual and inseparable from the being of God, for prior to creation God immutably and perfectly existed as an individual personal-being.[8]

---

[5] Cf. 1 Cor 11:7; Gen 1:26.

[6] This is a conclusion necessitated by the doctrine of God's omnipresence (cf. Ps 139:7-12), as well as by the Scripture's teaching regarding the existence and activities of other personal-beings, namely the good angels (cf. Ps 34:7; Heb 13:2) and the angels who sinned (cf. 1 Pet 5:8; Eph 6:12).

[7] Some unitarians have attempted to argue that God's personal nature can be understood in complete isolation (see, for instance, Tuggy, Dale. "Are Persons Essentially Relational?," Trinities (02/07/2008), http://trinities.org/blog/are-persons-essentially-relational, Accessed 04/24/2018. However, this is in no way supported by the Scriptures. As we note in this chapter, even if completely isolated individual personal being were a reality— and it is not— it would nevertheless remain the case that individual personal being is necessarily virtually plural.

[8] Lest the reader miss this very important point, we offer some further clarity here. Given that God is immutable, he does not change in any way. He cannot view himself as virtually performing or not

Scripture's use of "singular-plurals" in reference to man and woman in Genesis 1 further highlights the fact that individual human personal-being is multipersonal, and that this reflects the multipersonality of God himself. As Thomas A. Keiser explains:

> One feature of the text which seems to have been overlooked in the discussion of the divine plural is that as soon as *Elohim* is associated with a plurality, humankind is presented in the same way. Throughout the creation account, third person singular verbs describe God's actions, clearly presenting him in the singular. But when the divine plural appears, thereby introducing the idea of plurality, it occurs along with the presentation of humanity as both singular and plural ('Let us create man...so that they...' [v. 26], and 'God created man in his own image, in the image of God created he him, male and female created he them' [v. 27]). Thus, both Deity and humanity are simultaneously presented as both singular and plural. This simultaneous introduction of both Deity and humanity in both singular and plural terminology provides a strong argument for understanding a connection between the two.[9]

---

performing some action. He is *actus purus*. There is no potentiality in God; there is no virtuality in God. God is always what he will always be. Consequently, God must always be actually multipersonal. Given that his multipersonality is not the result of his being a temporal and mutable creature, it is necessarily perfect. Our point here is not that this necessity of divine multipersonality proves he is a Trinity; rather, our point is simply that God's necessary multipersonality proves conclusively that uniartianism is false.

[9] 2009. "The Divine Plural: A Literary-Contextual Argument for Plurality in the Godhead," *Journal for the Study of the Old Testament* Vol 34.2, 135.

Finally, granting for the sake of argument that individual human personal-being can be isolated from other *actual* personal-beings, it is still the case that individual human personal-being can only comprehended in relation to other *virtual* persons. This is a truth which has long been recognized even by secular thinkers. Among secular philosophers, for instance, David Hume views the individual human being as a conglomerate of persons, going so far as to liken the individual human being's person (soul) itself "to a republic or commonwealth, in which the several members are united by the reciprocal ties of government and subordination."[10] Hume's anti-Cartesian postmodern heirs, Gilles Deleuze and Felix Guattari follow closely behind, claiming that individual personal-being is in constant flux, always piecemeal, and always virtually related to itself. As Steven Best and Douglas Kellner note, Deleuze and Guattari

> ...reject the modernist notion of a unified, rational, expressive subject [i.e. person/self] and attempt to make possible the emergence of new types of decentered subjects, liberated from what they see to be the terror of fixed and unified identities, and free to become dispersed and multiple, reconstituted as new types of subjectivities and bodies.[11]

Deleuze and Guattari, that is to say, believe that the Cartesian/modernist notion of a primordial absolutely individual person corresponding to an individual being is false; a superimposed mechanism of control created by philosophers, religionists, and psychologists. True personal-being is, they argue,

---

[10] *A Treatise of Human Nature*, (Oxford: Clarendon Press, 1888), 261.

[11] *Postmodern Theory: Critical Interrogations*, (New York: The Guilford Press, 1991), 78.

multiple, comprised of a variety of desires and functions and means of expression that may or may not have any form of unity between them.

Admittedly, Deleuze and Guattari's view is somewhat radical. Nevertheless, even among less radical secular thinkers the idea that individual personal-being is multipersonal finds clear expression in many fields of study. Nicholas Humphrey and Daniel C. Dennett, again following Hume's lead, use the idea of the individual personal-being as a conglomerate-of-selves in the field of psychology, arguing that multiple personality disorder (or Dissociative Identity Disorder) results from an individual's failure to elect one representative "Head of Mind" over the other internalized persons that he has created over the "normal" course of his development. They state that

> ...a human being does not start out as single or multiple - she starts out without any Head of Mind at all. In the normal course of development, she gets acquainted with the various possibilities of selfhood that "make sense" - partly through her own observation, partly through outside influence. In most cases, a majority view emerges, strongly favoring one version of "the real me," and it is that version which is installed as her elected Head of Mind. But in some cases the competing fictive-selves are so equally balanced, or different constituencies within her are so unwilling to accept the result of the elect, that constitutional chaos reigns - and there are snap elections (or *coups d'état* all the time).[12]

For Humphrey and Dennett, the individual human being who

---

[12] "Speaking for Our Selves: An Assessment of Multiple Personality Disorder," http://www.humphrey.org.uk/papers/1989mpd.pdf, Accessed 01/30/2018.

speaks in the first person singular voice is a figurehead/representative for the totality of simultaneously existent virtual selves (persons) one has become over one's normal course of development. Being a single entity does not entail that one is a single person. Rather, for these authors all personal-being is personally plural. The multiplicity of selves/persons in one being is not the disorder; it is the lack of a representative person to rule over and speak for the others that is the disorder. This theory echoes Sigmund Freud's earlier theory of psychoanalysis that views personhood in individual personal-beings as only superficially unipersonal. That which is expressed by the individual personal-being is the measured expression of the Ego as it stands in conflictual relationship to the Id and the Super Ego. We may press the matter further, noting that prior to the advent of Christ a theory of man similar to Freud's can be found in Plato's notion of the tripartite soul.

We ultimately reject these secular theories of individual personal-being, seeing as they are in many ways incompatible with the Christian worldview. However, we simply note that they serve to underscore that within the fields of secular philosophy and psychology the notion of a multipersonal individual personal-being is not only not unheard of, but has a long history that extends into the present.

A. *Individual Human Personal-Being is Virtually Multipersonal*

Thus, it is not only the case that individual personal-being does not imply being-person numerical identity, it is likewise not the case that the notion of multipersonal individual personal-being is irrational, or foreign to the history of reflection on the nature of individual personal-being among either Christian theologians or secular philosophers and psychologists. More than this, it is the case that individual human personal-being can only be properly understood in the context of multipersonality, a truth which we find among contemporary theories of multipersonal individual

341

personal-being. Chief among these theories is the dialogical self-theory which states that "[internally directed] dialogue is a core quality of the self."[13]

> Dialogical conceptualization of the self stems from William James' (1890) distinction between I and Me. According to this division, I refers to 'self-as-knower', whereas Me symbolizes 'self-as-known', which is acknowledged by the objective agent - I. In other words, I as a subject perceives I as an object (Me/Mine).
>
> [. . .]
>
> I as a subject moves along different I-positions and endows them with a voice, which represents their distinctive points of view.[14]

This theory of the individual human personal-being (self) as constituted by three persons (i.e. the subject-I, the object-I, and the mediatorial-I) is reflected in many places in Scripture, as man's personal-being is tripartite, in this sense: Individual human personal-being is comprised of (i.)consciousness of oneself in the past, (ii.)consciousness of oneself in the future, and (iii.)consciousness of oneself as related to oneself in the past and in the future.[15]

Additionally, Scripture teaches us that men relate to themselves as if to other persons. The Word of God teaches us that

---

[13] Batory, A., Bąk, W., Oleś, P.K., Puchalska-Wasyl, M., 2010. "The Dialogical Self: Research and Applications," *Psychology of Language and Communication*, Vol. 14, No. 1, 46.

[14] Batory *et al.*, *The Dialogical Self*, 46-47.

[15] Cf. Phil 3:12-16.

men take counsel in their own souls,[16] are taught by their own hearts,[17] pray for their own souls,[18] encourage their own souls to continue on in faith,[19] to worship God,[20] and to rest in God's beneficence.[21] Scripture also teaches that men can deceive,[22] examine,[23] and love themselves.[24] The Scriptures do not present personhood as absolutely isolated. Rather, in place after place, individual personal-beings are revealed to be members of a plurality of either actual or virtual persons who are in communicative exchanges with one another. The analogy of man, therefore, does not support the unipersonalist presupposition assumed by unitarians. If we are to see in individual men an analogy of the individual personal-being of God, we must conclude that God is not unipersonal but multipersonal.

B. *The Singular-Plural Dialectic*

Unitarians, nevertheless, will often claim that God's unipersonality is proven by his many uses of singular personal pronouns throughout the Bible. For example, unitarian Anthony Buzzard writes:

> Of Himself God repeatedly says, "I am God, and there is no other God besides Me. Biblical people address God by saying "Thou alone art God (in modern English, You alone are God). There is no other God except You."

---

[16] Cf. Ps 13:2.

[17] Cf. Ps 16:7.

[18] Cf. Ps 35:3.

[19] Cf. Ps 42:5, v. 11; 43:5.

[20] Cf. Ps 103:1-2, v. 22; 104:1, v. 35; 146:1.

[21] Cf. Ps 116:7.

[22] Cf. 1 Cor 3:18; Gal 6:3.

[23] Cf. 1 Cor 11:28.

[24] Cf. Lev 19:18; Matt 19:19; 22:39; Rom 13:9; Gal 5:14; James 2:8; Eph 5:28, v. 33.

"There is no God besides You." Biblical writers refer to God as He, Him, Himself. "He is God and there is no other besides Him." "He alone is God." These singular personal pronouns, describing God as a single divine Person occur constantly, repeatedly and uniformly across the pages of Holy Scripture. They ought to convince a Bible reader that God is a single Person, not two Persons, not Three or more Persons.[25]

Buzzard's argument here is that the singular personal pronouns God uses of himself demonstrates that he is a single person. However, Buzzard's reasoning is fallacious in several ways.

Firstly, Buzzard is guilty of stacking the deck by ignoring what we may call the singular-plural dialectic evident in key places in Scripture, as we will demonstrate below. Secondly, Buzzard's use of the axiom of unipersonality constitutes a category error as it fails to differentiate between the divine being of God and the created being of his creatures. Logically, this necessarily leads to the conclusion that God and his creatures constitute a great chain of being, of which God is the apex. This is pantheism, not biblical Christianity. Thus, the axiom of unipersonality and the biblical doctrine of monotheism are mutually exclusive, for if the former is true God is not ontologically unique, and if the latter is true then God does not occupy the same ontological category as his creatures. Thirdly, granting, for the sake of argument, that the axiom of unipersonality did not constitute a category error, it would nonetheless be the case that Buzzard is guilty of begging the question by assuming what he is claiming to prove, namely that God is unipersonal.

---

[25] "Let Us Reason Together: God is a Who, Not a What!," 21st Century Reformation, http://www.21stcr.org/multimedia/artitcles/ab-god_is_a_who_not_a_what.html, Accessed 01/27/ 2018.

Regarding the singular personal pronoun argument made by Buzzard, we note that while it is the case that the Scriptures are replete with such singular personal pronouns being employed by God, it is simply not the case that God does not use plural personal pronouns to refer to himself. In Genesis 1:26, God uses plural personal pronouns:

"Let *us* make man in *our* image, after *our* likeness."[26]

He then uses singular personal pronouns in Gen 1:29-30.

"Behold, *I* have given you every plant yielding seed that is on the face of all the earth, and every tree with seed in its fruit. You shall have them for food. And to every beast of the earth and to every bird of the heavens and to everything that creeps on the earth, everything that has the breath of life, *I* have given every green plant for food."[27]

God moves from using plural personal pronouns of himself to using singular personal pronouns of himself.[28] In Genesis 3, this

---

[26] Emphasis added.

[27] Emphasis added.

[28] Burgos' remarks in this volume are concise and to the point:

God spoke creation into existence saying "Let there be" and "Let us make." To whom exactly was God speaking? Given the above evidence, the only tenable answer to that question is that God was speaking to God. That is not to say that God was soliloquizing. Rather, given that the Old and New Testaments teach one divine person speaks to the other two divine persons, it is apparent that God's language in creation does not fall upon deaf ears. The Father, Son, and Spirit communicate with each other. The Angel of Yahweh (i.e., God the Son) and Yahweh

self-reference pattern is reversed, as God moves from using singular personal pronouns of himself to using plural personal pronouns. In Gen 3:11, God asks Adam:

> "Who told you that you were naked? Have you eaten of the tree of which *I* commanded you not to eat?"[29]

After Eve answers his question, the Lord God then says to the serpent:

> "*I* will put enmity between you and the woman..."[30]

He then proceeds to tell Eve:

> "*I* will surely multiply your pain..."[31]

Finally, he declares to Adam:

> "Because you have listened to the voice of your wife

(i.e., the Father) speak with each other (1 Sam 24:16; Zec 1:12; John 12:28), and the Spirit speaks with the Father and Son (John 16:13-15; Rom 8:26-27; Rev 22:17)...

The communication of God is not merely a convention of creation. God spoke before creation existed. "By the word of the LORD the heavens were made" (Psalm 33:6), and therefore divine language pre-existed creation. The earth was formed "by the word of God"—it was divine language that affected the creation of all created things. God's communication presupposes another party, and in the case of Genesis 1:26, another party who is also God.

[29] Emphasis added.
[30] Emphasis added.
[31] Emphasis added.

and have eaten of the tree
of which *I* commanded you,
'You shall not eat of it,'
cursed is the ground because of you;
in pain you shall eat of it all the days of your life..."[32]

Throughout the Fall Narrative thus far, God has used singular personal pronouns. However, when we arrive at verse 22, he states,

> "Behold, the man has become like one of us in knowing good and evil..."[33]

Similarly, in Gen 11:7 God refers to himself as "us," despite Moses' record indicating that only Yahweh came down to observe the rebellion of the builders of the tower of Babel. The singular being of God is joined to plural personal pronouns, once again demonstrating that God refers to himself as a plurality of persons. The singular-plural dialectic is very clearly on display, moreover, in Isaiah 6:8, where Yahweh asks:

> "Whom shall I send, and who will go for us?"[34]

The first and second parts of this question are parallels of one another, indicating that God is using "I" and "us" interchangeably, even as the Lord Jesus Christ does in John 3:11 where he states —

---

[32] Emphasis added.

[33] Emphasis added.

[34] Emphasis added. [N.B. The Lord Jesus Christ says that this prophecy is fulfilled in his giving of parables of the kingdom (cf. Matt 13:10-17). Christ is identifying himself as Yahweh, the Lord who promised that he would blind his enemies lest they come to be healed by him.]

> "Truly, truly, *I* say to you, *we* speak of what *we* know, and bear witness to what *we* have seen, but you do not receive *our* testimony."[35]

Note that the "we" being used by Christ in this text cannot refer to the other Jews, as it does in John 4:22, since Nicodemus is himself a Jew. Nor can it refer to the disciples, seeing as the disciples did not witness or see what Christ had witnessed and seen. Instead, the "we" has reference to the other two persons who are always with Christ, witnessing to the veracity of his teaching and claims about himself — namely, the Father[36] and the Holy Spirit.[37]

§ II. *An Examination of Mark 12:28-34*

Having established that being-person numerical identity is neither logically nor ontologically requisite to a proper understanding of individual personal being, we will now examine Mark 12:28-34, demonstrating that it is in no way supportive of unitarian monotheism.

> And one of the scribes came up and heard them disputing with one another, and seeing that he answered them well, asked him, "Which commandment is the most important of all?" Jesus answered, "The most important is, 'Hear, O Israel: The Lord our God, the Lord is one. And you shall love the Lord your God with all your heart and with all your soul and with all your mind and with all your strength.' The second is this: 'You shall love your neighbor as yourself.' There is no other commandment greater than these." And the scribe said to him, "You are

---

[35] Emphasis added.
[36] Cf. John 5:37; 8:18.
[37] Cf. John 15:16.

right, Teacher. You have truly said that he is one, and there is no other besides him. And to love him with all the heart and with all the understanding and with all the strength, and to love one's neighbor as oneself, is much more than all whole burnt offerings and sacrifices." And when Jesus saw that he answered wisely, he said to him, "You are not far from the kingdom of God." And after that no one dared to ask him any more questions. (Mark 12:28-34)

A. *Setting the Tone: Amicability or Hostility?*

The question of the manner in which the scribe approaches Christ is important, for it plays a part in understanding the nature of this theological encounter. Commentators are divided, with some believing that the scribe was a hostile questioner, and others believing that he was sincere. Having seen that Christ "answered [the Sadducees] well" (v. 28), the scribe approaches Christ. Unlike Matthew's account of this event,[38] Mark does not mention that the scribe's intention in approaching Christ is "to test him." James R. Edwards observes that Mark's account "does not contain the invective that Jesus otherwise experiences from the scribes," and therefore concludes that this is "the *one* story in Mark where a scribe approaches Jesus on *amicable* terms."[39] Similarly, Robert H. Stein lists four reasons as to why the scribe's questioning of Christ "cannot be seen as hostile in intent,"[40] namely —

> (1) the scribe is positively inclined toward Jesus, not insolent...; (2) he praises Jesus (12:32–33); (3) he is described as having answered Jesus "wisely" (νουνεχῶς,

---

[38] Cf. Matt 22:34-40.

[39] *The Gospel According to Mark*, (Grand Rapids: Eerdmans, 2002), 370. (emphasis added)

[40] Ibid. (emphasis added)

nounechōs; 12:34a); and (4) he is praised by Jesus for not being far from the kingdom of God (12:34b).[41]

Likewise M. Eugene Boring, although acknowledging that "the scribe belongs to the group *consistently hostile* to Jesus throughout Mark,"[42] maintains that the scribe "asks a sincere question...treats Jesus as neighbor, [and] transcends the party strife and us/them mentality of the narrative."[43] According to Boring, Christ's interlocutor, "unlike his fellow scribes...addresses Jesus as a colleague and accepts him as a participant in serious theological discussion."[44] Ben Witherington III also views the scribe as "someone who is a genuine seeker of knowledge who admires Jesus' responses under pressure to the Sadducees and others, and responds well and wisely to Jesus' teaching."[45]

Joel F. Williams states that "in contrast to the preceding questions of the religious leaders, which were intended to trap, the question of the scribe is sincere."[46] Edwards, similarly, argues that the scribe's

> ...personal interaction with Jesus, including the emphasis in the pericope on "hearing" (Gk. *akouein*; vv. 28, 29, 37), testifies to the scribe's sincerity. His sincerity, in turn, helps to account for his positive encounter with Jesus.[47]

---

[41] *Mark*, (Grand Rapids: Baker Academic, 2008), 558.

[42] *Mark: A Commentary*, (Louisville: Westminster John Knox Press, 2006), 343. (emphasis added)

[43] Ibid.

[44] Ibid.

[45] *The Gospel of Mark: A Socio-Rhetorical Commentary*, (Grand Rapids: Eerdmans, 2001), 330.

[46] *Other Followers of Jesus: Minor Characters as Major Figures in Mark's Gospel*, (Sheffield: T & T Clark, 1994), 174.

[47] Edwards, *The Gospel According to Mark*, 370.

This demonstrates that the scribe was "impressed with Jesus' wisdom in answering the Sadducees."[48] In agreement with Williams and Edwards, William L. Lane further states that,

> The scribe's openness and humility before God exhibited a favorable disposition, while his enthusiastic approval of Jesus' teaching revealed an attraction toward the one through whom God had brought the Kingdom near to men in an eschatological and messianic perspective.[49]

Yet despite the popularity of this particular view among commentators, we note that the gospel of Matthew clearly indicates that the scribe's intention is malevolent. Consequently, rather than treating Mark as an isolated text,[50] we must interpret this pericope in light of Matthew's parallel account in Matt 22:34-40, where we are informed that the scribe "asked [Christ] a question *to test him*."[51]

The reader familiar with Matthew's gospel will note that the language of "testing" Christ in Matthew in 22:35 is found in previous passages, all of which reveal Christ's testers to be hostile in intent.[52] Of particular importance in this regard is Matthew's

---

[48] Ibid.

[49] *The Gospel of Mark*, (Grand Rapids: Eerdmans, 1974), 434.

[50] Given the difference between Matthew and Mark, i.e. Mark's omission of the scribe's nefarious intentions, other solutions have been offered by scholars. For instance, textual-critical commentators typically view Matthew's statement about "testing" as a later addition addressing Matthean contemporary concerns (representative of this view is Camille Focant's *The Gospel According to Mark: A Commentary*, Trans. by Keylock, Leslie Robert, (Eugene: Pickwick Publications, 2012), 501-502).

[51] Matt 22:34. (emphasis added)

[52] Cf. Matt 16:1; 19:3; 22:18.

record of hostile interlocutors who, for the sake of entangling him in his speech, feign deference to Christ.

> Then the Pharisees went and plotted how to entangle him in his talk. And they sent their disciples to him, along with the Herodians, saying, "Teacher, we know that you are true and teach the way of God truthfully, and you do not care about anyone's opinion, for you are not swayed by appearances. Tell us, then, what you think. Is it lawful to pay taxes to Caesar, or not?"[53]

According to Luke's account, the scribes "watched him and sent spies, *who pretended to be sincere, that they might catch him in something he said*, so as to deliver him up to the authority and jurisdiction of the governor."[54] Feigning sincerity for the sake of ensnaring the Lord in his words is not out of character for these opponents of the Son of God. Thus, the praise lavished upon Christ by an interlocutor is by no means an indication that the interlocutor is sincere. Hypocritical praise for Christ's person, wisdom, and his special role as a prophet is underscored and rebuked throughout the gospels,[55] revealing that the scribe's praising of Christ's wisdom in Mark's gospel is not proof that he was positively inclined toward him.

Additionally, we observe in this pericope a pattern of behavior that is very similar to what we observe in Mark 12:28-34. The Pharisees first gather together and plot how to entangle Christ in his words. After this, they send questioners to praise his moral character ("you are true") and his adherence to the truth of Scripture ("you teach the way of God"). Thus, taking into

---

[53] Matt 22:15-17.

[54] Luke 20:20. (emphasis added)

[55] cf. Matt 21:14-17 & 27:15-26; John 2:23-24; 3:1-2; 6:22-33, vv. 41-42, 66; 8:28-30, vv. 41, 48, 52-53, 59.

consideration the Scriptures' characterization of the scribes as ungodly opponents of the truth,[56] Calvin asserts that the scribe's approaching of Christ

> ...show[s] that *it was done by mutual arrangement*, and that out of the whole sect one person was chosen who was thought to excel the rest in ability and learning...he makes a *deceitful* attack on Christ, that, if he can draw any thing from his lips that is at variance with the law, he may exclaim against him as an apostate and a promoter of ungodly revolt.
>
> [...]
>
> [The scribe] being an expounder of the Law...is offended at the doctrine of the gospel, by which he supposes the authority of Moses to be diminished. At the same time, he is not so much influenced by zeal for the Law, as by displeasure at losing some part of the honor of his teaching. *He therefore inquires of Christ to the hatred of the people.*[57]

The scribe's intention is not to truly understand Christ's doctrine, but to ensnare him in his words.

B. *The Question*

Edwards notes that "the scribes concerned themselves with proper exposition of the law and earned a reputation as experts in

---

[56] We may also add here that the scribes were not ethically ambiguous. The Lord Jesus excoriates the scribes throughout Matthew 23, characterizing them as hypocrites.

[57] *Commentary on Matthew, Mark, Luke*, Vol. 3, (Grand Rapids: Christian Classics Ethereal Library, 1999), 33. (emphasis added)

its interpretation."[58] The question was not unheard of during this time period, yet it takes on new significance in light of some of the claims that Christ has been making of himself throughout his ministry in general, and in the latter end of his ministry. The entrance of Christ into Jerusalem not only caused the people to identify him as the one who comes in the name of the Lord,[59] who is bringing forth the promised kingdom of David,[60] and the Son of David who has the authority to cleanse the temple of God,[61] but the eschatological Son of Man, the Last and Greater Adam.[62]

Central to the debates between Christ and his opponents is the question of authority. The enemies of Christ openly ask him

> "By what authority are you doing these things, or who
> gave you this authority to do them?"[63]

Seeing as they are unwilling to give him an explicit answer to his counter-question concerning the authority of John the Baptist,[64] he refuses to give an explicit answer. Instead, he answers with a parable. Mark 12:1-11 records *The Parable of the Tenants*, in which the Lord Jesus Christ identifies himself not as merely one servant of God among many, or even as one son of God among many,[65] but as the unique Son of God himself. It is this claim, again given emphasis in his immediately ensuing *Parable of The Wedding Feast*,[66] that drives Christ's enemies to seek to arrest

---

[58] Edwards, *The Gospel According to Mark*, 370.

[59] Mark 11:9.

[60] Mark 11:10.

[61] Mark 11:15-16.

[62] Cf. Ps 8.

[63] Mark 11:28.

[64] Mark 11:29-33.

[65] Cf. Matt 21:28-32; Luke 20:9-18.

[66] Cf. Matt 22:1-14.

him.[67] And it is their desire to have him arrested that drives them to present him with three theological tests.

The First Test: To Whom is Ultimate Allegiance, Honor, and Obedience Due?

> And they sent to him some of the Pharisees and some of the Herodians, to trap him in his talk. And they came and said to him, "Teacher, we know that you are true and do not care about anyone's opinion. For you are not swayed by appearances, but truly teach the way of God. Is it lawful to pay taxes to Caesar, or not? Should we pay them, or should we not?" But, knowing their hypocrisy, he said to them, "Why put me to the test? Bring me a denarius and let me look at it." And they brought one. And he said to them, "Whose likeness and inscription is this?" They said to him, "Caesar's." Jesus said to them, "Render to Caesar the things that are Caesar's, and to God the things that are God's." And they marveled at him. (Mark 12:13-17)

In this first test, the Pharisees present Christ with a moral dilemma, the goal of which is to force him to either make himself an enemy of the state (by refusing to pay taxes to Caesar) or an enemy of the people (by acquiescing to the demands of the pagan Gentile oppressors). The Lord's response ("render to Caesar the things that are Caesar's, and to God the things that are God's") leaves his opponents marveling. This is in part due to his intellectual prowess, which is on full display as he effortlessly splits the horns of what they thought was an insoluble moral dilemma. However, there is more that is at work in the Lord Christ's answer. For as Edwards notes,

---

[67] Mark 12:12.

In the saying of v. 17 the unmistakable *exousia* or authority of Jesus again emerges. Caesar and God were ultimate and uncontested authorities in the political and religious climate of Jesus' day, *and yet Jesus presumes to speak for both.* That ultimate authority resided with God is clearly implied in Jesus' use of the word "image"... which is the same word used in Gen 1:26 of humanity's creation in God's image. If coins bear Caesar's image, then they belong to Caesar. But humanity, which bears God's image, *belongs to God!*[68]

This reply is significant, given that the reason for the coming judgment on Jerusalem is her teacher's unwillingness to render unto God those things which are God's, namely the children of Jerusalem (i.e. God's people). Jesus makes this clear in his lament over the city, which Luke informs us he spoke prior to engaging in debate with the Pharisees, Sadducees, and scribes —

"O Jerusalem, Jerusalem, the city that kills the prophets and stones those who are sent to it! How often would *I* have gathered your children together *as a hen gathers her brood under her wings*, and you would not! Behold, your house is forsaken. And I tell you, you will not see me until you say, 'Blessed is he who comes in the name of the Lord!'"[69]

Christ openly identifies himself as the one whose wings provide salvation for Israel, a symbol used consistently by Yahweh in the Old Testament.[70] Jerusalem's children are Christ's people,

---

[68] *The Gospel According to Mark*, 364. (emphasis added)

[69] Luke 13:34-35. (emphasis added)

[70] Cf. Exod 19:4; Deut 32:11-12; Ps 17:8; 36:7; 57:1; 63:7.

the lost whom he has come to find. Hence, immediately after stating these things, in Luke 14:1-6 & 15:3-8 Christ likens the lost to *sons* (i.e. image bearers[71]), *sheep* (i.e. property of the shepherd[72]) whom he seeks to bring back to his fold,[73] and, most significantly, *coins* that he has come to find/collect.

If that which is God's belongs only to God, and Jesus is not God, then why is Jesus gathering the people of God to himself as though he were God? Whose image do the people of God bear? Given that "Jesus emphatically rejected [the pagan] confusion between man and God," and emphasized that "divine honors belong to God alone,"[74] if he were merely a man, he would not be claiming the bearers of the divine image as *his* coins. Yet he does this explicitly, identifying the people as *his* coins and, therefore, his image bearers. Consequently, Christ views himself as being the proper recipient of supreme, i.e. divine, allegiance, honor, and obedience. Men are required to honor him above even their parents, a requirement only Yahweh can righteously impose on mankind. Instead of owing supreme allegiance to a mere man like Caesar, Jesus argues that "because men bear the image of *God* they owe their total allegiance to *him*."[75]

The Second Test: Man's Covenant vs. God's Covenant

> And Sadducees came to him, who say that there is no resurrection. And they asked him a question, saying, "Teacher, Moses wrote for us that if a man's brother dies and leaves a wife, but leaves no child, the man must take the widow and raise up offspring for his brother. There

---

[71] Cf. Gen 5:3.

[72] Cf. Ps 23:1ff; 28:9; 74:1; 80:1; 95:6-7a; 100:1-3.

[73] Luke 15:3-7.

[74] Lane, *The Gospel of Mark*, 425.

[75] Ibid. (emphasis added)

were seven brothers; the first took a wife, and when he died left no offspring. And the second took her, and died, leaving no offspring. And the third likewise. And the seven left no offspring. Last of all the woman also died. In the resurrection, when they rise again, whose wife will she be? For the seven had her as wife."

Jesus said to them, "Is this not the reason you are wrong, because you know neither the Scriptures nor the power of God? For when they rise from the dead, they neither marry nor are given in marriage, but are like angels in heaven. And as for the dead being raised, have you not read in the book of Moses, in the passage about the bush, how God spoke to him, saying, 'I am the God of Abraham, and the God of Isaac, and the God of Jacob'? He is not God of the dead, but of the living. You are quite wrong." (Mark 12:18-27)

This second test may at first not appear to belong to the overall question of authority, but upon closer inspection it is seen to fit precisely within that context, making Christ's answer to the scribe a narrower articulation of what he has already set forth in Mark 12:13-17. For as Bradley R. Trick notes, "God's faithfulness to his continuing covenant with Abraham provides the key to understanding Jesus' line of reasoning."[76] The continued existence and eventual resurrection of the patriarchs rests upon the fact that the patriarchs, although dead, have to be alive in some sense, lest the covenant God be annulled. Trick explains:

...resurrection requires a death, but death annuls a covenant. To argue for resurrection based on God's

---

[76] 2007. "Death, Covenants, and the Proof of Resurrection in Mark 12:18-27," *Novum Testamentum* 49, 235.

covenantal faithfulness therefore requires a kind of preliminary death, a death sufficient to experience resurrection, yet not so complete as to annul the covenant....Jesus' argument requires a person's continued existence in a non-corporeal interim state after physical death. The assumption of such an interim state then enables the following distinction: whereas physical death suffices to annul covenants (such as marriages) between physical beings, it cannot annul covenants with God since all people—not just the patriarchs—continue living with respect to God even after physical death...[77]

Whereas the Sadducees imply that God can and does break his covenant with his elect people, Jesus states that this is false. God's people, as well as all of humanity, stand in an ongoing covenant relationship with him.

The Sadducees' challenge is more subtle, but it is not unrelated to the first, for Christ declares himself to be the One who will raise the elect from the dead, and who will bring them from the four corners of the earth to himself.[78] Christ's people are not only his possession by virtue of the image they bear (i.e. his image), they are also his people because they are covenantally bound to *him*.[79] Since covenants made between mere men are nullified upon death, but neither Christ's death nor the death of his people will nullify his covenantal promises to raise them from the dead and bring them into his eternal kingdom, it necessarily

---

[77] *Death, Covenants, and the Proof*, 255.

[78] Cf. Matt 11:4-5, 24:31; Mark 13:27; Luke 7:22; John 5:21& 24, 11:25-26.

[79] The covenantal nature of the language used by Christ at the Last Supper is explained by Paul in 1 Cor 11:25 as the establishment of the New Covenant. The author to the Hebrews implies the same in Heb 7:22-28; 9:11-24. Cf. John 6:52-58.

follows that Christ implies his deity when he speaks of any dead being raised by him— including, here, Abraham, Isaac, and Jacob.[80] He will fulfill his promise to raise his people, as well as all men from, the dead. John 5:24-29 —

> "Truly, truly, I say to you, *whoever hears my word and believes* him who sent me has eternal life. He does not come into judgment, but has passed from death to life.
>
> [...]
>
> Do not marvel at this, for an hour is coming when *all who are in the tombs will hear his voice and come out*, those who have done good to the resurrection of life, and those who have done evil to the resurrection of judgment.[81]

The people bear his image, and are in covenant with *him*, a covenantal relationship that cannot be broken by his death or theirs. This would not be the case if he were a mere man, for all merely human covenants are dissolved upon the death of either party.

The claims here being made by Christ are exceptionally clear—

1. He is the one whose image all of humanity bears.
2. He is the one whose image his elect people, in a distinct way, bear.
3. He is the one who will raise all mankind from the dead.

---

[80] This also implies that death can be neither "soul sleep" nor annihilation, seeing as either soul sleep or annihilation would imply that God the Son had broken his covenant with his people, which is an impossibility for God (cf. Heb 6:13-20; Titus 1:2).

[81] Emphasis added.

4. He is the one who will raise his people from the dead and, thereby, keep his promises to the patriarchs.

Upon whose authority does Jesus receive the praise of the people of Jerusalem, come boldly into the Temple, and cleanse it?

The Third Test: One Lord or More than One Lord?

> And one of the scribes came up and heard them disputing with one another, and seeing that he answered them well, asked him, "Which commandment is the most important of all?" Jesus answered, "The most important is, 'Hear, O Israel: The Lord our God, the Lord is one. And you shall love the Lord your God with all your heart and with all your soul and with all your mind and with all your strength.' The second is this: 'You shall love your neighbor as yourself.' There is no other commandment greater than these." And the scribe said to him, "You are right, Teacher. You have truly said that he is one, and there is no other besides him. And to love him with all the heart and with all the understanding and with all the strength, and to love one's neighbor as oneself, is much more than all whole burnt offerings and sacrifices." And when Jesus saw that he answered wisely, he said to him, "You are not far from the kingdom of God." And after that no one dared to ask him any more questions. (Mark 12:28-34.)

Given that Christ has already identified himself as superior in rank to *all* prophets, *all* men, and *all* authorities among men, has implied that *all* allegiance, honor, and obedience is owed to him, that *all* humans bear his image,[82] and seeing, finally, that he has

---

[82] Cf. Luke 20:25, vv. 37-38.

just implied that *he* is the One who will keep his promises to Abraham, Isaac, and Jacob, the scribe's question cannot be seen as a misplaced sincere question regarding Jesus' take on the Law of God. Rather, context requires us to view this question as yet another attempt to entangle Christ in his words. The question at hand cuts to the issue immediately: Is Christ commanding men to depart from the one true God, the God of Israel?

The question must be asked, for while it is the case that Jesus is telling men to not worship Caesar, he is also commanding them to pay *him,* the Messiah, the same allegiance, honor, and obedience that is due to Yahweh *alone.* Failing to believe and follow Christ in this manner will bring about one's destruction. He states this in no uncertain terms, saying —

> "Everyone who comes to me and hears my words and does them, I will show you what he is like: he is like a man building a house, who dug deep and laid the foundation on the rock. And when a flood arose, the stream broke against that house and could not shake it, because it had been well built. But the one who hears and does not do them is like a man who built a house on the ground without a foundation. When the stream broke against it, immediately it fell, and the ruin of that house was great."[83]

Those who trust and follow Christ's word will not face this devastating end and, therefore, it is imperative that those who claim to be his disciples and servants do what he says. To those who rightly call him "Lord" (Κύριος),[84] but do not do all that he says, he asks—

---

[83] Luke 6:47-49.
[84] John 13:13.

"Why do you call me 'Lord, Lord,' [Gr. Κύριος, *kurios*] and not do what I tell you?"[85]

Words echoing those of Yahweh in Malachi 1:6b —

"...if I am a master [Gr. Κύριος], where is my fear?"

Christ declares that those whose profession of faith in him as Κύριος is not absolute will see their house brought to ruin, just as Yahweh promised to bring destruction to those who called him Κύριος but did not fear him. And this teaching of Christ continues on into our present text, for immediately following upon his interaction with the Pharisees, Sadducees, and scribes, the Lord Jesus declares that the temple will be destroyed because its greedy[86] elite rulers fail to acknowledge Israel's Κύριος on the day of their visitation.[87]

To whom do men owe absolute obedience, then, if Christ is Κύριος? If Christ is the one whose image all men bear, whose authority surpasses that of all men, whose covenant bond with men cannot be broken by his own death or the deaths of those in covenant with him, if he is owed absolute honor, allegiance, and obedience, and is *rightly* called Κύριος, does not this imply that he either *is* or is in competition with Yahweh? What does Christ believe in this matter? He states his doctrine very clearly —

> "The most important is, 'Hear, O Israel: The Lord our God, the Lord is one. And you shall love the Lord your God with all your heart and with all your soul and with all your mind and with all your strength.' The second is this:

---

[85] Luke 6:46.

[86] Cf. Mal 3:6-12; Mark 12:38-42.

[87] Cf. Malachi 3:1; Luke 19:20.

'You shall love your neighbor as yourself.' There is no other commandment greater than these."[88]

Christ is not leading men away from worshiping the one true God who revealed himself to Abraham, and to Isaac, and to Jacob. He teaches that loving Yahweh above all is of greater importance than all of the other commandments. The scribe agrees, saying —

> "You are right, Teacher. You have truly said that he is one, and there is no other besides him. And to love him with all the heart and with all the understanding and with all the strength, and to love one's neighbor as oneself, is much more than all whole burnt offerings and sacrifices."[89]

Mark then reports that "when Jesus saw that he answered wisely, he said to him, 'You are not far from the kingdom of God.'"[90]

The scribe's reply places an emphasis on the fact that there is no other Κύριος besides Yahweh. Unitarian interpretations of text, therefore, believe it teaches "strict" monotheism (i.e. U^{mt}). Yet the Hebrew of the *Shema* in Deuteronomy 6:4-5 presents translators with several interpretive difficulties that make the unitarian's interpretation implausible. "The essential challenge [scholars face]," notes Judah Kraut, "is [breaking] down the four Hebrew words in 6:4b—YHWH *'elohenu YHWH 'eḥ ad*—into subject(s) and predicate(s)."[91] This is a challenge that has resulted in "a dizzying array of grammatical, exegetical, and text-critical

---

[88] Mark 12:29-31.

[89] Mark 12:32b-33.

[90] Mark 12:34.

[91] 2011. "Deciphering the Shema: Staircase Parallelism and the Syntax of Deuteronomy 6:4," *Vetus Testamentum* 61, 583.

suggestions"[92] offered by scholars. Of the many differing suggestions offered by scholars, Daniel I. Bock lists five main translational possibilities, none of which teaches or implies U^{mt}. These are —

> "Hear, O Israel, Yahweh our God, Yahweh is one."
> "Hear, O Israel, Yahweh our God is one Yahweh."
> "Hear, O Israel, Yahweh is our God; Yahweh is one."
> "Hear, O Israel, Yahweh is our God; Yahweh is One/Unique."
> "Hear, O Israel, Yahweh is our God; Yahweh alone."[93]

These translational possibilities share the same emphasis, namely the absolute uniqueness of God. Yahweh alone is the Κύριος of Israel, a fact that is to be met with Israel's absolute allegiance, honor, and obedience toward Yahweh.

In contradiction to the unitarian use of this passage, Bock argues that

> The Shema should not be taken out of context and interpreted as a great monotheistic confession. Moses had made that point in 4:35, 39: "For Yahweh (alone) is God; there is none beside(s) him."

> [...]

> This is *a cry of allegiance, an affirmation of covenant commitment in response to the question, "Who is the God of Israel?"* The language of the Shema is "sloganesque" rather than prosaic: "Yahweh our God! Yahweh alone!"

---

[92] Ibid.

[93] 2004. "How Many is God? An Investigation into the Meaning of Deuteronomy 6:4," *JETS*, 47.2, 195-196.

or "Our God is Yahweh, Yahweh alone!" This was to be the distinguishing mark of the Israelite people; they are those (and only those) who claim Yahweh alone as their God.[94]

What is being asserted in the *Shema* is the absolute uniqueness of Yahweh, an assertion intended to prompt Israel's entire allegiance to him in all areas of life. Lane captures this well—

> [The *Shema* indicates] that the command to love God is an obligation which stems from his uniqueness as God and his gracious favor in extending his covenant love to Israel. It is the Lord our God who is to be loved with a completeness of devotion which is defined by the repeated "all." Because the whole man is the object of God's covenant love, the whole man is claimed by God for himself. To love God in the way defined by the great commandment is to seek God for his own sake, to have pleasure in him and to strive impulsively after him. Jesus demands a decision and readiness for God, and for God *alone*, in an unconditional manner.[95]

Yahweh's people are to only be *his* servants, for "adherence to many gods," as Robert Gundry explains, "results in divided loyalty."[96]

The scribe and Christ agree regarding the answer to the question "Which commandment is the most important of all?," and Christ goes on to state that the scribe is not far from the kingdom of heaven. Unitarians have taken this response to be indicative of

---

[94] *How Many is God?*, 211. (emphasis added)

[95] Lane, *The Gospel of Mark*, 432. (emphasis added)

[96] *Mark: A Commentary on His Apology for the Cross*, Vol. 2, (Grand Rapids: Eerdmans, 1993), 715.

Christ's approval of the scribe's U^{mt}, but as noted above, the *Shema* is not concerned with establishing U^{mt} or even monotheism proper. In a word, "the account does not concern a rabbinic discussion about the heart of the Mosaic Law [and by implication monotheism proper], but a proclamation of the demands of the messianic Kingdom."[97]

C. *Christ's Counter Test*

Lane notes that Christ's reply concerning the scribe's proximity to the kingdom of God is actually "deliberately ambiguous and...undoubtedly intended to provoke reflection"[98] on the requirements of the citizens of the kingdom of God. However, that he intends to have the scribe reflect on yet another aspect of the kingdom of God is made clear by the question he asks immediately afterward.

> "How can the scribes say that the Christ is the son of David? For David himself, in the Holy Spirit, declared,
>
>> 'The Lord [κύριος] said to my Lord [κύριος],Sit at my right hand, until I put your enemies under your feet.'
>
> David himself calls him Lord. So how is he his son?" And the great throng heard him gladly.[99]

What is being argued here is not unrelated to the last test, for the scribe had not seen or entered the kingdom of heaven, he had only been told that it was not far from him. The reason seems to be that the scribe failed to recognize Jesus as the King of that

---

[97] Ibid.

[98] Lane, *The Gospel of Mark*, 432.

[99] Mark 12:35-37.

kingdom. The scribe believed that the Messiah would merely be a descendant of David. We are not told why explicitly, but it is implied by the scribe's prior test concerning who is to be the proper recipient of absolute allegiance, honor, and obedience, and his emphasis on the fact that Yahweh *alone* is Israel's Κύριος. If there is only one Κύριος of Israel, and he alone is to be the recipient of all obedience, allegiance, and honor, then no other besides him can demand these things of men. No creature can demand these things from men. Yet this is exactly what Christ, who is Κύριος, has done repeatedly throughout his ministry. By divine revelation, David recognized that Christ was Κύριος, his superior in all things prior to, during, and after his (i.e. David's lifetime). Thus, rather than properly understanding the Messiah to be Κύριος, worthy of absolute allegiance, honor, and obedience, Jesus' enemies believed him to be exercising an authority that was unlawful not only for their opponents to exercise, but for *any* man to exercise.[100] The scribe's answer, then, was only formally correct. Yes, man is to worship *only* Yahweh. Yes, Yahweh *alone* is God. However, Scripture identifies the Father and his Son as Κύριος, as *one* Κύριος, equally worthy of the same honor, obedience, and allegiance.[101]

Whereas the Pharisees, Sadducees, and scribes sought, but ultimately failed, to catch Christ on the horns of an insoluble dilemma,[102] he now effortlessly forces them to deal with a dilemma of their own making. For if the Father *only* is the one Κύριος worthy of absolute allegiance, honor, and obedience, then the Christ cannot be David's Κύριος, since as Κύριος he demands the same from David. However, if the Christ is David's Κύριος, then Father *alone* is not the one Κύριος worthy of absolute allegiance, honor, and obedience, but *with the Son* occupies the

---

[100] Cf. Mark 2:1-7, vv. 23-27; John 5:1-18; 8:48-59; 10:22-38.
[101] Cf. John 5:23.
[102] Cf. Mark 12:13-17.

unique category reserved for the one true God, and he alone. Yahweh is one Κύριος, but he is personally plural.

D. *The Persons Delineated by Mark*

According to David and Jesus, therefore, the Father and the Son have been, and now are, the one Κύριος of Israel. What is more, by prefacing his citation of David's prophecy by the words "David...in the Holy Spirit, declared," Christ is acknowledging that the Spirit of God gives David's words authority above that of any man. David was under the authority of the Father and the Son, and the Holy Spirit. The Lord Jesus Christ's authority, however, comes from the Father who sent him, *from himself* as the Son of God who is equal to the Father, and from the same Holy Spirit who authorized David and *all* the prophets to speak the Word of God.[103] Although the personhood of the Holy Spirit is not mentioned explicitly in Christ's counter test, this is not necessary given the overall pneumatology of the gospel of Mark. For from the first chapter of the gospel, the Holy Spirit is personally differentiated from the Father and the Son. He descended from heaven, from where the Father's voice sounded forth, rested upon Christ at his baptism,[104] and *drove* him into the wilderness.[105] The Father and the Son and the Spirit are here seen unfolding and fulfilling the divine plan of redemption. More clearly than this is the testimony of Mark 3:22-30, where Christ warns his enemies of the unpardonable sin. In the narrative, Christ is said to be possessed by the unclean, *personal* spirit, Beelzebub. Christ informs his opponents that the Spirit they have spoken against is not a demon but the Holy Spirit of God. This necessarily implies that the Spirit of God is *personal*, not impersonal. Moreover, the Lord Jesus

---

[103] The Holy Spirit's inspiration of *all* the prophets implies his co-equality with the Father and the Son.

[104] Cf. Mark 1:9-11; also, cf. John 1:32-34.

[105] Cf. Mark 1:12.

states that his opponents have blasphemed neither himself nor the Father, but the Holy Spirit. This also necessarily implies that the Holy Spirit is personal, for if the Holy Spirit were an *attribute* or *power* or *force* from the Father, then it would follow that blasphemy against the Holy Spirit would be equivalent to blasphemy of the Father. If the Holy Spirit were an *attribute* or *power* or *force* from the Father and the Son, the same would be true. However, blaspheming the Father and the Son are forgivable sins, whereas blaspheming the Holy Spirit is not forgivable. Therefore, it follows that the Holy Spirit, according to Christ himself, is a distinct divine person.

Hence, whereas Mark 12:1-12 reveals that the Father has sent the Son into the world to die by the hands of sinners, and Mark 12:13-34 reveals that the Son has come into the world to retrieve those with who bear his image, and who are covenantally bound to him, Mark 12:35-37 reveals that the personal Holy Spirit authorized David to write Scripture, granting his (i.e. David's) words a divine authority they did not otherwise possess. Christ is not teaching U^{mt}; the Lord Jesus is openly acknowledging that the Father and the Spirit, who are always with him, are equally authoritative with him over the affairs of men. These three divine persons belong to a single category that only Yahweh occupies, and are the one Κύριος together. Contrary to the claims of U^{mt}'s, Jesus was a Trinitarian.

Conclusion

As we began our study, we noted that the unitarian use of Mark 12:28-34 to support the idea that Jesus was a U^{mt} is not merely implausible but impossible. The foregoing study has established this through several arguments that are all interlinked. In the first part of this paper, we noted that being-person numerical identity is not a necessary logical or ontological assumption when considering the nature of individual personal-being. Any attempts to claim that such an assumption is necessary to understanding personal-being is, therefore, false. There are numerous examples of other disciplines that also recognize this, *viz.* secular psychology and philosophy, rendering any appeals to a "common-sense" understanding of personal being, qua the axiom of unipersonality, inadmissible. What is more, we argued, that because individual personal-being is only analogically reflected by humans and, because humans are always in relation to other *actual* individual personal-beings (namely God and other men), this means that individual personal-being can only be understood in the context of multipersonality. God being the source of this analogy of his individual personal-being, he must, therefore, be multipersonal. This is further confirmed even when we consider the impossible scenario of there existing a human being in complete isolation from all other individual personal-beings. For in such a context, it is still the case that man relates to his past and future virtual selves as to *others;* man is tripartite, in this sense, serving in the present as the mediator between himself in the past and himself in the future. This is not philosophical speculation; rather, the Scriptures present man as standing in such a relationship to himself. Finally, the Scripture's use of the singular-plural self-reference dialectic underscores the fact that God is multipersonal. There is no place in Scripture that represents the individual personal-being of God or his analogues as unipersonal.

In the second part of this paper, we examined Mark 12:28-34 in its larger context, closely looking at the details of the narrative. We established that the exchange between Christ and the scribe was not amicable, but conflictual. Rather than seeking to understand Jesus' doctrine, the scribe was feigning deference to Christ in order to entangle him in his words. We established that the scribe's approaching of Christ, in fact, constituted the third test in a series of tests seeking to have Jesus explicitly state his source of authority. We then analyzed the tests, pointing to their underlying shared goal with more specificity, *viz.* getting Christ to say that there is another Κύριος other than Yahweh.

The first test established Christ as the one to whom the people of Jerusalem belong, the one whose image the people bear. This implies that he is Yahweh, the Creator who made mankind in his image, and who redeems his people to be his image bearers. The second test established that the patriarchs are in covenant with Yahweh and will, therefore, be raised from the dead, for death cannot break God's covenant with his people. We underscored the fact that if Christ has claimed to be the one who will raise the patriarchs, then it follows that he is here implying that he is Yahweh. The people of Jerusalem *and* the patriarchs, therefore, are Jesus' covenant people who have been, and who always will be in covenant with him. The third test established that Yahweh alone is to be the recipient of man's absolute honor, allegiance, and obedience— and no one else. There is only one Κύριος, Yahweh the God of Israel. After this we established that Christ's argument against the scribe's Christology raises the problem of there being more than one Κύριος, if the scribe's theology is correct. Their theology, however, is incorrect, for there are three who are David's absolute authority, and they are yet one Κύριος. The Spirit reveals the Father's commissioning of the Son to rule and reign not only over David, but all of humanity forever. Thus, the Father and the Son and the Holy Spirit, though personally distinct, are the one Κύριος over David and, by implication, over all humanity.

Thus, given that the concept of unipersonal individual personal-being is not a necessary logical or ontological assumption when considering the nature of individual personal-being, and given that the Scriptures teach that man, whose individual personal-being is never absolutely isolated but always stands in relation to either actual or virtual others, engaging in communicative exchanges with them, is the analogue of God, the archetypal individual personal-being, it cannot be the case that God is unipersonal. Moreover, given that Mark 12's overall context is concerned with Christ's authority, repeatedly implying that he is Yahweh, and given that Christ identifies himself as Κύριος, equal to the Father and the Spirit prior to his incarnation in the prophecy of king David, it cannot be the case that the scribe and Christ agree as to the nature of the one Κύριος of Israel. For the scribe, the one Κύριος of Israel is the Father only; for Christ, and for David and *all of the prophets*,[106] the one Κύριος is the Father and the Son and the Holy Spirit.

According to the Word of God, Jesus was, is now, and will always be a Trinitarian.

---

[106] Cf. Matt 22:40.